ing the biblical witness to divine determinism. It is quite well written, deals equitably with opponents, and presents a balanced argument. It is a handy tool for an introduction to the issues. In this regard, I found it a wonderful addition to the conversation from a practical and informative perspective, with a forthright presentation of the argument for Christensen's point of view while showing the weakness of opposite opinions. I can recommend it highly as a worthy presentation of the argument that neither culpability nor human freedom need be surrendered to embrace praise, blame, and sovereignty."

> —**John D. Hannah**, Distinguished Professor of Historical Theology; Research Professor of Theological Studies, Dallas Theological Seminary

"Just as there seems to be no end of books (so the Preacher in Ecclesiastes), so there seems to be no end to the discussion about human free will and divine sovereignty. Pelagius and Augustine, Erasmus and Luther, Wesley and Whitefield—the discussion is certainly not a new one. But this simply means that every generation needs to wrestle afresh with what Scripture teaches on this subject. This new popular work by Scott Christensen helpfully lays out the major positions and seeks to show what Scripture teaches on this enormously important subject. A good primer!"

> —**Michael A. G. Haykin**, Professor of Church History and Biblical Spirituality, The Southern Baptist Theological Seminary, Louisville

"The perennial debate over free will and divine sovereignty often gets off on the wrong foot. More popular treatments can verge on caricature, while more serious treatments are often inaccessible to the average believer. This book is different. Careful in description and argument, it is also eminently readable. Scott Christensen doesn't take anything for granted, but defines the major terms as he goes. Most important of all, it breathes a spirit of wonder and gratitude before the face of a God who is not only all-powerful but good."

> —**Michael Horton**, J. Gresham Machen Professor of Theology, Westminster Seminary California

"This concise little volume is a clear, intelligent, immensely helpful overview of one of the most confusing conundrums in all of theology: the perennial debate over divine sovereignty and human free will. While avoiding the dense philosophical prose found in most works on this subject, Scott Christensen doesn't sidestep the hard questions. The answers he gives are thoughtful, biblical, satisfying, and refreshingly coherent. Lay readers and seasoned theologians alike will treasure this work."

> —**John F. MacArthur Jr.**, Pastor-Teacher, Grace Community Church, Sun Valley, California

"Many think that free will is the silver-bullet answer to some of theology's most difficult questions. But do we have a free will? Short answer: It depends on what you mean by free. Long answer: Read this book."

> —**Andy Naselli**, Assistant Professor of New Testament and Biblical Theology, Bethlehem College & Seminary, Minneapolis

"Christensen has provided an admirably clear and succinct defense of the compatibilist view of human freedom and divine sovereignty. Scholars and laypersons alike will benefit from this well-researched and carefully argued book. I recommend it highly!"

> —**James S. Spiegel**, Professor of Philosophy and Religion, Taylor University, Upland, Indiana

"Compatibilism is not a word with which most Christians are familiar, but it represents a truth apart from which neither the Bible nor the Christian life can be properly understood. Can God be sovereign and man still be free? Can God foreknow our choices without undermining our accountability to him? These sorts of questions have troubled souls for centuries. Scott Christensen's treatment of compatibilism, the notion that divine determinism and human freedom are harmonious, speaks to this issue with biblical clarity and practical wisdom. I am thoroughly persuaded that God knew infallibly from eternity past that I would freely and without reservation endorse this excellent book!"

> —**Sam Storms**, Lead Pastor for Preaching and Vision, Bridgeway Church, Oklahoma City

"Scott Christensen has made an important contribution to the perennial conversation in Christian theology about God's sovereignty and free will. He pushes beyond the mutual stereotypes that so often derail this important conversation, charitably engaging the major objections raised against Calvinism. Scott fuses clearheaded philosophy with helpful everyday life examples and significant insights for Christian living, all under the final authority of Scripture. *What about Free Will?* is an important work for anyone who seeks to champion God's awesome sovereignty over the full scope of reality without reducing humanity to the level of meaningless robots."

—**Thaddeus J. Williams**, Assistant Professor of Biblical and Theological Studies, Talbot School of Theology, La Mirada, California

WHAT ABOUT
FREE WILL?

WHAT ABOUT FREE WILL?

Reconciling Our Choices
with God's Sovereignty

SCOTT CHRISTENSEN

P U B L I S H I N G
P.O. BOX 817 • PHILLIPSBURG • NEW JERSEY 08865-0817

ISBN: 978-1-62995-186-7 (pbk)
ISBN: 978-1-62995-187-4 (ePub)
ISBN: 978-1-62995-188-1 (Mobi)

Printed in the United States of America

Library of Congress Cataloging-in-Publication Data

Christensen, Scott, 1965-
 What about free will? : reconciling our choices with God's sovereignty / Scott Christensen.
    pages cm
 Includes bibliographical references and index.
 ISBN 978-1-62995-186-7 (pbk.) -- ISBN 978-1-62995-187-4 (epub) -- ISBN 978-1-62995-188-1 (mobi)
 1. Free will and determinism--Religious aspects--Christianity. 2. Providence and government of God--Christianity. 3. Libertarianism. 4. Calvinism. 5. Arminianism. I. Title.
 BT810.3.C47 2016
 233'.7--dc23
                                    2015024880

To my wonderful wife, Jennifer, who is a
helpmate beyond compare.

Contents

Foreword

For some time I have been toying with the advisability of committing myself to writing two books on compatibilism. That possibility has now been reduced to one, for Scott Christensen has written the other. And you are holding it in your hand.

Many of the theological disputes of almost any day, including ours, revolve around compatibilism—that is, the view that God's sovereignty on the one hand and human freedom and responsibility on the other are mutually compatible. Veer too much to one side and it is difficult to avoid fatalism (a mechanical form of determinism) and, apparently, the destruction of meaningful human responsibility. Veer too much to the other side and it is difficult to avoid serious loss of confidence in God's sovereignty and goodness: the future laid out in Scripture seems assured only to the extent that the statistical probabilities make room for it. In the West during the last two centuries, these theological issues have often been associated with the name of Calvin on the one hand and with the names of Arminius and of Wesley on the other. Each side has been known to dismiss the other with considerable zeal and enthusiasm.

Both sides discern how much pastoral theology is at stake: the debate focuses not only on theological issues of considerable complexity, but on a plethora of practical issues with which all Christians wrestle: Does prayer change things? If not, why pray? If so, why should we believe that God's plan is already fixed? If God is sovereign, why doesn't he intervene a little more dramatically and clean up the mess? Or is he sovereign, but not reliably good? Or if he is invariably good, how can we believe that he is doing the best he can—unless, of course, we hold that he is not quite sovereign after all? Is it possible to believe that everything is determined, without being driven to what is commonly meant by (a pretty mechanical) determinism? How does this topic bear on such massive and biblically unavoidable topics as election, the freedom of grace, the assurance of faith, even questions about what the cross achieved?

Enter Scott Christensen. This fine discussion, written in the Reformed heritage of Jonathan Edwards, is characterized by several outstanding virtues. First of all, considering the complexity of the subject, this book is wonderfully accessible. I do not mean to suggest that a reader can skim it: that is not possible, for the flow of the argument is often tight and requires alertness to details. Nevertheless, the illustrations are contemporary and pointed, and the demands made of the reader are considerably less challenging than what is expected of readers of Edwards, who is widely recognized as being a rather "user-unfriendly" author. Second, Christensen is immaculately fair with his opponents. He valiantly attempts to present their positions in the categories and with the empathy that they would use to present their own cases. And third, he has come as close to doing this subject justice—that is, to handling it in a way that is both faithful to and submissive to Scripture—as anyone else who has written on the subject in recent memory. Only those who know the literature will appreciate how many traps and misconceptions he has skillfully avoided in constructing his argument.

This is a serious book for serious Christians, whether they initially agree with Scott Christensen or not. Best of all, the cast of the book is not to turn readers into theological pundits who can gain points over opponents in theological debate, but to engender deeper faith in the God of sovereign goodness, while avoiding the temptation to abuse God's sovereignty by blaming him for sin. Rightly used, this book will not foreclose on future discussion—indeed, each chapter ends with useful questions for group study—but will build up many believers in their most holy faith.

D. A. Carson
Research Professor of New Testament
Trinity Evangelical Divinity School
Deerfield, Illinois

Preface

It was never my intention to write this book. It just sort of happened. Well, maybe not. That would undermine my thesis. The fact is, I had been wrestling with and writing about divine sovereignty and the notion of free will for a long time. It seemed only natural to organize my thoughts into a book.

My own head-on collision with the problem occurred in 1984 on a beautiful spring day in the parking lot of Union County College in Cranford, New Jersey. For some time I had cautiously pondered this new doctrine called *divine election* that a friend had introduced to me. Even though I had been a Christian for many years, I had never encountered such teaching before; and like many others, I was immediately repulsed by it. I was convinced that the Bible never taught such a radical and reprehensible doctrine. But there I sat in my Plymouth Horizon, transfixed by the words of Romans 9:15–16: "'I will have mercy on whom I have mercy, and I will have compassion on whom I have compassion.' So then it depends not on human will or exertion, but on God, who has mercy." Divine sovereignty hit me squarely on my frontal lobe. But I was perplexed. If my salvation is wholly dependent on a merciful God, then what happens to my choices? Am I a listless marionette who descends silently through the relentless cogs of divine fate?

One reality reached a crescendo of certainty. I was gripped with the truth of God's meticulous determination of all that transpires in time, space, and human history, including my salvation. I have never turned back from the light that shined squarely on my Bible through the window of my vehicle on that bright day. But something was still amiss, and a new quest unfolded before me. I had to make sense of the other side—the human act of willing, desiring, purposeful choosing. And I just couldn't be satisfied with a wall of isolation separating God's actions from those of his creatures. There was no resignation to chalk up the two ideas to impenetrable mystery or what the venerable theologian J. I. Packer calls "antinomy."[1] Thirty years later I am still peering deeply into this theological enigma, but the thick dust darkening the opposite window in my car has gotten a lot clearer. I hope to reveal now what I didn't see then.

Much of my thinking on God's sovereignty was solidified during my seminary years, but questions about free will remained. I continued to grapple with them for years. Around 2004 I was compelled to start collecting my thoughts about these issues on paper—actually, in a Word file on my hard drive. The file started out as a modest collection of verses, quotes, and my scattered personal reflections. Slowly it grew and became a little more organized. Every time I read a passage from my Bible or something from a pertinent book on the subject, I entered the data into the running file. Eventually the file splintered, and I created separate documents looking at the issues from slightly different angles. Soon a rough outline of my more articulate thoughts began to emerge.

In December 2011, I began a series of sermons from Ephesians 1 on the doctrine of election. Of course, the matter of free will became an issue of importance. I turned to my files and the outline I had developed, which was given a little more polish for the sermon series. To date, those sermons have been the most well received messages I have preached. It was a year and a half later that the thought occurred to me to write a book on the subject. I soon embarked on the quest to make this conundrum a little more comprehensible—first for myself, and maybe for a few others as well.

---

1. J. I. Packer, *Evangelism and the Sovereignty of God* (Downers Grove, IL: InterVarsity Press, 1991), 18–25.

Acknowledgments

This book would not have been possible without a great deal of help from a great number of people. I want to thank Rick Kress for giving me the initial encouragement to tackle this project and the elders of Summit Lake Community Church, who graciously supplied me with a five-week sabbatical in which I completed the first draft. I want to thank Jay Wegter, Josh and Gretchen Rank, Paul Russell, Daniel Cameron, and Dan Phillips, who read portions of the initial draft and made many helpful suggestions. I owe a special thanks to John D. Wilsey, Leonard G. Goss, Irv Busenitz, Jade Greenfield, Phil Johnson, and Jeff and John Crotts for their help, advice, and encouragement at different stages of the project.

I want to thank the fine scholars Matthew Barrett, Thaddeus J. Williams, and James S. Spiegel, who each reviewed later versions of the manuscript and made many invaluable suggestions for improvement. I especially thank James N. Anderson, who thoroughly read the final manuscript. His keen eye for careful arguments and minor details has been indispensable. The time and energy that these generals have given to such a lowly foot soldier has been a kindness that I could never repay. Any errors in my work that remain are, of course, my own. Thinking biblically and soundly about such a difficult and complex topic as divine sovereignty and human free agency is a daunting task. For that reason, I am grateful for my professors and the solid biblical training I received at The Master's Seminary.

I am extremely grateful to D. A. Carson and his willingness to write the foreword to this book. Dr. Carson's writings have been immensely influential in my thinking on this topic. It is a privilege to have him honor me in this way.

I thank the wonderful folks at P&R Publishing for taking an interest in this project. I am especially indebted to John J. Hughes for his expert guidance throughout the publishing process and his many kindnesses to me. Likewise, Karen Magnuson is a fantastic editor, and it has been a pleasure to work with her.

I appreciate the prayers of my church family as I labored to write this book. It is a privilege to serve as their shepherd. I also thank my beloved wife, Jennifer, and my four boys, Daniel, Andrew, Luke, and Matthew, who endured long hours while I was holed up in my office chained to my computer. My son Daniel deserves credit for helping me with the illustrations in the book. My family is a blessing from the Lord. Finally, I thank my Lord and Savior, Jesus Christ, for the indescribable gift of salvation and his providential direction and care.

Introduction:
The Free-Will Problem

Biblical Christianity makes two indisputable affirmations, yet not without generating fierce controversy. First, God controls in some sense all that transpires in time, space, and history, including the course of human lives. Second, human beings are responsible moral agents who freely choose the direction that their lives take. Our ability to make meaningful choices that impact history as it unfolds is what separates us from every other creature.[1] On the surface, these two truths appear to be in conflict with each other. How can God direct the path of human history and yet humans remain free to choose their own course of action?

This question has plagued philosophers and theologians throughout the ages. The problem perplexes us no less today. Even popular culture has tuned in to the vexing question. Anyone who has watched the *Matrix* trilogy or *Groundhog Day* is confronted with daunting notions about free will and whether events are predetermined. The comic strip *Foxtrot* by Bill Amend tackled the matter with a dry wit befitting the ponderous nature of the subject. In the first frame of a strip composed in 2003, the main protagonist of the comic, ten-year-old Jason Fox, holds a football over his head. He calls out to his best friend, Marcus Jones, to "go deep."[2]

1. Mark R. Talbot, "All the God That Is Ours in Christ," in *Suffering and the Sovereignty of God*, ed. John Piper and Justin Taylor (Wheaton, IL: Crossway, 2006), 56.
2. FOXTROT © 2003 Bill Amend. Reprinted with permission of UNIVERSAL UCLICK. All rights reserved.

Marcus deadpans, "How can free will coexist with divine preordination?"[3]

In the next frame, Jason silently ponders the question. In the third frame he replies, "Too deep."[4]

Marcus then alleviates the moment with lighter fare: "If Batman died, would the Joker be happy?"[5]

Is Reconciliation Possible?

Since free will and divine sovereignty seem irreconcilable, one or the other is usually denied or limited in some degree. Historically, some Christians say that God has purposely limited his sovereignty in order to uphold man's free will. This is most often associated with Arminianism and the teachings of the theologian Jacob Arminius (1560–1609). Other Christians have emphasized God's sovereign determination of what transpires while either limiting human freedom or denying it altogether. This is generally associated with *Calvinism*, a term derived from the Protestant Reformer John Calvin (1509–64). Of course, both views date to the early history of the church.[6]

The matter seems straightforward. Either man has a free will that limits God's sovereignty or God is absolutely sovereign and man is not really so free. But is it possible to somehow reconcile God's sovereignty with human freedom? It is my quest to answer that question in the affirmative.

This is no easy task, for several reasons. First, the issue has generated no small amount of controversy within the history of the church, including the present. Second, confusion is often generated by the controversy because of caricatures on both sides of the debate. Third, the issues can get complicated, especially because of the apparent contradictory nature of the two basic propositions. Fourth, the claim that we have free will is usually assumed to be true and its meaning

---

3. Ibid.

4. Ibid.

5. Ibid.; also reprinted in Peter J. Thuesen, *Predestination: The American Career of a Contentious Doctrine* (New York: Oxford University Press, 2009), 222.

6. For the history, see R. C. Sproul, *Willing to Believe: The Controversy over Free Will* (Grand Rapids: Baker, 1997).

self-evident. But if pressed, few are able to articulate a definition. The idea of free will becomes muddled very quickly. Finally, Scripture itself doesn't provide straightforward answers to questions about free will.[7] For that reason alone, one must approach the subject with great care.

My purpose is to try to clear up some of the murkiness that is commonplace and to provide biblical answers to the questions that free will raises. Most Christians have no problem accepting God's control over the big picture of history. When it comes to God's preordaining our actual choices, however, we often entertain a different perspective. Many assume that God's actions have little bearing on our personal choices. We like to reserve a degree of autonomy for ourselves. God's sovereignty provokes nightmares "that we are like puppets being jerked around against our wills by a malevolent master puppeteer."[8]

For many, to deny free will is anathema—we have no choice (!) but to believe in free will. This is understandable. It appears intuitively obvious that we make our own independent choices.[9] They are usually made unhindered and seemingly apart from any outside causes other than our own freedom to choose. This is where confusion sets in. Many readily accept that God chooses us for salvation and directs our lives for his purposes, but don't we freely choose what we want as well? How can both notions be true? The burden of this book is to answer such questions.

Why Bother?

Does it really matter what one believes about such a contentious subject? Why is it so important? Well, it certainly generates lively debate, but there are reasons why believers need clarity about the matter. A biblical view of divine sovereignty and human freedom highlights a host of important matters in the Christian life. It helps us in the following ways:

---

7. John S. Feinberg, *No One Like Him* (Wheaton, IL: Crossway, 2001), 679.

8. Gerhard O. Forde, *The Captivation of the Will: Luther vs. Erasmus on Freedom and Bondage* (Grand Rapids: Eerdmans, 2005), 31.

9. Jerry L. Walls and Joseph R. Dongell, *Why I Am Not a Calvinist* (Downers Grove, IL: InterVarsity Press, 2004), 104; Clark H. Pinnock, "Responsible Freedom and the Flow of Biblical History," in *Grace Unlimited*, ed. Clark H. Pinnock (Minneapolis: Bethany House, 1975), 95.

- Sorting out God's role and our role in matters of salvation.
- Making sense of how regeneration, conversion, and sanctification work.
- Understanding how we should engage in evangelism and discipleship.
- Building greater confidence in God's providential purposes for both history and our individual lives.
- Navigating crucial questions about the existence of evil and whether God or man or even Satan is responsible for it.

The questions can be quite personal:

- If God determines the course of events in my life, how can I be responsible for my actions?
- How can I have a meaningful relationship with God? Doesn't his sovereignty undermine my choice to freely love him?
- Why should I pray, if God has already determined the future? Can my prayers change God's mind? Do my choices have any bearing on the course of the future?
- Do God's commands really matter? If he is sovereign, can't I do whatever I want?
- Isn't divine determinism—another way of speaking of God's absolute sovereignty—really fatalism, so that it doesn't matter what choices I make? Shall I resign myself to "what will be will be," since I can do nothing about it?
- How can I know whether my choices are in or out of the will of God?

The questions are endless, and the unbridled speculation about the answers threatens to wreak havoc on our limited brain capacity.

I am not writing another book about the doctrine of predestination or the problem of evil and suffering. It will become necessary to touch on these topics, but full treatments of them are to be found elsewhere.[10]

10. Good accessible treatments of the doctrine of predestination include R. C. Sproul, *Chosen by God* (Wheaton, IL: Tyndale, 1986); Sam C. Storms, *Chosen for Life* (Wheaton, IL: Crossway, 2007); and David N. Steele, Curtis C. Thomas, and S. Lance Quinn, *The*

Yet few books treat the issue of free will exclusively, especially from a distinctively biblical perspective. Older treatments on the topic are so ponderous that they leave the average reader bewildered—works such as Augustine's *On Free Choice of the Will* and Martin Luther's *The Bondage of the Will*. Other treatments of free will engage in discussing heavy philosophical concepts that make matters worse.

Compatibilism and Libertarianism

I approach this subject from what I believe the Scripture, rightly interpreted, teaches. Nonetheless, it corresponds historically to what Calvinism has taught. Furthermore, the approach taken here is often labeled *compatibilism*. Although the term *compatibilism* is part of the parlance of modern philosophical discourse on this issue, it accurately reflects what the great American colonial pastor and theologian Jonathan Edwards taught. He was the first to thoroughly articulate the ideas of compatibilism in his magisterial tome *Freedom of the Will*, written in 1754.[11] The common alternative view to compatibilism held among theologians is known as *libertarianism*, which is in no way related to the political ideology of the same name. This is the view held by Arminians and open theists.[12] This subject matter is not confined to the domain of theology. Secular philosophers engage

---

Five Points of Calvinism (Phillipsburg, NJ: P&R Publishing, 2004). Good accessible treatments of suffering and evil include chapters 6 and 7 in John M. Frame, *Apologetics: A Justification of Christian Belief* (Phillipsburg, NJ: P&R Publishing, 2015); D. A. Carson, *How Long, O Lord? Reflections on Suffering and Evil* (Grand Rapids: Baker, 2006); and Joni Eareckson Tada and Steven Estes, *When God Weeps* (Grand Rapids: Zondervan, 1997). For a more advanced philosophical and theological treatment, see John S. Feinberg, *The Many Faces of Evil: Theological Systems and the Problem of Evil* (Wheaton, IL: Crossway, 2004).

11. Jonathan Edwards, *The Freedom of the Will*, vol. 1 of *The Works of Jonathan Edwards*, ed. Paul Ramsey (New Haven, CT: Yale University Press, 1957). On Edwards as a compatibilist, see Paul Helm, *John Calvin's Ideas* (Oxford: Oxford University Press, 2006), 164–71; Paul Helm, "Edwards and the Freedom of the Will," available at http://paulhelmsdeep.blogspot.com/2011/02/edwards-and-freedom-of-will.html. Compatibilist beliefs are not monolithic. One need not follow all that Edwards taught to be a compatibilist.

12. Open theism is a radical brand of Arminianism that has been rejected as unorthodox by Calvinists and many Arminians. Open theists virtually deny God's sovereignty as clearly spelled out in Scripture, including his omniscience and other attributes accepted by orthodox Christianity. See the treatment of this movement by Bruce A. Ware, *God's Lesser Glory: The Diminished God of Open Theism* (Wheaton, IL: Crossway, 2000); John M. Frame, *No Other God: A Response to Open Theism* (Phillipsburg, NJ: P&R Publishing, 2001).

in these discussions as well, and the viewpoints span a wide and complicated spectrum.[13] Generally, I will not concern myself with non-Christian viewpoints, even though some significant overlap in ideas occurs.

A distinctly biblical form of compatibilism holds that there is a dual explanation for every choice that humans make. God determines the choices of every person, yet every person freely makes his or her own choices. Thus, divine sovereignty is compatible with human freedom and responsibility. In this model, people are free when they voluntarily choose what they most want to choose as long as their choices are made in an unhindered way. In either case, what people actually choose, whether hindered or not, is determined by a matrix of decisive causes both within and without. Biblical compatibilism says that our choices proceed from the most compelling motives and desires we have, which in turn is conditioned on our base nature, whether good or evil. The more voluntarily and unconstrainedly our choices are made, the more freedom and responsibility we have in making them. Sometimes this is called the *freedom of inclination* because a person is always inclined to make particular choices.

Conversely, libertarianism teaches that free will is incompatible with divine determinism (i.e., God's meticulous decreeing of all things), since this undermines human freedom and responsibility. It should be noted that Arminians do not espouse the incompatibility of human freedom with divine sovereignty. Rather, they hold that divine sovereignty is exercised so that God does not *causally determine* human actions.[14] Libertarian freedom of choice comes about when we have the ability to choose contrary to any prior factors that influence our choices, including external circumstances, our motives, desires, character, and nature, and, of course, God himself. If these prior influences decisively determine choices, then the freedom and responsibility of those choices are hindered. God is in control of history, but he exercises that control

---

13. See Robert Kane, *A Contemporary Introduction to Free Will* (New York: Oxford University Press, 2005); Joseph Keim Campbell, *Free Will* (Malden, MA: Polity Press, 2011).

14. Steve W. Lemke, "A Biblical and Theological Critique of Irresistible Grace," in *Whosoever Will: A Biblical-Theological Critique of Five-Point Calvinism*, ed. David L. Allen and Steve W. Lemke (Nashville: B&H Publishing Group, 2010), 150–51.

so as not to interfere with man's free will. Libertarian free will is often called the *freedom of contrary choice*.

If the libertarian definition of *free will* is correct, then God is limited in his sovereignty. On the other hand, if the compatibilist view of man's will is correct, then it not only is compatible with a robust view of divine sovereignty, but also preserves human freedom and responsibility. I will seek to show how the libertarian view of free will falls short of making sense of human experience and what Scripture teaches. Throughout the book, the main object of my critique is classic Arminianism and its appropriation of libertarian arguments. In contrast, I will devote the larger part of the book to defending a compatibilist perspective on the human will, which I believe is more faithful to Scripture and makes far better sense of our actual experience.

In making the case for compatibilism and against libertarianism, I run up against some unavoidable philosophical concepts and arguments. But my primary goal is not to assess all the complex philosophical arguments, but to show that a broad compatibilist framework better fits the scriptural evidence. The Bible is our decisive authority for judging ultimate truth claims.[15]

The organization of this book is as follows: Chapters 1 and 2 will lay out the libertarian viewpoint and its shortcomings. Chapter 3 will examine what the Bible teaches about God's absolute sovereignty in determining human affairs, including our choices. This chapter precedes the overview of compatibilism in chapter 4, since God's sovereignty is foundational to understanding biblical compatibilism. Chapters 5 and 6 will look at two prominent sets of compatibilistic patterns in the Bible to demonstrate the truth of this perspective. The chapters that follow will seek to flesh out the compatibilist view of the human will, freedom, and responsibility. Along the way, I will discuss how this perspective makes sense of many theological and practical issues that affect our everyday lives. The book is designed to facilitate further study of the topic. With that in mind, I close each

---

15. Many philosophers believe that the arguments for various views on free will and determinism have reached an impasse. But philosophical argumentation is not our final recourse—Scripture is (John 17:17; Col. 2:8).

chapter with a chapter summary and study questions. Most chapters also include a glossary of terms[16] and resources for further study. There is also a full glossary of terms at the end of the book, as well as two appendices. The first appendix is a chart that compares libertarian beliefs with compatibilist beliefs. The second appendix is a review of Randy Alcorn's recent book *hand in Hand: The Beauty of God's Sovereignty and Meaningful Human Choice*, which tackles the same topic. Although Alcorn promotes a compatibilist position, I seek to point out that his perspective differs considerably from traditional biblical compatibilism.

To sort through all the thorny questions and befuddled ideas that surround this topic is daunting, but the rewards are worth the effort. When we enhance our understanding of God's role and our own roles as his plan unfolds for history and our personal lives, it gives us confidence and hope that God is good and wise and powerful and that our choices have meaning and purpose. We are a vital part of what he does in the world. Our choices matter, and what makes this true has everything to do with the manner in which his sovereignty manifests itself in our lives. I trust that this book will be a faithful guide in understanding this truth.

Glossary

Arminianism. A theology associated with the teachings of Jacob Arminius (1560–1609). Arminianism teaches five basic ideas. First, God has predestined to save those whom he foreknows will exercise faith in Christ. Second, Christ's death was an atonement for all mankind regardless of who believes on Christ for salvation. Third, humans in their natural state do not have *free will* or the capacity for saving faith. But, fourth, God has supplied *prevenient grace* to all humans so that they can recover free will and exercise saving faith. This prevenient grace enables them to either cooperate with God's saving grace or resist it if they choose.

16. When unique terms first occur in this volume, they are usually italicized, which means that they are defined in the glossary at the end of the chapter where they occur. Furthermore, most italicized terms in each chapter's glossary are cross-references to other entries, either in the chapter glossary or in the full glossary at the end of this volume.

Fifth, the grace of God assists the believer throughout his life, but this grace can be neglected. Subsequently, the believer can incur the loss of salvation.

Calvinism. A theology that embraces a broad spectrum of ideas associated with the teachings of the Protestant Reformer John Calvin (1509–64). Calvinism, however, is often identified by the five points of Calvinism, traditionally represented by the acronym *TULIP*. The *T* stands for *total depravity*, which indicates that humanity is in bondage to sin. The *U* stands for *unconditional election*, which indicates that God chooses people for salvation wholly apart from anything they do. The *L* stands for *limited atonement*, which indicates that Christ's death secured atonement only for the elect. The *I* stands for *irresistible grace*, which indicates that God draws chosen sinners to salvation irresistibly. The *P* stands for *perseverance of the saints*, which indicates that the elect will certainly persevere in their salvation until the end.

compatibilism. The biblical view that divine *determinism* is compatible with human *free will*. There is a dual explanation for every choice that humans make. God determines human choices, yet every person freely makes his or her own choices. God's causal power is exercised so that he never coerces people to choose as they do, yet they always choose according to his sovereign plan. People are free when they voluntarily choose according to their most compelling desires and as long as their choices are made in an unhindered way. While God never hinders one's choices, other factors can hinder people's freedom and thus their responsibility. Furthermore, moral and spiritual choices are conditioned on one's base nature, whether good or evil (i.e., regenerate or unregenerate). In this sense, one is either in bondage to his or her *sin nature* or freed by a new spiritual nature. See also *soft determinism*.

divine sovereignty. The biblical doctrine that God controls time, space, and history. Calvinists usually hold that God meticulously determines all events that transpire, including human choices. Arminians teach that God limits his sovereign control of events, giving humans significant freedom of choice, which is defined as *libertarianism*. See also *determinism*.

free will (free agency). The idea that humans are designed by God with the capacity for freely making choices for which they are responsible. Most Calvinists and Arminians agree that some kind of free agency is necessary for *moral responsibility*. But each branch of theology defines it differently. Arminians embrace a libertarian notion of free agency. Many Calvinists embrace a compatibilist notion of free agency. See also *compatibilism* and *libertarianism*.

human responsibility. See *moral responsibility*.

libertarianism. The view that *free will* is incompatible with divine *determinism* (i.e., God's meticulous decreeing of all things), which undermines human freedom and *moral responsibility*. God's sovereignty is exercised so that he does not causally determine human actions. Freedom of choice comes about when one has the ability to choose contrary to any prior factors that influence the choice, including external circumstances, one's motives, desires, character, and nature, and, of course, God himself. If these prior influences decisively determine choices, then the freedom and responsibility of those choices are undermined.

moral responsibility. Humans' culpability for their moral choices. A person who does good deserves praise or reward. A person who does evil deserves blame or punishment. Most Calvinists and Arminians believe that some kind of human freedom is necessary for moral responsibility. Also termed *human responsibility*.

Resources for Further Study

F. Leroy Forlines, *Classical Arminianism: A Theology of Salvation* (Nashville: Randall House, 2011). A very readable defense of Arminianism.

Roger E. Olson, *Arminian Theology: Myths and Realities* (Downers Grove, IL: InterVarsity Press, 2006). One of the better defenses of Arminianism.

R. C. Sproul, *Chosen by God* (Wheaton, IL: Tyndale, 1986). A classic defense of the Calvinist view of election.

———. *Willing to Believe: The Controversy over Free Will* (Grand Rapids: Baker, 1997). A survey of the debate over free will in the history of the church.

David N. Steele, Curtis C. Thomas, and S. Lance Quinn, *The Five Points of Calvinism* (Phillipsburg, NJ: P&R Publishing, 2004). An excellent source for Scripture's defense of the five points of Calvinism.

Sam C. Storms, *Chosen for Life* (Wheaton, IL: Crossway, 2007). An engaging defense of the Calvinist view of election. Also treats libertarian and compatibilist views of free agency.

Jerry L. Walls and Joseph R. Dongell, *Why I Am Not a Calvinist* (Downers Grove, IL: InterVarsity Press, 2004). A popular defense of Arminianism and critique of Calvinism.

1

A Road Map for Libertarianism

Walk down Main Street and conduct an informal survey: "Do you believe in free will?" The answer is axiomatic: "Of course; who doesn't?" The rich and the poor, the schooled and the unschooled, the famous and the forgotten, the pretty and the pedestrian—nearly everybody believes in the freedom of choice.

But what does this really mean?

The default answer usually lies along the lines of what is commonly known as *libertarianism*. The word sounds delightful, enlightening, positively liberating. But how many know what it means? What does this elusive ideology about the human will espouse?

Mapping the Debate over Free Will

In order to answer that question, we need to unfold a bigger map of the debate over free will (see fig. 1.1 below). Libertarianism falls within a broader landscape of ideas about freedom and determinism. These ideas can be categorized as *incompatibilist* and *compatibilist* theories.[1] Incompatibilist theories state that freedom and responsibility are incompatible with *determinism*. *Determinism* refers to the idea that all things that occur in our world are necessarily and causally determined by prior conditions. Thus, given specific prior conditions, only one outcome could possibly take place. We live in a cause-effect universe. This is particularly true in the natural world. Gravity causes apples to

1. For overviews of these theories, see Steven B. Cowan and James S. Spiegel, *The Love of Wisdom: A Christian Introduction to Philosophy* (Nashville: B&H Publishing Group, 2009), 226–41; J. P. Moreland and William Lane Craig, *Philosophical Foundations for a Christian Worldview* (Downers Grove, IL: InterVarsity Press, 2003), 265–83.

fall. The right combination of oxygen, fuel, and heat causes fires. When the temperature cools to 32 degrees Fahrenheit, it causes water to freeze.

Few people deny that the natural world follows this strict cause-effect principle.[2] But when it comes to human choosing, there is not so much agreement. In this case, many accept that the act of choosing isn't part of the material world of natural laws. This is true of both libertarians and compatibilists. We should interject here that the sort of determinism that Calvinists hold to is not a physical determinism because God is not a physical being. Furthermore, all Christians hold that our thoughts, beliefs, feelings, conscience, imagination, and so forth reside in the immaterial realm. This comports with Scripture, which speaks of the souls or spirits of persons as being distinct from their material bodies (1 Thess. 5:23). For the Christian, to be "away from the body" is to be "at home with the Lord" (2 Cor. 5:8; cf. 1 Cor. 5:3). At the resurrection, our bodies will be rejoined with our spirits. Accordingly, the act of choosing is not the result of material processes, as a materialist or naturalist might conclude.

Now, among these incompatibilist theories are *hard determinism* and *libertarianism*. Hard determinism holds that human choices are causally determined but incompatible with human freedom and responsibility, which are regarded as illusions. Secular hard determinists (including some materialists) hold that human choices are the result of environmental factors, genetics, brain chemistry, psychological and social conditioning, and so forth.[3] Conversely, libertarianism holds that humans must be free and responsible, which means that our choices cannot be causally determined by forces outside our own control. Libertarianism denies determinism (i.e., choices are indeterministic). See fig. 1.1.

---

2. Some theorists point to the uncertainty principle in quantum mechanics, which seems to support indeterminism at the level of subatomic particles, as support for libertarian free will. See Robert Kane, *A Contemporary Introduction to Free Will* (New York: Oxford University Press, 2005), 132–35. It is unclear whether physicists know enough to say that the uncertainty principle supports indeterminism. Furthermore, it is a leap to suggest that this has anything to do with human choosing.

3. The popular atheist author Sam Harris argues that our choices are the result of mysterious "neurophysiological events" in the brain. We *feel* that we have freedom, but we don't. See *Free Will* (New York: Free Press, 2012).

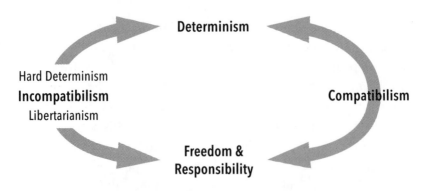

Determinism

Hard Determinism
Incompatibilism
Libertarianism

Compatibilism

**Freedom &
Responsibility**

Fig. 1.1. Incompatibilist and Compatibilist Theories of Free Will

This, then, leaves us with the *compatibilist* theory, which states that determinism is compatible with human freedom and responsibility. Sometimes compatibilism is called *soft determinism*, in contrast to *hard determinism*. In this regard, both hard determinism and soft determinism are deterministic theories, while libertarianism is an indeterministic theory. Human moral responsibility is a matter that virtually all Christians have affirmed and that the Bible clearly teaches. Furthermore, both libertarians and compatibilists would agree that some kind of freedom is necessary in order for human responsibility to make sense. Christian brands of hard determinism affirm human responsibility but reject human freedom. Very few Christians have explicitly embraced this perspective, but some of its thinking creeps into otherwise inconsistent beliefs.[4]

While libertarians and compatibilists agree on the necessity of human freedom, they have fundamental differences about what sort of freedom is necessary for human responsibility. Furthermore, while both Arminians (who are libertarians) and Calvinists (who are compatibilists) affirm the sovereignty of God, they differ in how God exercises his sovereignty in the providential governance of the world. Calvinists believe that God causally determines all that transpires in

4. Many strong Calvinists could be categorized as hard determinists. Hyper-Calvinists would fall into this category as well, but hyper-Calvinism denies not only any sort of human freedom, but also human responsibility. See Phillip R. Johnson, "A Primer on Hyper-Calvinism," available at http://www.spurgeon.org/~phil/articles/hypercal.htm; Timothy George, *Amazing Grace: God's Pursuit, Our Response* (Wheaton, IL: Crossway, 2011), 103–6. For a thorough critique, see Iain H. Murray, *Spurgeon v. Hyper-Calvinism: The Battle for Gospel Preaching* (Carlisle, PA: Banner of Truth, 1995).

the world, whereas Arminians believe that God's providence does not employ causal determinism except in rare cases.

With the scope of the debate set forth, let us now focus our attention on libertarianism. This model of human freedom embraces many nuances, and philosophers advance sophisticated arguments in support of it. Furthermore, not all libertarians agree on the particulars. I will not canvass the thicket of these differences.[5] Rather, I will seek to lay out the basic parameters of what the majority of libertarians hold to—particularly Christian libertarians, who are generally Arminians. Reduced to its core, this concept of free will teaches two fundamental ideas.

Contrary Choice

First, libertarianism teaches that humans are fully capable of making choices contrary to the choices they actually make. This is called the *power of contrary choice*. Arminian theologian Roger Olson declares, "Free agency is the ability to do other than what one in fact does."[6] Norman Geisler states that morally free creatures are able to respond in more than one way in a given situation: "When we did evil we could have *not* done it."[7] Good and evil are both fair game, and each alternative makes itself an equal-opportunity employer for the liberated will.

A person can choose to do what he wants to do, but he can equally choose to do what he *doesn't* want to do. Little Jimmy really doesn't want to eat his broccoli, but he can also choose to go against this prevailing desire and eat it anyway. Libertarianism is far less concerned than compatibilism about the specific reasons *why* Jimmy makes one choice over another. Libertarianism prefers to focus on the rainbow of options in the pantry of human choices. It champions one's power to explore any color he chooses and its multiple variations without being hampered by particular prevailing reasons.

5. See Kane, *Free Will*. For an advanced survey, see Randolph Clarke and Justin Capes, "Incompatibilist (Nondeterministic) Theories of Free Will," in *Stanford Encyclopedia of Philosophy*, ed. Edward N. Zalta, 2014 Spring ed., available at http://plato.stanford.edu /entries/ incompatibilism-theories/.

6. Roger E. Olson, *Arminian Theology: Myths and Realities* (Downers Grove, IL: Inter-Varsity Press, 2006), 71.

7. Norman L. Geisler, *Chosen but Free: A Balanced View of Divine Election* (Minneapolis: Bethany House, 1999), 30 (emphasis in original).

My brother-in-law's family lived in New Zealand for a time. What a life of limitations. When you go to the store in New Zealand to buy shampoo, you don't have long aisles of options to choose from. Selecting shampoo is made simple. By virtue of its extremely narrow options, your purchase is virtually determined for you already. If you like freedom of choice, you don't live in New Zealand; you live in America.

You want to buy shampoo? What kind? Aveda or Aveeno? Maybe Nexxus or Neutrogena will suit you? If not, try Pert or Pantene. The options are bewildering by design, and you get to choose whatever you like—or don't like. That is the triumph of libertarian free will.

Self-Determining Choice

Second, libertarianism teaches that when we have the ability to make alternative choices, they cannot be determined by anything outside the person making those choices. "The essence of this view is that a free action is one that does not have a sufficient condition or cause prior to its occurrence."[8] Olson states that free will is the power of self-determining choice and that "it is incompatible with determination of any kind." This idea amounts "to belief in an uncaused effect—the free choice of the self to be or do something without antecedent."[9] In other words, a self-determining choice is not sufficiently caused by anything prior to the agent who makes a choice. Each person is the "unmoved mover"[10] who alone puts his choices in motion. We might say that he is the first cause (originator) of his own actions.[11]

It is important to note that libertarians don't deny that reasons stand behind our choices. Many things can influence those choices, including both internal and external conditions. For example, we have internal beliefs, values, desires, preferences, motivations, and any number of odd inclinations that can influence the choices we make.[12] But in the end, our strength of will has an unequaled power

8. Jerry L. Walls and Joseph R. Dongell, *Why I Am Not a Calvinist* (Downers Grove, IL: InterVarsity Press, 2004), 103.

9. Olson, *Arminian Theology*, 71.

10. Moreland and Craig, *Philosophical Foundations*, 270.

11. Geisler calls our choices "self-caused." *Chosen but Free*, 30. Philosophers refer to this as *agent-causation*. See Kane, *Free Will*, 44–47.

12. Moreland and Craig, *Philosophical Foundations*, 270.

to overrule all our inner dispositions. Jacob Arminius observed that humanity enjoys "a freedom from necessity, whether this proceeds from an external cause compelling, or from a nature inwardly determining absolutely to one thing."[13]

As strong as Jimmy's hatred for broccoli is, in the end that hatred cannot be said to determine his refusal to eat the dreaded vegetable. He could act against this most powerful desire, slaying it like a dragon, and devour the broccoli with defiance—if he chooses to do so. Thus, human freedom is a fiercely independent enterprise. If Jimmy chooses to eat the broccoli that he doesn't want to eat, his decision isn't determined by anything other than the power and freedom of Jimmy's own will.

We are also affected by external conditions, such as our upbringing, our education, people who exert psychological power, favorable or unfavorable circumstances, rules or laws to govern behavior, persuasive arguments in defense of a particular choice, the lure of the culture, and so forth. While all these internal and external influences can serve as reasons for the choices we make, libertarianism states that no particular reason or set of reasons is *sufficient* to *determine* our choices. Libertarian Bruce Reichenbach notes, "Freedom is not the absence of influences, either external or internal," but "we can still act contrary to those dispositions and choose not to follow their leading."[14] In most cases, compelling reasons might appeal to a person, who then chooses to follow its leading. What cannot happen is that a set of reasons becomes "strong enough to move the [person] decisively to choose one thing over another. Even if a person agrees in light of various reasons and arguments presented that one course of action is preferable, that in no way guarantees that it must be followed."[15] Free will means that we always have alternative choices at our disposal and that we exercise complete control over which alternative we choose. Christian libertarians believe that God endows his creatures with this freedom and that he steadfastly refuses to interfere with it except in rare cases.

---

13. Quoted in Matthew Barrett, *Salvation by Grace: A Case for Effectual Calling and Regeneration* (Phillipsburg, NJ: P&R Publishing, 2013), 226.

14. Bruce R. Reichenbach, "Freedom, Justice and Moral Responsibility," in *The Grace of God and the Will of Man*, ed. Clark H. Pinnock (Minneapolis: Bethany House, 1989), 286.

15. John S. Feinberg, *No One Like Him* (Wheaton, IL: Crossway, 2001), 630.

It is important to note that many libertarians distinguish between reasons and causes. We can have reasons for the choices we make, but those reasons cannot be causal in nature.[16] In either case, if a libertarian agrees that reasons can be construed as causes, we can still act contrary to any such causes. Furthermore, if libertarians maintain that desires, preferences, and so forth determine one's choices (as compatibilists say), then those internal dispositions cannot themselves be determined by any prior conditions, either internal to the person (genetics, nature, etc.) or externally (circumstances, people, etc.). In other words, such desires and inner inclinations must themselves be freely conceived by the choosing agent and able to go in alternative directions. Thus, both our inner inclinations and our subsequent choices are indeterminate. We have the power to exercise control over both.[17]

Necessary and Sufficient Conditions

In order to clarify matters, it is useful to explain the difference between *necessary* and *sufficient* conditions in understanding the libertarian notion of free will. A necessary condition is a prior condition that is necessary in order for something to come about. For example, it is necessary for your car to have gasoline in order to run. Without it, the car will not run. But gasoline is not sufficient to make your car run. Many other conditions must be met as well.

On the other hand, a sufficient condition is that which guarantees that something will come about, but this condition may not be necessary. For example, rain that pours from the sky is sufficient for your front yard to get wet, but it is not necessary. You could turn on your spigot and hose down your yard with water until it is wet, or you could buy hundreds of gallons of gasoline intended to make your car run and pour it out on the yard instead; but that wouldn't be recommended, especially on a hot, dry summer afternoon.

Now, in some cases, for something to come about, the conditions are both necessary and sufficient. For example, how do I know that my brother is in fact my brother? It is a necessary condition that he

16. Ibid., 629.
17. Ibid., 630.

be a male. If he is not a male, he can't possibly be my brother, since the notion of what a brother is includes maleness. His being a male, however, is not a sufficient condition for him to be my brother. There are billions of males in the world, and most of them are not my brothers. It is also a necessary condition that my brother be my sibling. But again, that is not a sufficient condition. Females can be siblings as well, but I have no female siblings. In order for my brother to be my brother, it is necessary that he be both a male and my sibling. These two conditions are both necessary and sufficient in order to secure the fact that my brother is indeed my brother.

How do these matters relate to libertarian freedom? Libertarianism argues that some conditions (reasons, causes) may be necessary for a choice to be made, but they are never sufficient for that choice to be made; otherwise, we are not free. Nonconstraining circumstances, internal desires, available options, persuasive actions of others, and so forth may be necessary conditions for a choice to be made, but they are not sufficient. Only our own power of willing is sufficient to guarantee freely made choices. Even if certain necessary conditions are present, it does not guarantee that a choice will be made.

Same Past, Different Futures

With choices that are indeterminate, given exactly the same conditions, which exist before the point of choosing, multiple futures are possible, depending on the course of action that a person takes.[18] The past in no way determines the future. We cannot change the past, but our free will shapes the future by opening whatever door lies before us.

Suppose that Jane wants her husband, Terry, to buy her a bottle of shampoo at the store because she has run out. She wants to present herself in as good a light as possible in her upcoming job interview. Jane's hair can get really frizzy, and she prefers not to take any chances. Before she lost her job, she bought an expensive brand of shampoo at the hair salon. She has found that nothing works better to tame her hair. But now the money is tight, so without appearing anxious, she

18. See Robert Kane's "garden of forking paths" in *Free Will*, 7.

leaves the choice of which shampoo to buy up to Terry. Terry knows that Jane is on edge about her appearance for the interview, and he has always struggled to please her.

What will Terry do?

All these conditions (in addition to others) form contributing factors in whatever choice he might make. With free will, he can allow all, some, or none of them to influence his decision. The settled conditions of the past and all its powerful forces that shape present circumstances cannot hold a free person hostage. Whatever Terry decides to do is not *necessitated* by his circumstances, his wife's feelings, or even his own feelings. He can make whatever choice *he* decides on. There may be any number of reasons why Terry makes the choice to buy Jane her shampoo. One obvious reason may be her request. Another may be the fact that she asked him to buy shampoo specifically for frizzy hair. Finding the closest store for shampoo may be another reason. Looking for the least expensive shampoo may be yet another reason.

Now, even though these may be regarded as necessary causes for choosing the shampoo, none of them are sufficient for Terry to make the choice. For example, he may decide to drive to a different store from the one he first considered. After discovering three different types of shampoo for frizzy hair, he may decide to buy the most expensive brand. Or he might ignore his wife's request and buy shampoo for dry hair. Perhaps he feels constrained to make another choice because there are no shampoos for frizzy hair. Libertarianism says that Terry doesn't need to act on any of these reasons. For that matter, he could forget the shampoo and decide to buy spaghetti sauce instead. He is not chained to any particular choice for any particular decisive reason. Nothing is allowed to compel or determine the choice he makes.

Two points need to be made in light of this. First, libertarianism doesn't entail the idea that people can actually do *whatever* they want. The laws of nature constrain us. You can't lift a two-ton truck above your head. Standing in the open prairie won't stop that tornado from putting you into the next county. Furthermore, sometimes other forces hinder one's freedom. If your bank goes belly-up, you may not get your money back. You surely desire that pretty girl's attention, but she won't give you the time of day. You strive to understand what a difficult Bible passage means, but ferreting out the complications overwhelms you. And may God forbid that you should be a captain of a freight ship off the coast of Somali when pirates kidnap you and hold you for ransom. Thus, there are occasions when freedom is constrained or denied altogether. In that case, some antecedent conditions such as these do have varying degrees of power to *determine* what choice a person makes. People are free only when they can escape these constraining conditions.

Second, libertarians affirm that a person's character and even circumstances generally indicate the sorts of choices that the person is likely to nake. Terry is likely to choose based on the internal and external conditions that push him toward what is best. A girl whose life has been shaped by parents who taught her to remain chaste will likely choose to remain chaste in future situations. She has the option to rebel, of course, but that is less likely. In either case, she made the choices that led to the development of her chaste character in the first place. She could have resisted the outside influence of her parents, but she didn't. Now, even though choices are shaped by one's character, this doesn't limit such choices to only one option. A person who has a proclivity for acting horribly has many horrible options. Likewise, a person who is known for kindness has many kind options to freely choose from. Nonetheless, such a person could choose unkindness, and nothing prevents that from happening.

God's Providence and Our Freedom

How does this conception of free will relate to the Arminian view of God's providential power? Arminians embrace libertarian freedom, but they also affirm God's sovereignty. Arminian theologian Roger Olson says that God exercises sovereign control of events by means of his strong persuasion or influence. But he claims, "Free and rational creatures have the power to resist the influence of God. This power was given to them by God himself."[19] The thrust of the libertarian

---

19. Olson, *Arminian Theology*, 131; F. Leroy Forlines, *Classical Arminianism: A Theology of Salvation* (Nashville: Randall House, 2011), 47–51, 78–86.

argument here is simple. God cannot be in control of our choices while at the same time we are in control. Since it is intuitively obvious that we are in control of our choices, this rules out any notion that God controls what we do. This is not to say that God lacks the power to control our choices. It simply means that he doesn't, for the sake of maintaining our liberty.[20]

This is especially true in the matter of salvation. Arminians claim that the influence of God is a *necessary condition* for a person to exercise saving faith. Leroy Forlines rejects the idea that "man can choose Christ without the aid of the Holy Spirit." He says that "no matter how much or how strong the aid of the Holy Spirit may be, the 'yes' decision [to choose Christ] is still a decision that can be rightly called the person's decision. Also, he could have said no."[21] In other words, although the influence of God's grace is *necessary* for a person to make the choice of believing Christ for salvation, it is not *sufficient* for that choice to be made.[22] God's grace is critical for salvation in the Arminian view, but it cannot by itself guarantee that sinners will cooperate with it through their power of choosing. The notion of human cooperation with God indicates that salvation is synergistic, meaning "multiple agents (God and man) working (*ergon*) with (*syn-*) one another."[23] This is in contrast with Calvinism, which teaches that salvation is monergistic, meaning "one (*mono-*) agent working (*ergon*)." In this case, salvation is solely the work of God's grace.

This has important ramifications in other debates about salvation, sanctification, and eternal security. Classical Arminianism believes in the possibility of the loss of salvation. In order to procure salvation, a sinner must cooperate with God's grace by exercising his free will. Furthermore, he must continue to persevere in that grace as a Christian. If at some point he fails to do so, he can experience the loss of his salvation. Again Forlines states, "While there is divine aid [grace] for

20. Some Arminians argue that on rare occasions God intervenes so as to disable, as it were, the libertarian freedom of his creatures in order to accomplish some important purpose. For example, some would argue that Pilate was not free to disallow the crucifixion of Jesus.

21. Forlines, *Classical Arminianism*, 52.

22. Paul Helm, "The Augustinian-Calvinist View," in *Divine Foreknowledge: Four Views*, ed. James K. Beilby and Paul R. Eddy (Downers Grove, IL: InterVarsity Press, 2001), 169–70.

23. The Greek word *ergon* is the source of our word *energy*, which can also mean "work."

the Christian it is possible for him to resist this aid and make wrong choices. Among these wrong choices is the possibility of turning back to unbelief."[24]

Freedom Is the Absence of Coercion

Libertarianism holds that only indeterminate choices can be free of coercion. If external influences were sufficient to determine a person's choices, then those choices would be coerced, undermining freedom and responsibility. If we are to be free and responsible, then our choices must originate from our own autonomous power of willing unhindered by the force of any cause decisively directing us toward a particular choice. This doesn't mean that some choices might not be coerced. As mentioned before, many forces constrain freedom. For example, during World War II, many Japanese prison-camp guards and officers exhibited violent psychopathic behavior that left many veterans of these prison camps to suffer post-traumatic stress disorder (PTSD). For years after the war, flashbacks, nightmares, and the triggering of panic attacks (called *hyperarousal*) in which one suddenly relives the terror of his experiences became recurring plagues among these former POWs. They were unavoidable no matter how intensely the victims wished to resist them or make them go away.[25]

Even positively compelling influences constrain the will if they cannot be overcome. Benjamin asks, "Should I marry Joanna or not?" What liberates Benjamin is the power of the will to choose either option—to marry or not to marry. If Benjamin decides to marry Joanna, he must be free to determine that choice unhindered by prior factors. Of course, he may choose to marry her because her beauty and intelligence overcome him. But freedom is enhanced if he marries her *ultimately* because he could have resisted the compelling power of her desirable qualities. If only one option presents itself as the compelling

24. Forlines, *Classical Arminianism*, 314. See also Robert E. Picirilli, *Grace, Faith, Free Will* (Nashville: Randall House, 2002), 211–32; Grant R. Osborne, "Soteriology in the Epistle to the Hebrews," in *Grace Unlimited*, ed. Clark H. Pinnock (Minneapolis: Bethany House, 1975), 144–66.

25. See, for example, the story of the celebrated Olympian and World War II veteran Louis Zamperini in Laura Hillenbrand, *Unbroken: A World War II Story of Survival, Resilience, and Redemption* (New York: Random House, 2010).

choice, then it is not a choice at all. There must be equal alternative possibilities for a choice to be free and meaningful.

Biblical Support

In order to support this theory of free will, Christian libertarians appeal to the host of biblical passages that demand obedience to God's commands, invite responses to offers of blessing when the right choice is made, or warn of impending judgment when the wrong choice is made. When Joshua calls forth, "Choose this day whom you will serve" (Josh. 24:15), he appears to assume the power of contrary choice. When Paul encourages financial stewardship among the believers at Corinth, he states, "Each one must give as he has decided in his heart, not reluctantly or under compulsion, for God loves a cheerful giver" (2 Cor. 9:7). This statement suggests that options exist with our choices, and that the capacity to choose alternatives rests within our own self-determining power to will one choice or another. Furthermore, it suggests that if something other than our own power to will determined our choices, then we would be choosing under compulsion and not freely.

Contrary choice also appears to be present in the "whosoever will" texts that implore the indiscriminate masses of sinful human beings to place their faith in Christ for salvation.[26] The two quintessential verses in this regard come from the pen of the apostle John. In his Gospel he writes, "For God so loved the world, that he gave his only Son, that whoever believes in him should not perish but have eternal life" (John 3:16). Jerry Vines tells us that the Greek term for *whoever* (*pas*) is nonrestrictive. It demonstrates the possibility that "anyone . . . anywhere . . . anytime" has the power to believe. He claims, "To say otherwise is to make a travesty of this verse."[27] Revelation 3:20 pictures

---

26. Steve W. Lemke, "A Biblical and Theological Critique of Irresistible Grace," in *Whosoever Will: A Biblical-Theological Critique of Five-Point Calvinism*, ed. David L. Allen and Steve W. Lemke (Nashville: B&H Publishing Group, 2010), 122–27; Bruce R. Reichenbach, "God Limits His Power," in *Predestination and Free Will: Four Views of Divine Sovereignty and Human Freedom*, ed. David Basinger and Randall Basinger (Downers Grove, IL: InterVarsity Press, 1986), 104.

27. Jerry Vines, "Sermon on John 3:16," in *Whosoever Will: A Biblical-Theological Critique of Five-Point Calvinism*, ed. David L. Allen and Steve W. Lemke (Nashville: B&H Publishing Group, 2010), 24.

Christ as exhorting all within earshot: "Behold, I stand at the door and knock. If *anyone* hears my voice and opens the door, I will come in to him and eat with him, and he with me."[28] For many, it would appear superfluous for Christ to make such an invitation unless we had libertarian freedom.

More importantly, why would God put forth these open invitations if he had already determined the outcome of all human actions? Libertarianism is unequivocal—God would not issue commands and conditional promises if he had already set the future in stone. Reichenbach notes, "Commands to act properly and sanctions imposed on improper conduct only make sense if humans have freedom. God places before us his obligations and at the same time has created us free to accept or reject them."[29]

We also read about people's resisting God's commands and desires for us. Stephen cries out in his final sermon before being stoned to death: "You stiff-necked people, uncircumcised in heart and ears, you always *resist* the Holy Spirit. As your fathers did, so do you" (Acts 7:51; cf. Isa. 63:10).[30] After the Israelites made the dreaded golden calf, God complained to Moses: "And the LORD said to Moses, 'I have seen this people, and behold, it is a *stiff-necked* people. Now therefore let me alone, that my wrath may burn hot against them and I may consume them, in order that I may make a great nation of you'" (Ex. 32:9–10). Fearing God's fierce retribution, Moses prays fervently that God would not act on his word. So powerful was Moses' effect on God that we read: "And the LORD *relented* from the disaster that he had spoken of bringing on his people" (32:14). This episode suggests that God does not determine all things and that the force of one's freely exercised will can change God's mind and the subsequent course of the future.

Consider how Jesus' desires are thwarted by the resistance of the Jews when he laments: "O Jerusalem, Jerusalem, the city that kills the prophets and stones those who are sent to it! How often would I have

28. See also Isa. 55:1; Jer. 33:3; Joel 2:32; Matt. 7:24; 10:32–33; Mark 16:15–16; John 4:13–14; 6:40; 7:37–38; 11:26; 12:46; Acts 2:21; 8:36–37; Rom. 9:33; 1 John 2:23; 4:15; Rev. 22:17.
29. Reichenbach, "God Limits His Power," 104.
30. See also Pss. 78:10; 81:11–13; Matt. 23:37.

gathered your children together as a hen gathers her brood under her wings, and you would not!" (Matt. 23:37). God does not always see his desires fulfilled. He is "not wishing that any should perish, but that all should reach repentance" (2 Peter 3:9), while at the same time he "desires all people to be saved and to come to the knowledge of the truth" (1 Tim. 2:4). Libertarians argue that God never forces anyone to conform to his desires. They must come freely, and this means that God risks their rejection.

Another interesting passage of Scripture used to support libertarianism is 1 Corinthians 10:13, where Paul teaches, "No temptation has overtaken you that is not common to man. God is faithful, and he will not let you be tempted beyond your ability, but with the temptation he will also provide the way of escape, that you may be able to endure it." The assumption here is that in the midst of temptation, God helps us out by placing a detour in our path. On the one hand, we can succumb to the path of temptation, or we can take the alternative route that God graciously provides. It is up to us which choice we make.

From passages such as these, it is argued that the Bible presupposes libertarian free will; otherwise, they lose their force. C. S. Lewis asked the perennial question: Why would God make his creatures this way? "Because free will, though it makes evil possible, is also the only thing that makes possible any love or goodness or joy worth having. A world of automata—of creatures that worked like little machines—would hardly be worth creating."[31] Furthermore, in order to maintain such a world, God must purposely limit his sovereignty, intervening only when absolutely necessary.

What are we to make of libertarianism? Is it really the best way to make sense of how God created us and interacts with us? We will consider these questions in the next chapter.

Chapter Summary

Libertarianism teaches that free will is incompatible with God's meticulously determining all things, because this undermines human

---

31. C. S. Lewis, *Mere Christianity* (New York: Macmillan, 1952), 49.

freedom and responsibility. It posits that one has the ability to choose contrary to any prior factors that influence (but don't sufficiently determine) our choices, including external circumstances, our motives, our desires, and, of course, God himself. If divine determinism is true, then human freedom and responsibility are hindered. Choices are self-determined. We are the unmoved movers of our own actions. Our choices can go in alternative directions. Given exactly the same past conditions, different futures could result if we could choose again. God exercises his sovereign control so as not to interfere with this notion of free will. Libertarians believe that the Bible presupposes such free will when it issues commands that include blessings for obedience and consequences for disobedience.

Glossary

contrary choice. A basic idea in *libertarianism* that humans can always choose contrary to any prior influences that might direct their choices. Given exactly the same set of circumstances, no particular choice or outcome is guaranteed.

determinism. The idea that all events and human choices are necessarily and causally determined by prior conditions. The world operates in a definitive cause-effect reality. Calvinists believe that God's sovereignty is deterministic and stands behind all that transpires in the world. Arminians deny that God's sovereignty is deterministic. See also *divine sovereignty* and *hard determinism*.

hard determinism. The concept that all human choices are necessarily determined by prior conditions, which may include God's sovereignty. Hard determinists believe that human freedom is incompatible with *determinism* and that it is therefore an illusion. Some hard determinists reject *moral responsibility*, while others say that human freedom is not necessary for responsibility. See also *hyper-Calvinism*.

hyper-Calvinism. A deviant form of *Calvinism* that denies any human freedom or *moral responsibility*, usually with respect to matters of faith and repentance. Hyper-Calvinists embrace *hard determinism* and discourage open invitations to sinners to believe on Christ for salvation. God's love is restricted only to the elect.

incompatibilism. The idea that human freedom is incompatible with *determinism. Hard determinism* and *libertarianism* are incompatibilist views. Hard determinists believe that every human choice is determined and that this is incompatible with human freedom, which is an illusion. Libertarians say that human choices are free and that this is incompatible with determinism of any kind.

monergism. In *Calvinism*, the idea that salvation is the result of "one (*mono-*) agent working (*ergon*)." In this case, salvation is solely the work of God's grace. See also *synergism*.

necessary condition. A prior condition that is necessary in order for something to come about. While something may be necessary in order to bring about a particular outcome, it may not be sufficient. Gasoline is necessary for a car to run, but it is not sufficient, since other conditions are also necessary. See also *sufficient condition*.

self-determining choice. The idea in *libertarianism* that choices are self-determined or self-caused. Nothing outside the person making the choice can be the decisive cause for choices made. Humans are the sole originators of their own choices.

soft determinism. Another name for *compatibilism*, the idea that choices are necessarily determined, yet compatible with human freedom and responsibility.

sufficient condition. A prior condition that is sufficient in order for something to come about. While something may be sufficient in order to bring about a particular outcome, it may not be necessary. A rainstorm may be sufficient to wet a lawn, but it is not necessary. Gasoline can wet a lawn as well. See also *necessary condition*.

synergism. In *Arminianism*, the idea that salvation is the result of "multiple agents (God and man) working (*ergon*) with (*syn-*) one another." Humans must cooperate with God's grace in order to be saved. See also *monergism*.

Study Questions

1. Without consideration to what the book says, how would you define *free will* for human beings? What does it mean to make free choices?
2. What is the meaning of *determinism*?

3. What is the difference between incompatibilist and compatibilist theories regarding determinism and ideas about human freedom and responsibility?

4. What is *hard determinism*?

5. *Soft determinism* is another name for what?

6. What two fundamental ideas does libertarianism teach?

7. What is the difference between a *necessary condition* and a *sufficient condition*? Provide your own examples of each.

8. Given that the same past conditions exist, will the future always be the same? Why or why not?

9. What do Christian libertarians believe about God's determination of human choices? Does God have limited power to control the future? Does God impose self-limitations on his power?

10. What does libertarianism believe about the relationship between choices that are determined and the idea of coercion? Do you agree with this assessment?

11. Does the Bible support libertarian freedom? Why or why not?

Resources for Further Study

Steven B. Cowan and James S. Spiegel, *The Love of Wisdom: A Christian Introduction to Philosophy* (Nashville: B&H Publishing Group, 2009), 226–41. Good overview of the free-will debate from a Calvinist perspective.

Robert Kane, *A Contemporary Introduction to Free Will* (New York: Oxford University Press, 2005). Good overview of the free-will debate from a secular perspective.

J. P. Moreland and William Lane Craig, *Philosophical Foundations for a Christian Worldview* (Downers Grove, IL: InterVarsity Press, 2003), 265–83. Good overview of the free-will debate from an Arminian perspective.

Roger E. Olson, *Arminian Theology: Myths and Realities* (Downers Grove, IL: InterVarsity Press, 2006). One of the better defenses of Arminianism and libertarian freedom.

Jerry L. Walls and Joseph R. Dongell, *Why I Am Not a Calvinist* (Downers Grove, IL: InterVarsity Press, 2004). A popular defense of Arminianism and libertarianism.

2

Assessing the *Whys* of Libertarianism

People entertain an intuitive sense that our actions originate within ourselves and that we enjoy a freedom to choose in any direction we wish. This explains why libertarian free will seems so obviously true to most people. For example, if you go to McDonald's to buy a Big Mac, are you committed by some mysterious force to make only that choice? Surely you could have chosen Chicken McNuggets instead. What's the big deal? Why can't little Jimmy just as easily choose to eat his broccoli as refuse it? It doesn't appear to require the redirecting of planetary orbits for Jimmy to make one choice or the other.

But do we have this power of contrary choice? Compatibilists argue that every choice has reasons that are absolutely determinative. You can choose Chicken McNuggets instead of a Big Mac *only* if you have a *different* and *compelling* reason for doing so. Jimmy doesn't refuse his broccoli without a sufficient set of reasons before making this choice. If libertarianism were true, then factors that supply reasons for one choice could also lead to an opposite choice.[1] Poor ole Jimmy hates the color, the taste, and the feel of broccoli as it wedges its way down his ever-constricting throat. This sensory repulsion drives the reason why he refuses to eat it. But can this hatred be the same reason he eats it anyway? This idea should raise anyone's suspicious eyebrows.

1. Bruce A. Ware, *God's Greater Glory: The Exalted God of Scripture and the Christian Faith* (Wheaton, IL: Crossway, 2004), 85–86.

People are rarely indifferent to the choices they make. Libertarianism risks choices that verge on being made randomly. To strip choices of sufficient causes (reasons) is to strip them of all meaning.[2] And this leaves us with a world of chance.[3] You might get lucky. Then again, you might not. According to R. C. Sproul:

> In a technical sense nothing occurs by chance, for chance has no being and can exercise no power. . . . It is one thing to say that we do not know what causes a given effect; it is quite another to say that nothing causes the effect. Nothing cannot do anything because it is not anything.[4]

Libertarians would dispute this claim. Most would argue that choices do have sufficient causes—they are self-caused (i.e., by agent-causation). In other words, the people who choose are the "irreducible causes of their actions."[5] But to say that choices are self-caused does not answer the question about what causes our choices. It is self-evident that our choices in some way originate with ourselves.[6] Rather, it is hard to see that choices somehow spring whole cloth out of the person's choosing without having other prior causes that become part of the necessary and sufficient causal nexus if those choices are to be made. If no other decisive reasons exist for the choices we make, what distinguishes them from being random acts? If Terry can sever himself from all the reasons that influence his decision about Jane's shampoo,

2. R. C. Sproul, *Willing to Believe: The Controversy over Free Will* (Grand Rapids: Baker, 1997), 164.

3. John Byl, *The Divine Challenge: On Matter, Mind, Math and Meaning* (Carlisle, PA: Banner of Truth, 2004), 201–9, 211–12, 215. *Chance* refers to the factor involving occurrences that have no sufficient causes. For a more detailed response to the problem of choices involving chance, see Steven B. Cowan and James S. Spiegel, *The Love of Wisdom: A Christian Introduction to Philosophy* (Nashville: B&H Publishing Group, 2009), 233–36.

4. Sproul, *Willing to Believe*, 162.

5. Joseph Keim Campbell, *Free Will* (Malden, MA: Polity Press, 2011), 74. Philosophers say that there are three main kinds of libertarianism: (1) noncausal; (2) event-causal; and (3) agent-causal theories. Ibid., 74–86. It seems that most Arminians fall into the third category, and thus my critique focuses on that view.

6. John Feinberg, "John Feinberg's Response [to Norman Geisler]," in *Predestination and Free Will: Four Views of Divine Sovereignty and Human Freedom*, ed. David Basinger and Randall Basinger (Downers Grove, IL: InterVarsity Press, 1986), 87.

what compels him to buy shampoo at all? He might come home with a jar of spaghetti sauce instead.

Thus, if people had libertarian free will, they wouldn't resemble free persons at all. We can't go so far as to say that they would resemble "erratic and jerking phantom[s], without any rhyme or reason at all," as one critic announced,[7] but the control that they exercise over their choices would appear to be severely hampered. People could never really be certain of why they chose as they did, nor could they predict with any amount of certainty what they might choose next. A pilot who must land his airliner has multiple and complex decisions to make, each following a specific sequence and protocol. But if his choices always involved the possibility of chance, who would ever board that plane?[8]

Yet matters are worse than this.

If our choices have the possibility of being cut off from our circumstances, desires, motives, beliefs, and so forth, then in what sense can we say that choices come from ourselves at all?[9] The response of many libertarians to this dilemma is that our choices in the end cannot be fully explained.[10] The whole matter becomes a mystery.[11]

The power of contrary choice is dubious on the face of it, but many Christians have championed libertarianism for other reasons. Namely, it appears to provide an attractive solution to a number of thorny issues that Christians face. There are three principal reasons why libertarians think this account of human action makes sense. They claim that free will is what (1) establishes a meaningful relationship with God; (2) undergirds moral responsibility; and (3) rescues God from being culpable for evil. Let us consider each of these points and some of the problems they pose.

7. Richard Taylor, *Metaphysics* (Englewood Cliffs, NJ: Prentice-Hall, 1974), 51, quoted in Byl, *The Divine Challenge*, 216.

8. This illustration is borrowed from Byl, *The Divine Challenge*, 216.

9. James S. Spiegel, *The Benefits of Providence: A New Look at Divine Sovereignty* (Wheaton, IL: Crossway, 2005), 69.

10. Cowan and Spiegel, *The Love of Wisdom*, 236.

11. Robert Kane, *A Contemporary Introduction to Free Will* (New York: Oxford University Press, 2005), 42, 44, 48. It seems that most of the sophisticated philosophical versions of libertarian free will go to great lengths to avoid these charges. In my opinion, they involve equivocating definitions and perplexing arguments involving unrealistic hypothetical conditions that render the theories unpersuasive.

Libertarianism Establishes a Meaningful Relationship with God

According to libertarians, only if we are free to accept or reject God can we have a meaningful relationship with him. Roger Olson states, "The main reason Arminians reject the Calvinist notion of monergistic salvation, in which God unconditionally elects some to salvation and bends their wills irresistibly, is that it violates the character of God and the nature of a personal relationship."[12] If our love for God is determined, this must mean that it is either mechanistically programmed or coerced against our will. If either notion were true, then love would be stripped of its value. Greg Boyd muses, "If love is the goal [of creation], what are its conditions? . . . The first condition of love [is] that it must be freely chosen. It cannot be coerced. Agents must possess the capacity and opportunity to reject love if they are to possess the genuine capacity and ability to engage in love."[13]

While persuasive on the surface, this argument is problematic. It seeks to counter a caricature of what a determinist God would have to do in order to get his creatures to love him. Thaddeus Williams has answered this charge.[14] Suppose that someone is necessarily compelled by God to tell him, "I love you." Williams indicates that this can result from one of only three possible conditions.[15]

The first condition is mechanistic programming. Williams notes that the popular Christian radio personality Hank Hanegraaff often uses this caricature. Hanegraaff argues that if God determines our love, then we are like the old Chatty Cathy dolls that say "I love you!" when God pulls the string.[16] How can love be expressed toward

---

12. Roger E. Olson, *Arminian Theology: Myths and Realities* (Downers Grove, IL: Inter-Varsity Press, 2006), 38.

13. Greg A. Boyd, *Satan and the Problem of Evil* (Downers Grove, IL: InterVarsity Press, 2001), 52, quoted in Mark R. Talbot, "True Freedom: The Liberty That Scripture Portrays as Worth Having," in *Beyond the Bounds*, ed. John Piper, Justin Taylor, and Paul Kjoss Helseth (Wheaton, IL: Crossway, 2003), 87.

14. See Thaddeus J. Williams, *Love, Freedom, and Evil: Does Authentic Love Require Free Will?* (New York: Rodopi, 2011).

15. Ibid., 27ff.

16. See also Steve W. Lemke, "A Biblical and Theological Critique of Irresistible Grace," in *Whosoever Will: A Biblical-Theological Critique of Five-Point Calvinism*, ed. David L. Allen and Steve W. Lemke (Nashville: B&H Publishing Group, 2010), 156.

God if he mechanically dictates what his creatures will do? Such a person is no more than a computerlike entity programmed to perform automatic functions. The second condition is divine coercion. In this case, a person is forced to mouth the words against his or her will. This is tantamount to theistic totalitarianism. The third condition is a powerful heart desire. Here the person says "I love you" because of such strong internal affections for God that he or she cannot fathom acting any other way.

Note that in each scenario, the statement "I love you" is *necessarily* determined by the response of the three prior conditions. In the first scenario it results from purely mental programming—a kind of cultic mind control. In the second scenario, it results from pure coercion and an inescapable fear of consequences. In the third scenario, it results from a compelling heart desire. Libertarians and compatibilists agree that the first two scenarios are illegitimate responses for a truly loving and meaningful relationship with God. To suggest that either is the view of Calvinists is to set forth a straw man. Yet that is not true of the third scenario. Such a person loves voluntarily and without coercion and yet does so as a necessary result of deterministic causes. Libertarianism rejects this because it teaches that we must be free from the compelling force of all desires, motives, inclinations, passions, and the like. Thus, as Williams argues, libertarianism entails freedom from our own hearts.[17]

Let me explain. In libertarianism, Rachel could never say that she chose Christ because in her heart she was compelled to love him and accept his claims (John 8:42). Neither can she say that she didn't choose Christ because she was compelled to hate him and reject his claims (vv. 37, 44). Rather, all Rachel can say is that she chooses to either love him or hate him. Either choice can be made with equal ease because neither love nor hate is allowed to determine the will one way or another without interfering with one's freedom. If Rachel has a desire to place her faith in Christ, she cannot act on her heart's desire without first entertaining the equally legitimate option of *not* desiring to do so. If she entertains *only* the desire but not the lack of such a desire, then her desire is a hindrance to her freedom.

17. Williams, *Love, Freedom, and Evil*, 41.

Libertarianism would have us believe that such indeterminate choices are the basis for meaningful relationships. Truly meaningful relationships, however, are compelled out of a necessity driven by one's heartfelt desire to love. True love does not act with indifference to options but with headlong devotion in a single direction. In fact, all meaningful choices spring from such singular zeal to pursue the one choice that is clearly better than any other. In the doctrine of regeneration, God softens our hearts (Ezek. 36:26) and by his kindness leads us to repentance (Rom. 2:4). This produces a compelling inner desire to love him. And while this is a necessary result of God's determination, in no way can it be construed as a forced response against one's will. In fact, the voluntary nature of the response is what makes love meaningful, not that one could act differently. In heaven, the believer will love God with undeterred devotion without the possibility of even the slightest hint of acting contrarily (see chapter 12).

Intra-Trinitarian Love

This relational dynamic is demonstrated by intra-Trinitarian love (see John 17:22–26). According to Thaddeus Williams:

> There is a reason that the Trinitarian formula was never Uncle, Nephew, and Holy Spirit, or Boss, Employee, and Holy Spirit, or President, Citizen, and Holy Spirit. None of these capture the magnitude of interpersonal love that exists between the divine Persons. "Father and Son" shows something of the vast and beaming love relationship of which even our best father-son relationships are only a small blurry reflection.[18]

God the Father and his Son, Jesus, do not have the freedom to hate each other. They love each other necessarily because their nature and character compel them to do no other. Both *willingly* love with *irresistible* intentions, and that is precisely what makes their relationship significant.

18. Thaddeus Williams, "What Does Nicea Have to Do with Geneva?" (unpublished paper, n.d.), 2, available at http://www.monergism.com/thethreshold/sdg/Nicea%20and%20 Geneva.pdf.

Furthermore, it is out of this intra-Trinitarian love that we come to understand God's love for the elect. We read this in John 6:37: "All that the Father gives me will come to me, and whoever comes to me I will never cast out."[19] God's love for us stems from the fact that he loved the Son and desired to give a people to him as a gift of his love. Williams says, "Peer behind your decision to come to Jesus and you will find a Father generously in love with His divine Son."[20] He further explains how John 6:37 enhances our view of the Trinitarian work of salvation and its compatibilistic nature:

> Once it sinks in that our belief in Jesus originates because of the Father's love for His Son, we can never again think of the Trinity as some kind of abstract, black-and-white, strange math equation where three somehow equals one. Rather, the doctrine becomes something precious and practical. It bursts with color. It becomes a cool ocean to plunge into after we have followed John's map upstream from our rivers of faith and discovered their ultimate Source in the Triune God of love. Non-Calvinism cannot lead us to this ocean. Non-Calvinism reverses John's verbs. All who come (present) to the Son [with their autonomous free power] will be given (future) by the Father. For John, however, we do not believe to become love-gifts; we believe because we are gifts. "All" the Father gives will come to the Son. For John it lies beyond the scope of possibility that anyone the Father wants to give His Son as a living, conscious, worshipping "I love you" would not, in fact, come to the Son.[21]

Yet here we encounter a profound irony. In order for God to extend his love to the elect, he had to "crush" (Isa. 53:10) his beloved Son under the weight of his wrath. Imagine the grief that this brought the Father, even as the Son cried out on the cross, "My God, my God, why have you forsaken me?" (Matt. 27:46). In that brief moment of

19. Note that *gives* is a present-tense verb that secures the fact that whoever is given *comes* (future).

20. Williams, "Nicea," 5.

21. Ibid.

time, Jesus was separated from his Father, whose holiness could not look on the Son while he absorbed the full mass of our unholy sin (2 Cor. 5:21). This divine abandonment reaches such disconcerting depths that it stands far beyond our cognitive pay grade. While it seemed that the universe might shatter in that awful moment, we must realize that it took place on our behalf.

A steep price was paid in order for the triune God to secure this love-gift of a people for Christ. It was not a frivolous plan. Rather, it was the only plan that could achieve redemption, and God willingly designed and executed it on our behalf because of his love for the Son and then for us. Likewise, Jesus embraces the work of redemption because of his love for the Father (John 14:31) and then for us. He saw "the joy set out for him" and willingly "endured the cross, disregarding its shame" (Heb. 12:2 NET). The joy set before Christ was knowing the reward that he would receive after making the supreme sacrifice. The love-gift of the redeemed are his reward, the ones whom he brings to glory (Heb. 2:10).[22]

These redemptive acts can mean only that once the triune God's love has been extended to us in salvation, it is unfathomable to imagine that he would rescind it (John 14:21; Rom. 8:32, 35–39) or that we could resist it. Williams makes the point clear:

> The atonement is effective because intratrinitarian love is not defective. Why is grace irresistible? Because if we could shun the Father's grace as He draws us to worship His Son, then we have the power to thwart God's expression of love within the Trinity. Grace cannot be resisted because His Trinitarian love cannot be frustrated. . . . The saints are preserved because the Divine Persons perfectly fulfill one another's will.[23]

What is more, the love that exists between God and his chosen children is magnified when we realize that his grace transformed his recalcitrant enemies so that we would freely love him in turn (Rom. 5:6–11; 1 John

---

22. John Piper, *Desiring God* (Sisters, OR: Multnomah, 1996), 117.
23. Williams, "Nicea," 8.

4:19). Grace reveals that we were previously *unwilling* and *unable* to love him. We deserved nothing but wrath. Thus, it is not a freedom of indifference that provides the basis for a meaningful relationship with God, but rather a freedom of irresistible inclination initiated by the tender mercies of the Almighty and the love that forges an unbreakable bond within the Godhead. That same unbreakable love flows freely into the hearts of the redeemed.

Libertarianism Provides the Foundation for Moral Responsibility

Arminians teach that only libertarian free will can adequately allow moral responsibility. When a person acts with moral good, he deserves praise. When he acts with moral evil, he deserves blame. Libertarianism believes that praise or blame is meaningful only when a person is able to act in a contrary way.[24] Suppose that Mary drives 20 mph over the speed limit. She is responsible for breaking the law, but only because she had the choice to obey the speed limit instead. If Mary's breaking of the law was somehow determined by anything other than her own choosing, she is not liable for her actions. On another occasion, Mary is praised for stopping alongside the highway to help a stranded motorist, but only because she had the choice to keep driving on by. What gives Mary moral responsibility is that nothing compelled her to act with such kindness outside her self-determined act of will.

This argument is unpersuasive. Mary is held liable for speeding not because she could have done otherwise, but because her *intention* to drive above the speed limit broke the law.[25] In Western jurisprudence—influenced as it is by a Judeo-Christian ethic—crimes are assessed based on one's motives, not contrary choice. In this regard, libertarians confuse necessity with coercion. As we saw previously, compatibilism demonstrates that to act in love is a necessary result of strong desires, yet it is not something forced against one's will. Now, if Mary was forced against her will to exceed the speed limit, then of course her

24. Jerry L. Walls and Joseph R. Dongell, *Why I Am Not a Calvinist* (Downers Grove, IL: InterVarsity Press, 2004), 104; Norman L. Geisler, *Chosen but Free: A Balanced View of Divine Election* (Minneapolis: Bethany House, 1999), 31.
25. Byl, *The Divine Challenge*, 228–29.

liability is considerably lessened. No disagreement exists here. Maybe her estranged boyfriend Jerry was chasing her down to do her harm, so she began to speed up to avoid a confrontation. But to act necessarily as a result of compelling motives is not in most cases coercive.

The problem is that in the libertarian scheme, motives don't determine choices. Every act must be free not from motives per se, but from the sufficient causal power of motives. But that is not how the law works. If Mary commits a crime with no discernible compelling motive or sufficient reason, but it appears to be an arbitrary act, then it is hard to assess her liability for the crime. In a court of law, such individuals usually make an insanity plea. Guilt and culpability are applied only when a driving motive is uncovered. Unfortunately, in the libertarian perspective of free will, everybody would risk acting out of insanity.

Furthermore, consider that our system of jurisprudence makes distinctions in various cases of one person's killing another. First-degree murder, which carries the greatest consequences, is applied to homicides that proceed from malice aforethought. Suppose that Mary hated her estranged boyfriend Jerry and ran him down in her car while he walked to work. She would be guilty of first-degree murder. Second-degree murder applies if one acted with intent to harm but not to kill. There was no planned intention to carry out murder; rather, it happened as a matter of course. Suppose that Mary wanted to maim Jerry with her car but didn't want to kill him, yet he died anyway. In this case, the punishment is less severe because of the absence of a precalculated intent to kill Jerry.

From here we move further down the criminal-intent ladder. Voluntary manslaughter is a lesser crime in which harm may or may not have been intended but death resulted because of extenuating circumstances. Here the perpetrator acted "in the heat of the moment," usually with some kind of provocation. Suppose that Jerry started to pound the hood of Mary's car as it slowly approached him; Mary got mad and pushed the accelerator, which caused the car to run Jerry down and kill him. Conversely, one is charged with involuntary manslaughter when no intent to harm at all is determined. In this case, suppose that Mary hit and killed Jerry with her car because she didn't notice him in her blind spot while turning the corner.

In libertarianism, to be free is to express a certain degree of indifference about the choices that one makes. You must have the power to choose one action or another such that no action carries any particular compelling preference. If this is true, then no action carries any consequence worthy of notice either. Bad choices could not be justly blamed and good choices could not be justly praised because neither would be preceded by sufficient causal intentions of the person making the choice.

Sam Storms illustrates the problem:

> How could a man be praised for preferring charity or stinginess, for example, if both deeds were equally preferable to him, or more accurately, lacking any preferability at all? Do we not praise a man for giving generously to the poor because we assume he is of such an antecedent character that such a deed appears more preferable to him than withholding his money? If there is nothing about the man that inclines him to prefer generosity, if the act of giving money is no more preferable to him than the act of withholding it, is he worthy of praise for giving?[26]

The answer: Of course not. We praise a man's good actions because they proceed from a heart with good intentions. Likewise, we blame him for his wicked actions because his heart harbors wicked intentions. In meaningful relationships, love is praised not because it is expressed as an indifferent duty but because it comes from a heart overflowing with affectionate desires. Loraine Boettner said, "If after every decision the will reverted to a state of indecision and oscillation equipoised between good and evil, the basis for confidence in our fellow man would be gone."[27]

In Scripture, God holds sinners liable because of their intentions, not because of their freedom to choose otherwise.[28] "All the ways of

---

26. Sam C. Storms, "The Will: Fettered Yet Free," in *A God Entranced Vision of All Things*, ed. John Piper and Justin Taylor (Wheaton, IL: Crossway, 2004), 205.

27. Loraine Boettner, *The Reformed Doctrine of Predestination* (Philadelphia: Presbyterian and Reformed, 1932), 220.

28. Scott J. Hafemann, *The God of Promise and the Life of Faith* (Wheaton, IL: Crossway, 2001), 136.

a man are clean in his own sight, but the LORD weighs the *motives*" (Prov. 16:2 NASB; cf. 1 Sam. 16:7). "I the LORD search the heart and test the mind, to give every man according to his ways, according to the fruit of his deeds" (Jer. 17:10; cf. 20:12). The global flood was divinely orchestrated to destroy mankind because "every *intention* of the thoughts of his heart was only evil continually" (Gen. 6:5). Jesus locates the source of our sin not in our actions, but in our hearts. Thus, a man commits adultery in his heart long before he commits it in deed (Matt. 5:28). Jesus excoriated the Pharisees, who sought to justify themselves before others by their external behavior. But Jesus says, "God knows your hearts" (Luke 16:15; cf. Acts 1:24; Rom. 8:27). Consider David's counsel to his son: "And you, Solomon my son, know the God of your father and serve him with a whole heart and with a willing mind, for the LORD searches all hearts and understands every plan and thought" (1 Chron. 28:9). Solomon is held responsible for the intentions of his heart and the degree of his willingness to serve God. God is not interested in mere obedience. He wants our hearts. True Christianity is exercised by way of the affections of the heart, not mere conformance to a standard of ethics.

On the surface, Simon the sorcerer wanted something good, the power to bestow the Holy Spirit upon others. Yet he sought to buy this power with money. Note the response of the apostle Peter:

> May your silver perish with you, because you thought you could obtain the gift of God with money! You have neither part nor lot in this matter, for your heart is not right before God. Repent, therefore, of this wickedness of yours, and pray to the Lord that, if possible, the *intent* of your heart may be forgiven you. For I see that you are in the gall of bitterness and in the bond of iniquity. (Acts 8:20–23)

Simon's moral responsibility rested with the intentions of his heart. But notice something else in Peter's reply. He indicates that Simon is "in the bond of iniquity." The implication is that Simon sinned because he could do no other. He acted out of necessity because he was a slave of sin (John 8:34; Rom. 6:16–22). Sin is a root problem of the heart, which is the person's mission-control center directing the will (Prov. 4:23; Matt. 7:17–20; 12:33–35). Accordingly, people are not sinners because they choose to sin; rather, they choose to sin because they are sinners. The sinful heart is the cause of sinful choices, not the unfettered freedom of the will.

Ought Implies Can

Norman Geisler repeats a variant argument for moral responsibility. He writes, "Moral obligations imply that we have self-determining moral free choice. For *ought* implies *can*. That is, what we ought to do implies that we can do it. Otherwise, we have to assume that the Moral Lawgiver is prescribing the irrational, commanding that we do what is literally impossible for us to do."[29] For example, how can Simon the sorcerer repent of his sin if he is in bondage to it? Should God hold him culpable for that which he cannot do?

But suppose that Cory borrowed $500 from Corina and was unable to pay her back; that certainly doesn't excuse him from his obligation. Likewise, God is not obligated to dismiss our debt to him simply because we cannot repay it.[30] God demands our moral perfection (Matt. 5:48), and yet we are morally unable to do that which pleases him (Rom. 8:7–8). Humans are by nature in rebellion against God not just because we are under a curse (Rom. 5:17) and can do no other, but also because we heartily approve of our rebellious actions (Ps. 2:2–3; Rom. 1:32). One's inability to act contrary to his sinful nature does not abrogate his culpability, since he also acts voluntarily (intentionally).

Consider Paul's admonition in 1 Corinthians 4:5: "Therefore do not pronounce judgment before the time, before the Lord comes, who will bring to light the things now hidden in darkness and will disclose the *purposes* of the heart. Then each one will receive his commendation from God." The praise or blame that men receive from God is directly tied to the motives of their hearts, not their freedom of contrary choice or moral abilities. This applies to God's actions as well. The fact that God necessarily acts righteously and cannot sin doesn't mean that

---

29. Geisler, *Chosen but Free*, 30 (emphasis in original).
30. Robert L. Reymond, *A New Systematic Theology of the Christian Faith* (Nashville: Thomas Nelson, 1998), 454.

he is somehow undeserving of praise. We magnify God and praise his worthy deeds for the precise reason that he acts with unwavering righteousness and is incapable of acting any other way.

Libertarianism Rescues God from Instigating Evil

Libertarianism charges that if God is the ultimate determiner of human action, then he must be culpable for sin and evil, thus making God evil. This presents the most difficult challenge for determinists (and compatibilists) to answer. If God is all-good (omnibenevolent) and all-powerful (omnipotent), then why is there evil in the world? No one can escape the quagmire posed by this question. Whether you've lost a child in infancy, watched a drunken father abuse your mother, witnessed your house being wiped out by a hurricane, or wondered why thousands of innocent New Yorkers lost their lives on September 11, 2001, we all wrestle with deeply troubling aspects of this question.

The problem is illustrated this way. Imagine the senseless beating of a homeless man to death on the streets of the city. In this case, the Calvinist God is likened to a Mafioso-styled mayor who calls for this sort of evil.[31] Even though the mayor didn't directly conduct the beating, he is responsible because he called for one of his thugs to do it. Here God is a cosmic Vito Corleone, the evil mastermind of villainy. This picture represents libertarians' coup d'état, from which they believe Calvinists can never recover. Roger Olson observes that such a God "is at best morally ambiguous and at worst a moral monster hardly distinguishable from the devil."[32]

Conversely, Olson seeks to show how libertarianism rescues God from evil: "He values the liberty he gave his human creatures, and he will not abrogate it even though it means sin and evil enter creation. God permits, but does not will or cause, sin and evil."[33] Evil was a risk that God had to allow in order to preserve human freedom and responsibility. But Olson's account doesn't solve the dilemma. If God merely "permits" evil and knows that it will take place, then the

31. John M. Frame, *Apologetics: A Justification of Christian Belief* (Phillipsburg, NJ: P&R Publishing, 2015), 170.

32. Roger E. Olson, *Against Calvinism* (Grand Rapids: Zondervan, 2011), 84.

33. Olson, *Arminian Theology*, 106.

Arminian God is like a police officer who stands by idly while the homeless man in our illustration is being beaten to death. He didn't order the killing, but neither does he stop it.

It is important to understand that Arminianism doesn't deny God's omnipotence. Olson states, "God is sufficiently powerful to stop anything from happening, but he does not always exercise that power, because to do so would be to rob his free and rational creatures, created in his image, of their distinct reality and liberty."[34] Thus, libertarian freedom is a greater virtue for God to maintain than the prevention of evil. If the police officer is asked why he doesn't stop the beating, he has to say, "I am sorry, I can't do that; otherwise, I would violate the perpetrator's free will, and that would be a greater crime than stopping his senseless violence."

The Arminian supposes that God limits his sovereign power over evil, and yet somehow this doesn't abrogate his loving concern for those who suffer. Scott Hafemann responds:

> To limit God's love to empathy is to leave the evil of our world unchecked and beyond God's control and hence without an ultimate purpose. If God enters into the affairs of history only after they take place, or merely empathizes with them from afar, then evil itself remains meaningless. From this perspective, all we can say when evil strikes is that we happened to be in the wrong place at the wrong time under the wrong circumstances, all of which has nothing to do with God's will. Moreover, since evil is not just an occasional event but also characterizes the human heart, this means that God, for all intents and purposes, is fenced off from our entire lives.[35]

Libertarianism fails to exonerate God from liability for evil. The point is inescapable for both Arminians and Calvinists: if God permits evil, then at some level he concurs with its existence. Now, maybe God is powerless to prevent evil. But then evil or the source of evil would

34. Ibid., 132.
35. Hafemann, *The God of Promise*, 140.

be more powerful than God. That is unfathomable to all Christians, Arminians and Calvinists alike. If evil prevailed unabated and God were powerless against its onward rush, then we would be a race to be pitied. Our world would be like a carousel uplifted from its foundation, whirling out of control. Whom could we turn to for recourse?

No one.

Thus, if God doesn't prevent the evil that prevails, then he must have some purpose for its existence. But how does this exonerate God from the charge of being culpable for evil? Let us consider an answer.

The Good God's Purposes for Evil

One thing is certain for both parties in this dispute. Since God is perfectly benevolent, we know unequivocally that he cannot think or act in any evil manner. So the best way to respond to the question of who is culpable for evil is to return to what has already been stated. Evil proceeds from the motives and intentions of one's heart (James 1:14–15; cf. Gen. 6:5; Jer. 17:9). We cannot overestimate the importance of this truth. God *never* has evil motives or intentions; therefore, he cannot think or act with evil. The apostle John is clear: "This is the message we have heard from him and proclaim to you, that God is light, and in him is no darkness at all" (1 John 1:5).

Note carefully that this is not the same thing as saying that God cannot ordain evil to take place. As hard as it is to fathom, God can ordain evil without having evil intentions. James 1:13 affirms two important related propositions: "God cannot be tempted with evil, and he himself tempts no one." If God is not tempted to do evil, then it follows that he has no evil disposition whereby he can tempt others.

A key to understanding the apparent dilemma is found by considering the story of Joseph's enslavement by his brothers. When Joseph is promoted to be the prime minister of Egypt, many years after his brothers perpetrated their evil against him, they are providentially reunited with him. They stand shocked, suffering guilt and trembling with fear before their exalted brother. Then Joseph makes this iconic statement: "As for you, you meant evil against me, but God meant it for good" (Gen. 50:20). This is a dual (compatibilist) explanation for their actions. Joseph has already acknowledged that his brothers sold him into slavery in Genesis 45:4. But in the verses that follow, he says that God sent him to Egypt as well (vv. 5, 7–9; cf. Ps. 105:17). Which was it—his brothers or God? The answer: Both.

But a more profound point is revealed in the statement. Joseph's brothers acted with an evil *intention* ("you meant evil"), as they themselves rightly recognize (cf. Gen. 50:15, 17). Yet God brought about the same result, but with a different *intention*. His motive was good—"God meant it for good." Culpability can be attributed to Joseph's brothers because they intentionally purposed evil. God sovereignly purposed the same event, but his intention was good, and therefore he has no culpability for the evil that occurred.

The mechanics of how this is carried out remain a mystery that Scripture doesn't explain. D. A. Carson observes that God's causal relationship to good and evil is not identical or *symmetrical* as though he were amoral (i.e., neither good nor evil). Since God's fundamental nature is good, not evil, his relationship to good and evil must be *asymmetrical*. God stands behind what is good in such a way that it is always directly attributed to him. He stands behind evil only in a distant, secondary way so that it cannot be directly attributed to him, only to secondary agents or causes.[36] God wills good simply for the sake of good. But when he wills evil, he never does so for the sake of evil, but because it is necessary to achieve some good purpose. In speaking about the evil that befell Job, Scott Hafemann explains, "God is not sometimes good and sometimes evil, depending on his mood. God *always* acts in love, even when he was moved . . . to destroy [Job] without cause (Job 2:3)."[37]

When God decrees that which is righteous and good, it seems that he often directly "stirs up the spirits" (see Hag. 1:14) of those who act in accordance with his intentions.[38] In at least some cases in which God decrees evil, however, it appears to happen by sending evil spirits

36. D. A. Carson, *How Long, O Lord? Reflections on Suffering and Evil* (Grand Rapids: Baker, 2006), 189. See also Paul Helm, *The Providence of God* (Downers Grove, IL: Inter-Varsity Press, 1994), 190–91.

37. Hafemann, *The God of Promise*, 139 (emphasis in original).

38. See D. A. Carson, *Divine Sovereignty and Human Responsibility: Biblical Perspectives in Tension* (Atlanta: John Knox: 1981), 16.

to stir up people to act, as in the case of Satan and Job. According to 2 Samuel 24:1, God incited David to number Israel even as David acknowledged that doing so was a sin (v. 10). But the parallel passage in 1 Chronicles 21:1 indicates that Satan incited David to do this (cf. Ps. 105:24–25).

No matter how God carries out these decrees, we must be content in knowing that he doesn't always provide answers for every instance of evil. This is difficult, since we curious creatures want to know the secrets of God, and because prideful creatures demand answers. The message of the book of Job is very sobering on this count. When Job cries out, "Why?" in the midst of his intense suffering, the essence of the divine response takes our breath away—*I am God and you are not.* Those words can be easily choked on, and we should not be so blithe in stating them. There are depths to these matters that we simply cannot plumb. Much more will be said about the problem of evil and God's purposes for it in the next chapter.

The Foreknowledge Problem

Libertarianism faces another problem related to the foreknowledge of God. Classical Arminians affirm what is called *simple foreknowledge.* After God created the world, he obtained exhaustive foreknowledge of all future events, including human actions as well as his own actions. This sort of knowledge is what some call *precognition* or *prescience.* In other words, God looks at the future as if peering through a time telescope at what will actually happen, yet without determining what happens. In order to maintain the orthodox doctrine of omniscience, Arminians know this means that nothing could possibly happen apart from God's knowledge.[39] What is also of interest is how God's foreknowledge relates to his providential control of future events.

The Arminian position has several problems. First, if our choices are indeterminate and able to go equally in alternative directions, then they are unpredictable and therefore unknowable before they occur. Thus, how can God know our choices before they take place? If God

---

39. See Ps. 139:4; Isa. 42:9; 44:7; 46:10; Jer. 1:5; Dan. 2:28; Matt. 24:36; Mark 8:31; John 6:64; 18:4; Acts 2:23; Rom. 8:29; 1 Peter 1:20.

knows that you will choose to go to church this Sunday, is it possible for you to fool God and choose not to go at the last minute? Under libertarianism, you would have to say yes, and it is hard to see how this doesn't deny God's omniscience. In order to have libertarian freedom, you must be able to go to church or refrain from going to church, but God's foreknowledge could render only one of those choices certain. Therefore, one must dispense with either libertarian freedom or God's foreknowledge. Most orthodox Christians cannot imagine doing the latter. Martin Luther called this problem the "bombshell [that] knocks 'free will' flat, and utterly shatters it."[40]

Second, simple foreknowledge denies that God could have libertarian freedom, which Arminians regard as critical for meaningful relationships with his creatures. How could God deliberate about what he plans to do in response to our choices if he already knows what he will do?[41] That would be an empty exercise. But the problem doesn't end here. Suppose that God sees that you plan to skip church on Sunday and he doesn't like that idea. But he would not be able to intervene and try to persuade you otherwise, since this would change the future that he already infallibly sees. God could never use his knowledge of the future to adjust his plans in response to anything that his creatures do, since what he will do is already fixed by way of his foreknowledge.[42]

Of course, Arminianism holds that God could intervene in human affairs to prevent some evil from happening, but he chooses not to in most cases in order to preserve his creatures' libertarian free will. This may be the case with inexcusable church-skipping. But Arminianism faces an inescapable dilemma. If its view of foreknowledge is consistent, then God cannot intervene to prevent evil; for if God *infallibly foreknows* that some evil will occur in the future, then that evil *will* occur, and not even God can do anything to change it. This severely limits God's sovereignty beyond what most Arminians would favor. On the other hand, if the Arminian view of foreknowledge somehow does not prevent

---

40. Martin Luther, *The Bondage of the Will*, trans. J. I. Packer and O. R. Johnston (Grand Rapids: Fleming H. Revell, 1957), 80.

41. John S. Feinberg, *No One Like Him* (Wheaton, IL: Crossway, 2001), 744–45.

42. Ibid., 746.

God from intervening when he knows that evil will occur, then what stops him from doing so? Can he not be accused of condoning evil?

Open theists embrace libertarian freedom for many of the reasons Arminians do. But they have acknowledged these problems, and thus they deny that God can know the future choices of human beings. They believe that God has exhaustive knowledge of the past and present but not the future. Open theism has rightly come under serious fire from both Calvinists and Arminians for its denial of God's omniscience and cannot be regarded as orthodox at all. If libertarianism is true, however, then open theism appears to have developed more consistent and logical arguments in its favor than classical Arminianism has.[43]

Who Determines the Future?

Another problem arises for this view of foreknowledge. Arminians claim that God knows the future but doesn't causally determine the future. If God knows the future, however, then it is necessarily fixed and therefore causally determined by something. It can't be determined by the future choices of humans because those choices on the basis of divine foreknowledge are also necessarily fixed before they occur. If God didn't determine the fixity of the future, then some other force independent of God did. In this case, two options are left open.

First, some other being or beings have determined what the future will be, making it or them more powerful than God. This, of course, amounts to idolatry and must be rejected (Isa. 46:9–11). Second, if someone other than God didn't determine the future, then we are left with some impersonal force (e.g., fate) that has no plan or purpose. This position leads to fatalism, which teaches *que sera sera* ("what will be will be").

In both these cases, not only is God's absolute power and knowledge undermined, but also his status as absolute Creator of all things is

---

43. Other libertarians who reject open theism have also acknowledged these problems and have adopted a view called *Molinism*, or *middle knowledge*. I cannot assess their arguments here, but suffice it to say that it faces some of the same basic problems of the simple foreknowledge view. See ibid., 747–52; Bruce A. Ware, *God's Lesser Glory: The Diminished God of Open Theism* (Wheaton, IL: Crossway, 2000), 38–42; John M. Frame, *The Doctrine of God* (Phillipsburg, NJ: P&R Publishing, 2002), 501–5.

toppled. Nothing stands outside of God in power or purpose. This is why no faithful Christian will want to orient himself toward any other horizon. And so libertarianism finds itself on the horns of a dilemma when faced with the problem of God's foreknowledge.

Ironically, some believe that theistic determinism leads to fatalism itself. But this is untrue. Fatalism is an aberrant form of determinism,[44] and most forms of determinism hold that particular causes lead to particular effects. The ends are directly tied to the means to those ends. But James Anderson observes that in a fatalist worldview, "events will turn out a certain way *no matter what we do*. The central idea here is that future events (at least the major life-impacting ones) are fixed in such a way that *our choices are irrelevant*; those events aren't dependent on, or affected by, our decisions or actions to any significant extent."[45]

If a soldier's fate is to suffer a deadly bullet wound in battle, it doesn't matter what precautions he takes; the bullet will kill him regardless. Compatibilism says that one's actions have both *immediate* and *ultimate* causes and that they are not in contradiction to one another. In other words, if God *ultimately* determines that a bullet will kill a soldier, it will also be true that the *immediate* temporal circumstances conspire in such a way that it will happen. But if the circumstances were different—the bullet took a slightly different path or the soldier wore bulletproof armor or he acted alertly against the enemy—then the outcome would be different as well: the soldier would survive. And that, too, would correspond to God's determined plan.

Concluding Thoughts on Libertarianism

Libertarian freedom seems intuitively true because we aren't always consciously aware that God is determining our actions. Rather, we are aware that our actions are willingly made as a result of our own deliberations. We are indeed the tangible initiators of our own actions and thus fully responsible for them. Because we are always conscious of this reality, it appears to preclude any notion that God

44. Some philosophers say that fatalism should not be considered a form of determinism at all.

45. James Anderson, "Calvinism and Determinism," available at http://www.proginosko.com /2014/07/calvinism-and-determinism/ (emphasis in original).

could simultaneously determine the same actions. The two notions seem incompatible and contradictory. How can there be two separate explanations for the same act? How can Pharaoh harden his heart and yet God harden his heart at the same time? It seems that either some form of incompatibilist (hard) determinism must be true or libertarianism must be true.

Instead, we will see that the data of Scripture point us toward compatibilism. If we are reflective Christians, then we rarely make choices without some consciousness of God's presence and activity in our personal lives. When human events transpire, especially those that have significant implications for life, we readily and rightly attribute them to God's power and control. We draw comfort from a sovereign God because we instinctively know that he is good and powerful and has a wise plan. We have no reason to think that history will spiral out of control. Christians don't barter in arbitrariness.

Yet many bristle against God's sovereignty the moment it interferes with a desire for personal autonomy. Many prefer to think that we creatures know what is in our best interest, and they can't be (or don't *want* to be) sure that the Creator knows any better. They want to be the captains of their own souls, to control their own destiny, to escape the lordship of God. Such people seek to live independently and to take credit for any achievements they attain. Even as Christians, we are sometimes tempted to take credit for our belief in Christ and our spiritual growth, even though we should sense something amiss about this desire.

Herein lies a subtle pride that veers dangerously close to works-righteousness and self-sufficiency. Does libertarianism degenerate into this sort of thinking? Of course, no careful Christian, libertarian or otherwise, wishes to affirm a man-centered gospel. Nonetheless, without presuming the motive behind libertarianism, I fear that such a gospel is being sneaked through an obscure opening at the back of the stage. I believe that a biblically framed compatibilism eviscerates any subtle boasting that mitigates the force of genuine saving theocentric grace. God's thoroughgoing sovereignty fully complements his self-sufficing grace, and neither denies the freedom and responsibility of man. I will now turn to a defense of this perspective.

Chapter Summary

Libertarians claim that their definition of *free will* makes the best sense of three crucial realities. First, it says that only if we are free to accept or reject God can we have a meaningful relationship with him. If love for God is determined by God, then that love would be exercised by some sort of mechanical manipulation or sheer coercion. But meaningful love for God is exercised voluntarily and without coercion and yet as a necessary result of deterministic causes. People love God because they *want* to love him more than not. At the moment of choosing, they cannot act otherwise. Singular headlong devotion for the person one loves is the only basis for a meaningful relationship.

Second, libertarians argue that the freedom of contrary choice underscores moral responsibility. Only if one could have acted otherwise in a given situation is he morally responsible for his actions. Yet the Bible locates human culpability in the intentions of the heart, not contrary choice.

Third, libertarians argue that self-determined choices rescue God from being culpable for evil. But the Bible teaches that God ordains evil actions without being culpable because he always has good intentions for them.

Libertarianism also suffers from another problem. If our choices are indeterminate, then they are unpredictable and therefore unknowable before they occur. Thus, how can God know our choices before they take place? If God foresees that you will make a particular choice in a particular circumstance, is it possible for you to fool God and choose otherwise? Under libertarianism, you would have to say yes, and it is hard to see how this doesn't deny God's omniscience.

Glossary

fatalism. An aberrant form of *determinism* stating that future events are fixed in such a way that human choices are irrelevant. What will be will be, and there is nothing that anyone can do about it.

foreknowledge. In classic theism, God's exhaustive knowledge of all future events before they transpire. Arminians embrace simple foreknowledge or divine prescience: God looks down the corridors of time and sees all that will happen. Calvinists agree, but add that God predetermines all that he foresees.

open theism. A radical form of *Arminianism* that embraces *libertarianism* but denies orthodox doctrines that classical theism embraces. Namely, open theists deny that God has exhaustive *foreknowledge* of the future. The future is "open." God acts and reacts in response to what humans do and changes his plans accordingly.

Study Questions

1. Why does the libertarian view of human freedom seem so intuitively true?

2. Are people ever indifferent about the choices they make? Explain why or why not.

3. If choices do not have sufficient prior causes, are they real choices? Explain why or why not.

4. Can anything occur by chance? Explain why or why not. Does libertarian free will embrace the possibility of chance?

5. What are the three principal reasons why Christians have embraced libertarian free will?

6. Libertarians would say that if a Christian's love for God is determined, then it must be the result of one or the other of what two conditions? If these conditions were true, do you agree that love for God would be meaningless? Why or why not?

7. Thaddeus Williams argues that there is another way to think about love for God that is determined, yet also meaningful. Explain his argument.

8. How does the libertarian argument for moral responsibility go against most systems of Western jurisprudence?

9. What does the Bible teach about human culpability?

10. Why is the "*ought* implies *can*" argument faulty from a biblical perspective?

11. Why is the "problem of evil" difficult to solve for both Arminians and Calvinists?

12. Why does Roger Olson believe that libertarianism rescues God from being culpable for sin and evil? Is his argument persuasive? Why or why not?

13. From a Calvinist and compatibilist perspective, how can God determine evil and yet not be culpable for it? Do you agree? Why or why not?
14. How is the issue of God's foreknowledge a problem for Arminian libertarians?
15. Is divine determinism the same thing as fatalism? Why or why not?

Resources for Further Study

D. A. Carson, *How Long, O Lord? Reflections on Suffering and Evil* (Grand Rapids: Baker, 2006). A thoughtful, theological, and pastoral perspective on the problem of evil.

John S. Feinberg, *The Many Faces of Evil: Theological Systems and the Problem of Evil* (Wheaton, IL: Crossway, 2004). A thorough theological and philosophical treatment of the problem of evil for the advanced student.

———. *No One Like Him* (Wheaton, IL: Crossway, 2001). One of the best critiques of libertarianism. See especially chapters 13 through 16. More philosophical.

John M. Frame, *Apologetics: A Justification of Christian Belief* (Phillipsburg, NJ: P&R Publishing, 2015). Chapters 7 and 8 provide a good treatment of the problem of evil.

———. *No Other God: A Response to Open Theism* (Phillipsburg, NJ: P&R Publishing, 2001). Chapter 8 provides a seventeen-point critique of libertarianism.

Joni Eareckson Tada and Steven Estes, *When God Weeps* (Grand Rapids: Zondervan, 1997). A very encouraging biblical response to evil and suffering from one who has experienced it firsthand.

Thaddeus J. Williams, *Love, Freedom, and Evil: Does Authentic Love Require Free Will?* (New York: Rodopi, 2011). Excellent critique of the libertarian argument that free will is necessary for a meaningful relationship with God.

3

How Big Is Your God?

Some years ago J. B. Phillips wrote a cleverly titled book, *Your God Is Too Small*. This captures reality for far too many Christians. Our view of God has everything to do with how we view ourselves. John Calvin opens his magisterial work *Institutes of the Christian Religion* with these words: "True and sound wisdom consists of two parts: the knowledge of God and of ourselves."[1] Later he says, "It is certain that man never achieves a clear knowledge of himself unless he has first looked upon God's face, and then descends from contemplating him to scrutinize himself."[2] Before we can achieve a genuine view of our humanity, we must come to grips with the majesty of God. We must gaze upon the greatness of his person as he has revealed himself in Scripture.

If we are to understand biblical compatibilism, we must uncover the depth and breadth of its foundation—God's absolute sovereignty. This is where we begin our exploration.

A Portrait of God's Sovereignty

The sort of sovereignty envisioned by Arminians and other libertarians is one in which creation enjoys a strong independence from its Creator. God exercises his control in a way that is conditioned on his creatures' activities as he acts and reacts according to their freely exercised choices. His providence does not require predetermination of what happens in history. He purposely limits his power in order

1. John Calvin, *Institutes of the Christian Religion*, ed. John T. McNeill, trans. Ford Lewis Battles (Philadelphia: Westminster, 1960), 1.1.1.1, 35.
2. Ibid., 1.1.1.2, 37.

to preserve human free will.[3] He maintains a general plan for the future, but that future is significantly affected by what humans decide to do. Only on occasion does God directly intervene in the course of history.[4] Arminians would say that God is a macromanager, not a micromanager. Unfortunately, mankind is placed at the center of God's orbit in this scenario.

A careful perusal of the Bible, however, unveils a stark and stupendous portrait of a God that is far more magnificent. The Creator is at the center of Scripture's conceptual universe, exercising unyielding lordship over all that he has made, which exists to serve and glorify him. A. W. Pink offers this definition of God's sovereignty: "To say God is sovereign is to declare that he is the Almighty, the Possessor of all power in heaven and earth, so that none can defeat his counsels, thwart his purpose, or resist his will."[5] When the Bible unfolds God's supreme control, it speaks of a glorious choreographer who causally determines the course of history in a way that is not conditioned on anything that his creation or creatures do. Rather, the whole panorama of the cosmos is entirely dependent on his meticulous guidance. His foreordination of all things was forever settled before the foundations of the earth were laid, and nothing can change this fact. He neither established his plan by consulting the future choices of his creatures nor alters it by considering what they have already done.

The Scripture is replete with passages that paint just such a portrait of God. As the psalmist exults, "The LORD has established his throne in the heavens, and his kingdom rules over all" (Ps. 103:19). And again: "Our God is in the heavens; he does all that he pleases" (115:3). Moses declares God's ownership rights over the vast expanse of the universe: "Behold, to the LORD your God belong heaven and the heaven of heavens, the earth with all that is in it" (Deut. 10:14). Note the comprehensiveness. It includes the earth and all its material

---

3. Roger E. Olson, *Arminian Theology: Myths and Realities* (Downers Grove, IL: Inter-Varsity Press, 2006), 131.

4. Jack W. Cottrell, "The Nature of the Divine Sovereignty," in *The Grace of God and the Will of Man*, ed. Clark H. Pinnock (Minneapolis: Bethany House, 1989), 106–13.

5. A. W. Pink, *The Sovereignty of God* (Grand Rapids: Baker, 1984), 19.

substance, every living creature, and the whole host of humanity, as Psalm 24:1 indicates.

We can be certain that nothing stands outside the overarching hands of an omnipotent God. The apostle Paul is emphatic on this point: God "works all things according to the counsel of his will" (Eph. 1:11).[6] In other words, nothing escapes discussion and planning by the Godhead in the divine boardroom, nor the Trinity's thorough execution of those plans in the theater of play. The "all things" that Paul speaks of is qualified in the previous verse. It refers to "things in heaven and things on earth" (v. 10). This speaks of the two all-encompassing domains of God's rule.[7] In other words, God's sovereign execution of his blueprint for history is comprehensive and exhaustive.

As R. C. Sproul often quips, not a single atom or "maverick molecule" is out of place in God's universe. He determines the outcome of every occurrence extending from the broad panorama of history (Dan. 2:21; Acts 1:7)[8] to the minutest detail of everyday existence (Ps. 139:16; James 4:13–16).[9] Jesus notes, "Are not two sparrows sold for a penny? And not one of them will fall to the ground apart from your Father" (Matt. 10:29). Solomon proclaims, "The lot is cast into the lap, but its every decision is from the LORD" (Prov. 16:33). Nothing happens by chance; even the throw of the dice is determined by God.

Paul pours a sobering thought on the Athenian philosophers, who were known to be inebriated in the arrogance of their intellectual powers:

> The God who made the world and everything in it, being Lord of heaven and earth, does not live in temples made by man, nor is he served by human hands, as though he needed anything, since he himself gives to all mankind life and breath and everything. And he made from one man every nation of mankind to live on all the face of the earth, having determined

6. See John S. Feinberg, *No One Like Him* (Wheaton, IL: Crossway, 2001), 680–93, for an extensive exposition of Ephesians 1:11.

7. Peter O'Brien, *The Letter to the Ephesians* (Grand Rapids: Eerdmans, 1999), 112.

8. See also 1 Kings 12:15; 1 Chron. 29:10–12; 2 Chron. 36:22; Pss. 33:8–11; 135:6; Isa. 14:24, 27; 40:13–17, 21–26; 41:2–4; 44:6–8; 45:9–10; 48:3; Jer. 18:1–11; Lam. 3:37–38; Dan. 2:44; Acts 2:22–23; 4:27–28; Rom. 4:17; 11:36; Eph. 1:11; Rev. 3:7.

9. See also Prov. 21:1; Jer. 1:5; Matt. 20:23; Rom. 9:20–21.

allotted periods and the boundaries of their dwelling place, that they should seek God, in the hope that they might feel their way toward him and find him. Yet he is actually not far from each one of us, for

"In him we live and move and have our being";

as even some of your own poets have said,

"For we are indeed his offspring." (Acts 17:24–28)

Not a single breath we take or a twinge of the tiniest muscle in our body or the faintest hint of activity within could support signs of life without the hand of God resting directly on our frail little frame. We are wholly dependent on him for the fact that we move, breathe, think, hear, speak, see, touch—for the fact that we live, period.

When the Bible speaks of God's actions, it is clear that they are made freely and unconditionally. No outside forces determine or even influence the choices he makes. That which he decrees he also executes. He is both architect and builder. The Sovereign Lord boldly proclaims through the prophet Isaiah:

> Remember the former things of old;
> for I am God, and there is no other;
>   I am God, and there is none like me,
> declaring the end from the beginning
>   and from ancient times things not yet done,
> saying, "My counsel shall stand,
>   and I will accomplish all my purpose,"
> calling a bird of prey from the east,
>   the man of my counsel from a far country.
> I have spoken, and I will bring it to pass;
>   I have purposed, and I will do it. (Isa. 46:9–11)

An indelible portrait of Yahweh was revealed earlier to Isaiah: a potter reserving the right to mold the lump of clay as he pleases (Isa. 45:9).

The clay finds no voice to reprimand the potter for making it as he did or to pretend that the divine craftsman never sat at the molder's wheel in the first place.

God's lordship is supreme. The ruler Nebuchadnezzar entertained stratospheric thoughts of exaltation about himself (Dan. 4:30). But soon he acquiesced to this earth-grounding truth. The humbling revelation occurred only after the ruler was brought down by God below the horizon of the grass—to the level where cattle eat (vv. 31–33) and insects play. The now-lowly king declares:

> For his dominion is an everlasting dominion,
>   and his kingdom endures from generation to generation;
> all the inhabitants of the earth are accounted as nothing,
>   and he does according to his will among the host of heaven
>   and among the inhabitants of the earth;
> and none can stay his hand
>   or say to him, "What have you done?" (Dan. 4:34–35)

A Portrait of God's Care

No one has reason to imagine that God randomly exercises unbridled power just because he can. The all-powerful works of God are also executed by an all-wise and infinitely good God. Nor is God's providence detached and impersonal, leaving us with a dark and distant deity whose frigid disposition leaves us stranded in some arctic wasteland. This is important if we are to grasp the implications of God's sovereignty for his children's lives. A God who is all-powerful but stripped of his personal loving care is neither the God of the Bible nor a God that we could bear to live under.

Furthermore, at the heart of our comfort and assurance lies the knowledge that because God is fully sovereign, his care for us is meaningful. If God offers aid to us in the midst of crisis and yet is powerless to effectively institute it, then we are left with an impotent God and an impotent hope. He ever lives to employ his kind designs in the lives of his chosen ones, and no force under heaven can thwart them (Matt. 10:31; Rom. 8:28, 31–39). Charles Spurgeon affirmed that this doctrine is the source of great consolation:

There is no attribute of God more comforting to his children than the doctrine of Divine Sovereignty. Under the most adverse circumstances, in the most severe troubles, they believe that Sovereignty hath ordained their afflictions, that Sovereignty overrules them, and that Sovereignty will sanctify them all.[10]

His providential care is an especially deep cavern of hope when dark clouds gather and the tempest falls. Consider Jordan and Jessica.[11] Both are believers in Christ. Both were married in their early twenties around the same time. Then unexpectedly both lost their spouses at the same time, equally widowed and shattered and full of painful questions. Afterward, through a mutual acquaintance, Jordan was encouraged to friend Jessica on Facebook. She saw that they both had about a dozen mutual friends, so she accepted. After a carefully crafted message that Jordan sent Jessica, the two came together for their first face-to-face meeting. They talked, laughed, and cried for five hours, and they started to live again. Soon they were married, and God took the sorrow of mutual loss and turned it into joy.

Coincidence?

No one encounters a story like that, libertarian or not, and remains unconvinced of God's orchestration of our life story. He cultivates care for his children. In the libertarian view of free will, Jordan and Jessica's meeting barely falls short of being a chance encounter. In the compatibilist view, we can say that they were naturally drawn to each other as a result of mutual experiences while they discovered compelling reasons to join in matrimony. Nothing can detract from the intentional choices each made that moved them from loss to love restored. Nonetheless, something serious would be amiss if they denied God's providence in bringing them together. God inflicted their pain. But also, the reappearance of his kindness revived their lagging souls and united them in renewed love.

There are no bumbling misadventures here. God does not work things out in history as he goes along; rather, he established a careful

10. Quoted in Scott J. Hafemann, *The God of Promise and the Life of Faith* (Wheaton, IL: Crossway, 2001), 142.

11. Their story can be found here: http://www.youtube.com/watch?v=lFon14QjmFw.

blueprint before the foundations of the world were laid, and he does not deviate from it.[12] The plans of anyone less would indicate an inferior god that fails to stand before the matchless Creator. Such lesser gods are reared in the darkened halls of the human imagination and are unworthy of our worship. Thus, let us gaze in awe upon God's wondrously wise power and providence. Ongoing praise should flow from mouths that marvel at such a God:

> Blessed be the name of God forever and ever,
>   to whom belong wisdom and might.
> He changes times and seasons;
>   he removes kings and sets up kings;
> he gives wisdom to the wise
>   and knowledge to those who have understanding;
> he reveals deep and hidden things;
>   he knows what is in the darkness,
>   and the light dwells with him. (Dan. 2:20–22)

Evil Falls inside the Orbit of God's Sovereignty

None of this should lead us to become saccharine about God's sovereignty. If we are to grapple with its full dimensions, then we must peer deeper into the portals of evil and calamity in the world. When we consider Jordan and Jessica's story, it is easy to see how God was at work picking up the pieces of their shattered lives after their previous spouses suddenly died.

But was God sovereign in those deaths? Did he determine that the spouses should die?

These sorts of questions do not sit well in our daintily decorated theological parlor rooms. They are the kinds of thoughts that we prefer to hide behind shelves filled with lighter, more user-friendly theological fare.

Vexing questions about God and the problem of evil are, to say the least, very troubling. Charles Templeton was a close associate of

---

12. See Pss. 33:11; 139:16; Isa. 37:26; 46:10; Matt. 25:34; Acts 2:23; 1 Cor. 2:7; Eph. 1:4; Heb. 4:3.

Billy Graham. During the heady days of Youth for Christ International in the early 1940s, Templeton was believed by many to be the greatest evangelist since Dwight Moody and Billy Sunday. Of course, that recognition would soon belong to his friend Mr. Graham. Instead, Templeton's faith in the Christian God suffered an ongoing crisis, and he eventually abandoned Christianity altogether. In 1995 he wrote of his disaffection in a book entitled *Farewell to God: My Reasons for Rejecting the Christian Faith*.

A few years before Templeton died, he was interviewed by Lee Strobel for his book *The Case for Faith*. Strobel queried Templeton about the one thing that had finally drawn him away from his Christian beliefs. It was a photograph of a North African woman that he came across in *Life* magazine. "They were experiencing a devastating drought. And she was holding her dead baby in her arms and looking up to heaven with the most forlorn expression. I looked at it and I thought, 'Is it possible to believe that there is a loving or caring Creator when all this woman needed was *rain*?'"

With obvious dismay, Templeton continued: "Who runs the rain? I don't; you don't. *He* does—or that's what I thought. But when I saw that photograph, I immediately knew it is not possible for this to happen and for there to be a loving God."[13]

We must gird ourselves like warriors if we are to answer questions about God's sovereignty over natural and moral evil—over tornadoes, tidal waves, and terminal cancer; over wanton thievery, terrorism, and tyranny. In order to understand biblical compatibilism, God and evil must be squarely faced.

And here the Bible does not mince words.

Evil does not reside in a mysterious realm somehow untouched by God's plan, purpose, or power. If it did, we would have reason to fear, for then God would not in fact be sovereign. If God is genuinely in control, then he is Lord over good and evil, right and wrong, truth and error, blessing and curse, comfort and pain, life and death. Solomon speaks forthrightly: "The LORD has made everything for its purpose, even the wicked for the day of trouble" (Prov. 16:4).

---

13. Lee Strobel, *The Case for Faith* (Grand Rapids: Zondervan, 2000), 14.

Other passages are unequivocal as they make this point. Consider this from Isaiah:

> I am the LORD, and there is no other,
>> besides me there is no God;
>> I equip you, though you do not know me,
> that people may know, from the rising of the sun
>> and from the west, that there is none besides me;
>> I am the LORD, and there is no other.
> I form light and create darkness,
>> I make well-being and create calamity,
>> I am the LORD, who does all these things. (Isa. 45:5–7)

The word translated "calamity" in verse 7 is the standard Hebrew word for *evil*.[14] Furthermore, the word translated "create," used twice in verse 7, is the Hebrew word *bara'*, which is used exclusively of God in the Old Testament for bringing matter into existence. The word's most renowned occurrence is in Genesis 1:1—"In the beginning, God *created* the heavens and the earth."[15] In a similar passage Jeremiah writes: "Who has spoken and it came to pass, unless the Lord has commanded it? Is it not from the mouth of the Most High that good and bad come?" (Lam. 3:37–38).[16] Again, "bad" here is the word for "evil, harm, injure."[17]

The Bible draws a comprehensive picture of God's control over the entrance of natural and moral evil into human affairs. He determines life and death even when death involves injustice.[18] He is in control of mental and physical ailments and diseases.[19] He controls

---

14. William L. Holladay, *A Concise Hebrew and Aramaic Lexicon of the Old Testament* (Grand Rapids: Eerdmans, 1988), 341.

15. Ibid., 47; Bruce A. Ware, *God's Greater Glory: The Exalted God of Scripture and the Christian Faith* (Wheaton, IL: Crossway, 2004), 71.

16. See also Judg. 14:1–4; 1 Sam. 16:14–15; 2 Sam. 12:11–12; 1 Kings 11:14, 23; 22:23; Ps. 71:20; Jer. 11:17; 18:11; 19:3–15; 21:5–10; Amos 3:6; 9:4; John 9:1–3; Rev. 17:17.

17. Holladay, *Hebrew and Aramaic Lexicon*, 343.

18. See Gen. 38:7; Deut. 32:39; Pss. 90:3; 139:16; Jer. 15:2; Ezek. 24:16, 18; Luke 2:29; 12:4–5, 20; Acts 17:28; Rom. 4:17; Heb. 9:27; James 4:14–15; Rev. 1:18.

19. Ex. 4:11; 2 Sam. 12:15; 2 Chron. 21:18; John 9:2–3.

the weather and sends natural catastrophes.[20] Amos asks rhetorically, "Does disaster come to a city, unless the LORD has done it?" (Amos 3:6). Of course, such *natural* disasters in another sense stem from the fall of man into sin that resulted in a cursed creation (Rom. 8:20). Nonetheless, God often executes calamity specifically as a means of judgment.[21] In the same way, he appoints evil rulers and armies to judge others.[22] God decrees evil to transpire on multiple fronts in the course of human events.

Job's Calamity

The life of Job presents a test case for the relationship between God, evil, Satan, and mankind. Job is the recipient of all manner of sudden and unexpected evils—the murder of children, the theft of property, the death of other children by an apparent tornado, and a sickness that racked Job's body with acute pain. Note that as the scenario of Job's suffering unfolds, God never directly inflicts the adversities he encounters; rather, they proceed from Satan, the pawn of God.[23] Satan freely instigates his malintentions, yet he acknowledges God's sovereignty when he sneers, "Stretch out *your* hand and touch all that he has, and he will curse you to your face" (Job 1:11). Amazingly, Job is never inclined to attribute his misfortune to Satan; rather, he turns to the supreme Ruler of life.

The reader of Job is flabbergasted to see that God not only incites Satan to consider Job as a test for evil (Job 1:8; 2:3), but also commands him to put the calamitous designs into motion (1:12; 2:6). Satan has no sovereignty in the lives and affairs of human beings. He can do nothing except what God allows and purposes him to do.[24] For example, Satan entered Judas in order to betray Jesus (Luke 22:3; John 13:2), yet Judas's actions were ordained by God (John 17:12; Acts 1:16).

20. See 2 Sam. 24:15; 1 Kings 17:14; Job 38:8–11; Pss. 135:6–7; 147:15–18; Isa. 29:6; Jer. 10:13; 31:35; Nah. 1:5–6; Mark 4:39, 41; Luke 8:24; Rev. 11:13; 16:18.

21. See Ps. 78:44–48; Jer. 18:11; 19:3, 15.

22. See Deut. 28:48; 2 Kings 15:37; 24:2–4; 1 Chron. 5:26; 6:15; 2 Chron. 21:16; 24:24; 28:9; Ps. 78:60–62; Isa. 10:5–8; Jer. 43:10–13.

23. Compare 2 Samuel 24:1 with 1 Chronicles 21:1.

24. This is also true of other demonic entities who inflict evil on humans. See 1 Kings 22:21–23; 2 Thess. 2:11–12.

How often do sufferers cry out to Satan when they experience pain, evil, or injustice? Do they not instinctively direct their *whys* to God? They assume two things about God. First, he is all-powerful and could have prevented what took place or directed some other result. Second, they perceive that he must be good and therefore could not possibly desire that evil overtake their lives. People by nature acknowledge God's intrinsic control and his basic goodness (Rom. 1:19–20). Yet the experience of evil causes them to question these divine traits, and that was precisely what Satan thought Job would do. Of course, Job's response was quite contrary to Satan's intended purpose, but it fit fully with God's.

Consider this exchange between Job and his wife after all that befell him:

> Then his wife said to him, "Do you still hold fast your integrity? Curse God and die." But he said to her, "You speak as one of the foolish women would speak. Shall we receive good from God, and shall we not receive evil?" In all this Job did not sin with his lips. (Job 2:9–10)

Job's wife reacted as Satan wanted Job to react, but he refused. He passed God's test. The test reaffirmed his conviction that one cannot embrace the fullness of God's sovereignty while denying that he decrees both the good and the bad. As affirmation of this truth, we read that Job "did not sin with his lips" (Job 2:10). God is not the master over good while being a servant of evil.

Now, a word of clarification is necessary. When Job assigns responsibility to God for the evil that befell him, he is most certainly not saying that God is evil or the perpetrator of evil. God cannot entertain evil within himself; otherwise, he would not be God. The goodness of God is nonnegotiable. The psalmist declares, "The LORD is righteous in all his ways and kind in all his works" (Ps. 145:17). Moses writes, "His work is perfect, for all his ways are justice. A God of faithfulness and without iniquity, just and upright is he" (Deut. 32:4). David acknowledges, "For you are not a God who delights in wickedness; evil may not dwell with you" (Ps. 5:4). The apostle John adds to this testimony: "God is light, and in him is no darkness at all" (1 John 1:5; cf. Hab. 1:13). Absolutely nothing that God says or thinks or does can be attributed to some evil in him. For God to remain God, this is simply not possible.

Furthermore, because of God's intrinsic goodness, he cannot tempt people to act in evil ways (James 1:13). God can decree evil to occur, but relegates temptation to the work of Satan. This is difficult for us to get our arms around, and it leaves many mysteries unsolved. But we must allow the plain testimony of Scripture to speak with all the tension here juxtaposed. Only one conclusion is available to us. God always intends some good for the evil he decrees, and he does not always tell us what that purpose is (Gen. 50:20).

What can we say about this?

Let us circumspectly descend on our knees, lay our hands over our mouths in incomprehensible wonder, and with the apostle Paul declare: "Oh, the depth of the riches and wisdom and knowledge of God! How unsearchable are his judgments and how inscrutable his ways!" (Rom. 11:33). Such a God deserves our worship, not our scorn.

God's Goodness in the Midst of Evil

God's people, however, do find comfort. "Though he cause grief, he will have compassion according to the abundance of his steadfast love; for he does not willingly afflict or grieve the children of men" (Lam. 3:32–33). God has a good and wise purpose that transcends the immediate infliction of grief. Mysteriously, God decrees what he otherwise never prescribes. It doesn't bring delight to the heart of God (Ezek. 18:23; 33:11). Neither is it theologically wimpy to imagine that God sheds tears when inflicting necessary grief on his children, all in the service of achieving his greater good. Job understands: "Though he slay me, I will hope in him" (Job 13:15). Job embraces *everything* God does, even the hard providences, knowing that his Lord's compassions never fail. His faithfulness is great (Lam. 3:22–23).

In the libertarian scheme, many evils have no explanation, so that there is not only a sense of divine alienation but also a disconcerting senselessness to the presence of evil and especially personal suffering. The Bible does not paint such a dismal picture. Though God at times is silent, he never abandons his children, for whom he reserves the greatest care. A profound if mysterious coherence exists between his sovereign decrees of evil, his goodness, and the grief he bears alongside us. Thaddeus Williams explains: "A God who *both* predetermines *and* grieves evil replaces fears of cosmic alienation and absurdity with a sense of solidarity (because God authentically feels our suffering) and stability (because God authoritatively purposes our suffering)."[25]

Paul is unequivocal about the sovereign goodness of our Lord: "And we know that for those who love God all things work together for good, for those who are called according to his purpose" (Rom. 8:28). God does not cause *some* things to work out for the believer's well-being, but *all* things. Nothing that happens in the life of a believer can be attributed to some evil intention of God. It all has a purpose, fit with a concern for our full well-being in mind. Let this truth penetrate deeply and saturate our souls. Satan's temptation to Job through his miserable friends was to suggest that God was allowing him to suffer because he didn't love him. Or that God was punishing him for some egregious infraction.

It is true that as guilty sinners, we have incurred the wrath of God. We positively deserve divine punishment poured out in undiminished measure. To some, the thought of such wrath incurs a reciprocated wrath that embitters people toward God. It prompts them to lash out against him or to run away from him (and his people). For others who may actually be sensitive to the reality of their guilt, the wrath of God can be a crushing reality that brings despair. Judas despaired so much after he betrayed Christ to the authorities (Matt. 26:14–16, 47–50) that he committed suicide (27:1–6). He couldn't see that the God of wrath was also a God of mercy who receives those who are repentant. Judas could exercise remorse but not true repentance. As a result, it never entered his mind to seek Jesus' forgiveness.

The life-changing epiphany of hope for those who experience salvation comes not when they sag from the crushing burden of guilt before a just God, but when they see the smiling providence of the

---

25. Thaddeus J. Williams, *Love, Freedom, and Evil: Does Authentic Love Require Free Will?* (New York: Rodopi, 2011), 99–100.

God who forgives and relieves their burden. For the believer, God's wrath has been completely removed. We no longer stand under his condemnation (Rom. 8:1) because Christ diverted the Father's wrath from us to himself (5:8–9). No suffering, affliction, or evil is inflicted on us by God as punishment. Nothing can separate us from the love of God in Christ (8:31–39). God's children may experience pain and suffering because we still live in a fallen world that God controls, but he redeems our pain and suffering for his glory and our good. Sometimes he takes our pain away, and at other times he asks us to endure it. But he never brings it upon us capriciously or for some ill purpose.

In fact, the God of all comfort (2 Cor. 1:3–4) ministers to us in suffering. Richard Wurmbrand (1909–2001) was a Jewish believer in Christ living in Communist Romania. He was imprisoned and tortured for many years because of his faith in Christ.[26] At one time he suffered for three years in solitary confinement. In a short film, Wurmbrand described the suffering of his faith.[27] One might imagine that suffering unfathomable tortures would be to experience a glimpse of hell—not so for Wurmbrand. In hell, one is separated from Christ. But he says that while he languished in prison, Christ was present with him at all times, bringing hope and comfort.

What sort of God is it who works peace in the midst of terrors? Only the God who has revealed himself as the Ruler of good and evil.

Evil and the Glorious Grace of God

Evil—no matter how gratuitous, shameful, repugnant, or unjust—is never ultimately pointless, purposeless, or exercised apart from God's plan "to make known the riches of his glory" (Rom. 9:22–24; cf. Eph. 1:5–6). Scott Hafemann says:

> God is all-loving in his sovereignty over evil because he allows, guides, transforms, and even designs it for a good and loving eternal purpose that far transcends the evil itself but could not be accomplished without it. Herein lies the mystery of creation

26. See Richard Wurmbrand, *Tortured for Christ* (Bartlesville, OK: Living Sacrifice Book Company, 1998).

27. See http://www.youtube.com/watch?v=7_1j5FXC2Aw#t=561.

and redemption. Since God could have prevented evil from ever taking root in the world, we must conclude that evil is an essential part of God's overall plan for creation.[28]

Paul alludes to a singularly profound purpose for evil in Romans 5. After he describes how Christ reversed the effects of the fall of humanity, he goes on to make this statement:

> Now the law came in to increase the trespass, but where sin increased, grace abounded all the more, so that, as sin reigned in death, grace also might reign through righteousness leading to eternal life through Jesus Christ our Lord. (Rom. 5:20–21)

"The law" most likely refers to the Mosaic law. Nonetheless, it reflects the divine law written upon all human hearts (Rom. 2:14–15), which in turn reflects the very moral fabric of God's character. The more that God's character was revealed in divinely inspired codes for human behavior, the more that these laws became a light that exposed and increased the depth of people's disregard for it (Rom. 1:18ff.). Humans naturally think the wall of their moral uprightness is fairly straight. But the law of God comes along like an electronic laser level and reveals how crooked that wall really is. People don't like the scrutiny of that piercing red beam and seek to rebel against it all the more. Their transgressions increase before the Judge of their hearts.

But here is the remarkable point of the passage. When evil transpires at an increasing rate in the course of human history, God counters this rebellion by pouring out his grace upon ill-deserving sinners. With increased evil comes increased opportunity for the grace of God to be magnified. As Paul notes earlier, "Our unrighteousness serves to show the righteousness of God" (Rom. 3:5).

This grace came to its climax though the death of Christ. In leading up to his point at the end of Romans 5, Paul says in verse 8, "But God shows his love for us in that while we were still sinners, Christ died for us." Human sinfulness serves to highlight God's

---

28. Hafemann, *The God of Promise*, 139.

righteousness as nothing else does. Sin and evil form a mass of utter blackness. The law of God illuminates this darkness, exposing its repulsiveness. But the grace of God in the cross of Christ outshines even the light of his law. Its glory and magnificence penetrate deeply into that wretched core with the force of ten thousand suns dissolving sin and death. The dark and oppressive reality of evil can never outweigh the glory of the cross. As deep as evil seeks to dive, God's grace in the cross of Christ dives deeper still.

Consider further the divine paradox of the cross. Many rivals force their way to the top of the garbage heap of wickedness. One thinks perhaps of the Jewish Holocaust or the twenty thousand mass gravesites in Cambodia known as the Killing Fields of the despotic Khmer Rouge. Few things today compare to the wickedness of the international child sex slave trade. But there has never been a more unjust crime, a more heinous display of disregard, or a more despicable act of malice than this: the crucifixion of the perfectly righteous Son of God two thousand years ago.

Yet here we see something truly remarkable that highlights the uniqueness of the Christian faith. The focused rage of men against the one actually innocent person ever born into this world serves as a mirror for the wrath of God in that very same event. It seems inconceivable, but God did not spare his own beloved Son (Rom. 8:32) from the greatest display of divine wrath that history has ever witnessed. Yet at the same time, this wrath was commingled with God's greatest display of mercy. Christ, the precious unblemished Lamb of God, bore the fullness of the Father's judgment on sin (5:9) in order that many unworthy vessels would experience unprecedented mercy (9:23). Jesus' death satisfied the demands of God's justice leveled against us. He willingly absorbed the wrath of God meant for us because the Godhead loved us so much. Amazingly, without the planned entrance of evil into human souls epitomized in the unjust crucifixion of Christ, there is no grace, no mercy, no avenue for God to manifest his greatest glory.

This does not answer every question about the existence and purpose of evil. Nor does it always explain evil's immediate and tragic effects in the world or in our personal lives. The believer should never be sanguine about the inexplicable dimensions of suffering. The enigma of many afflictions cannot be untangled by uttering bare propositions of truth. What is needed most in those moments is simply the biblical injunction to offer compassion to those who suffer. Sometimes to shed silent tears in sympathy speaks louder than hundreds of erudite volumes on theodicy.[29] The same God who inflicts pain also applies a healing salve (cf. Job 13:15; 2 Cor. 1:3–5). And then once we are able to step away from the palpable and visceral impact that suffering and evil evoke, we can see the transcendent glory of God in the midst of it all. The glory that emanates from the cross casts a panoramic brilliance across the horizon of human existence that shimmers with untold riches of hope for humanity.

Pale Blue Dot

It is humbling to gaze on all these magnificent portraits of God's glory and sovereignty. I am reminded of the famous "Pale Blue Dot" photograph taken by the *Voyager 1* spacecraft in 1990. The photo captured Earth from some 3.7 billion miles away. Our planet appears as a tiny, almost indistinct speck no more than 0.12 pixel in size. It is easily missed in the vast expanse of the solar system. Yet the solar system itself is but a speck in the Milky Way, which in turn is a speck in the endless vista of galaxies stretched across the universe. Above and beyond it all stands a God of wonder, so powerful, so transcendent, and so glorious that attempting to describe him defies our words and imagination.

And yet here we are, creatures virtually undetectable by the lens of a spacecraft.

This is the sort of vantage point on which Calvin in his *Institutes* tries to get his readers to stand when contemplating who they are in the light of who God is. From this lofty and rarefied atmosphere, remarkably, God has focused his greatest attention on such lowly creatures. It is also the perspective from which we must understand how we relate to such a God. We dare not exalt ourselves as if God will somehow be confounded by his creatures. Whatever we embrace about

---

29. *Theodicy* is the term used by theologians and philosophers to discuss the problem of God and evil. It combines the Greek words for *God* (*theos*) and *justice* (*dike*). The term was coined by the German philosopher Gottfried Leibniz (1646–1716) in an attempt to explain how God can be "just" (good) while permitting evil.

the nature of our own power, our own freedom and independence, we cannot unhinge it from the God on whom we depend for our every breath. Anyone who has journeyed through this grand landscape of the Almighty One sees that he is the only basis of real hope and real confidence—and the only object worthy of our worship.

Chapter Summary

A careful perusal of the Bible unveils a portrait of a God who is at the center of Scripture's conceptual universe and exercises unyielding lordship over all that he has made. God's supreme control speaks of a glorious choreographer who causally determines the course of history in a way that is not conditioned on anything that his creation or creatures do. Rather, the whole panorama of the cosmos is entirely dependent on his meticulous guidance. Nothing escapes discussion and planning by the Godhead in the divine boardroom, nor the Trinity's thorough execution of those plans in the theater of play. From the broad sweep of history to the minutest movements of a bird, God controls all. Even the random casting of lots rests in the hands of God. As R. C. Sproul observes, there are no "maverick molecules" in the universe.

God's foreordination of all things—good and evil—was forever settled before the foundations of the earth were laid, and nothing that humans choose to do can alter this fact. The all-powerful works of God are executed by an all-wise and infinitely good God. His providence is not detached and impersonal, leaving us with a dark and distant deity whose frigid disposition leaves us stranded in some arctic wasteland. A God who is all-powerful but stripped of his personal loving care is neither the God of the Bible nor a God that we could bear to live under. Furthermore, God's sovereign purposes in the existence of evil serve to magnify the glory of his grace. Amazingly, without the planned entrance of evil into human souls epitomized in the unjust crucifixion of Christ, there is no grace, no mercy, no avenue for God to manifest his greatest glory.

Study Questions

1. Does God exercise a general sovereignty with a general plan for history? Or does he exercise specific control over everything with

a meticulous plan for history? Which view of divine sovereignty does the Bible support?

2. Does God control the big picture of history while letting small and insignificant details work themselves out on their own? Does the Bible support this idea of divine sovereignty?

3. Why is it unwise to isolate God's sovereignty from his other attributes, such as wisdom, goodness, justice, and love?

4. What is the difference between natural and moral evil?

5. Are there any instances of evil that fall outside of God's plan and purpose? If so, how does this affect God's sovereignty?

6. What role does Satan play in God's sovereign purposes?

7. How did Job respond to his suffering? What role did he see God playing in it? Was Job's perspective right or wrong? Explain your answer.

8. Read Romans 8:28. Why is it hard to imagine evil working out for the believer's good? How do you respond when calamity, adversity, or some form of evil befalls you?

9. How did Richard Wurmbrand cope with his unjust imprisonment? What lessons can the believer learn from his perspective?

10. How is the death of Christ the greatest display of God's wrath and at the same time the greatest display of his mercy? How does this shed light on the existence of evil in the world?

Resources for Further Study

D. A. Carson, *How Long, O Lord? Reflections on Suffering and Evil* (Grand Rapids: Baker, 2006). A thoughtful, theological, and pastoral perspective on the problem of evil.

John S. Feinberg, *The Many Faces of Evil: Theological Systems and the Problem of Evil* (Wheaton, IL: Crossway, 2004). A thorough theological and philosophical treatment of the problem of evil for the advanced student.

John M. Frame, *Apologetics: A Justification of Christian Belief* (Phillipsburg, NJ: P&R Publishing, 2015). Chapters 7 and 8 provide a good treatment of the problem of evil.

———. *The Doctrine of God* (Phillipsburg, NJ: P&R Publishing, 2002). One of the best modern treatments of the doctrine of God from a Calvinist perspective. See especially chapters 2 through 7 on the sovereignty of God.

————. *Systematic Theology: An Introduction to Christian Belief* (Phillipsburg, NJ: P&R Publishing, 2013). Chapters 8, 9, 16, 17, and 18 are especially helpful on the sovereignty of God.

Wayne Grudem, *Systematic Theology* (Grand Rapids: Zondervan, 1994). See chapter 16 on God's providence.

A. W. Pink, *The Sovereignty of God* (Grand Rapids: Baker, 1984). A classic Calvinist treatment of God's sovereignty.

Joni Eareckson Tada and Steven Estes, *When God Weeps* (Grand Rapids: Zondervan, 1997). A very encouraging biblical response to evil and suffering from one who has powerfully experienced it firsthand.

4

A Road Map for Compatibilism

Everyone has encountered "all-or-nothing" people. You ask them to turn down the TV because it's too loud, so they turn it off instead. They poke down the road when you are running late for an appointment. So instead of speeding up a little, they suddenly morph into Mario Andretti. Many Christians reflect this all-or-nothing approach to human choosing. The pendulum swings from unbounded personal autonomy to unbending divine totalitarianism. One is either the master of his destiny or the mindless slave of God. Many think that if you deny libertarianism, then you must embrace a model of divine sovereignty that amounts to fatalism.[1] God becomes a daunting dictator, and it matters not what we do. Our freedom of choice is stripped from us while suffering at the mercy of a capricious deity. This most certainly does not describe the God of Calvinism, nor does it represent the components of divine sovereignty of which biblical compatibilism is constructed.

To be sure, libertarianism has a certain appeal because God often goes undetected as we think, contemplate, dream, and choose in our day-to-day routines. But as the venerable Francis Schaeffer said, "He is there and he is not silent." While God and Satan were engaged in a celestial dialogue about Job's future, Job himself remained completely unaware of what course his life was about to take as the result of their deliberations. Yet in a rare glimpse for us, the curtain is pulled back in a special behind-the-scenes look at what precipitated all that Job experienced. Humans experience life and history primarily and almost exclusively

---

1. This sets up the logical fallacy of a false dichotomy.

from a visible earthbound perspective. We need special spectacles to see the invisible heavenly hand directing the scenes as they unfold.

So yes, it is true—God and his mighty acts *do* move the human story according to the plot line that he has determined. But if we don't consult the inspired biblical record, this is not always apparent. In some cases, the biblical narrative indicates that God directly peeks out from behind the curtain in a perceivable way—for example, when God sends plagues on Egyptian oppressors or raises grieving mothers' sons from the dead or speaks to his people through sage prophets. In due course, God came out fully from behind the curtain when the Son of God underwent the incarnation and took center stage for three critical decades before ascending back to his heavenly glory.

So where does compatibilism enter the story? Can there be another scenario besides our dangling as lifeless puppets at the end of the master puppeteer's strings? Yes—and this is where we now direct our attention.

Apples and Grub Worms

In order to illustrate the fact that compatibilism makes better sense of reality than libertarianism does, James Spiegel provides us with a memorable illustration:

> Consider the choice someone might give you to eat either apple pie or grub worm pie. Which would you choose? Presumably, you would select the former. Was your choice determined? Of course, this is apparent from the predictability of your choice. And what determined your choice was such causal influences as your desire to eat something you like and your natural aversion to eating worms. But, now, was your choice free? Again, the answer is yes. You were free because you were not externally compelled to give a pro-apple-pie response. However, had something so compelled you, such as the threat of physical violence or manipulation of your vocal cords, then you would not have acted freely.[2]

2. James S. Spiegel, *The Benefits of Providence: A New Look at Divine Sovereignty* (Wheaton, IL: Crossway, 2005), 70. Spiegel attributes this illustration to his mentor Wynn Kenyon.

This illustration demonstrates that our freedom of choice is not incompatible with antecedent causes that determine our choices. Of course, Spiegel has restricted such causes to those that emanate from our own internal desires. But can compatibilism of this sort also be squared with the fact that God is the ultimate determiner of our choices? Again, the answer is yes, which leads us to consider the unique perspective of *biblical* compatibilism.

Two Wills, One Outcome

Biblical compatibilism seeks to demonstrate one simple reality. Every human action in the course of history has a dual explanation, one divine and one human.[3] In this model of "double agency,"[4] the human side of the explanation is the more tangible, visible, and familiar side. The divine side is largely intangible, invisible, and less familiar. This juxtaposition is expressed simply and clearly by Solomon: "The heart of man plans his way, but the LORD establishes his steps" (Prov. 16:9; cf. 19:21; 20:24). The vast throngs of Earth's inhabitants contemplate, deliberate, and articulate their plans to pursue the paths that define their lives. Then they act on those plans. Yet God secretly stands behind them all, directing each set of footsteps along the specific course he designed. His guiding providence is like a transparent, colorless, odorless gas—the fuel that fires up the burners of human action. Yet he does so without undermining human freedom and responsibility.

When one reads the Scriptures with careful eyes, this dual explanation for the same human events begins to emerge with clarity. We will explore some of the more obvious instances of this pattern in a moment. In it we will see two wills at work in the same events: the will of God and the will of man. Although the intentions often differ, the outcomes of the exercise of these two wills never come into conflict. What God determines to occur in human events just so happens to coincide with the outcome of corresponding freely (voluntarily)

---

3. Angelic and demonic agents could be included as well. Yet Scripture is mainly concerned with the divine and human characters in the story.

4. Robert A. Peterson, *Election and Free Will: God's Gracious Choice and Our Responsibility* (Phillipsburg, NJ: P&R Publishing, 2007), 151.

made human choices. D. A. Carson has provided us with a careful explanation of compatibilism through two propositions:

> 1. God is absolutely sovereign, but his sovereignty never functions in such a way that human responsibility [and freedom] is curtailed, minimized, or maligned.

> 2. Human beings are morally responsible creatures—they significantly choose, rebel, obey, believe, defy, make decisions, and so forth, and they are rightly held accountable for such actions; but this characteristic never functions so as to make God absolutely contingent.[5]

A palpable tension exists between the two realities represented by Carson's propositions. Some think they speak of paradox,[6] but never involve contradiction. They can be viewed as converging links in a set of cause-effect relationships resulting in human actions. One cause is divine and the other is human. The divine cause is *primary* but *remote*. The human cause is *secondary* but *proximate* (i.e., the near cause). This is often called the doctrine of *concurrence*,[7] reflected in the 1646 Westminster Confession of Faith concerning "God's Eternal Decree" (3.1), which states: "God from all eternity did, by the most wise and holy counsel of His own will, freely and unchangeably ordain whatsoever comes to pass; yet so, as thereby neither is God the author of sin, nor is violence offered to the will of the creatures, nor is the liberty or contingency of second causes taken away, but rather established."[8]

5. D. A. Carson, *How Long, O Lord? Reflections on Suffering and Evil* (Grand Rapids: Baker, 2006), 179 (bracketed statement added). By *contingent* Carson means that God is not dependent on human choices for the actions he takes. Ibid., 182.

6. J. I. Packer calls the tension an "antinomy" that cannot be resolved until we reach heaven. See *Evangelism and the Sovereignty of God* (Downers Grove, IL: InterVarsity Press, 1991), 18–25. While some mysteries exist in the relationship between God's sovereignty and human action, I do not believe it is as incomprehensible as theologians such as Packer have insisted.

7. John M. Frame, *The Doctrine of God* (Phillipsburg, NJ: P&R Publishing, 2002), 287–88; R. C. Sproul, *The Invisible Hand* (Phillipsburg, NJ: P&R Publishing, 1996), 77–106.

8. Paul Helm notes that attributing a compatibilist view to the Westminster Confession is anachronistic, since the sorts of ways in which compatibilist and libertarian views of freedom

To speak of God's causal relationship to human action as *primary* is to reaffirm the biblical truth of absolute divine sovereignty. This means that he is the *ultimate* source of all human acts of choosing. To speak of his relationship as *remote* is to say that God does not make people's choices for them. He does not directly act on humans as automatons who have no independent heart, mind, or will. In this regard—and in some ways that we don't fully understand—God is exonerated from culpability for human choices. This also means that God never coerces a person to act against his or her will. Coercion can occasionally come from other sources—usually other humans—but never from God.

Furthermore, God employs *secondary* causes, which are the human side of the equation—the actual choices coming from people themselves. These are also the *proximate* causes—the more immediate sources of all human acts of choosing. These proximate human causes are primarily *internal* and include one's beliefs, personality, genetics, conscience, heart motivations, intellectual deliberations, and spiritual nature (moral character), whether dead or alive (see chapter 9). Alongside these personal inward causes are other complementary causes. These represent *external* influences that include other people, culture, upbringing, and education, as well as natural laws and spiritual forces (i.e., angelic/demonic forces). How all these things bear on human freedom and responsibility will be teased out in later chapters.

John Feinberg indicates exceptions to this general causal relationship between God and his creatures. He says that God sometimes acts in an immediate way to accomplish his purposes through human (or angelic) agents. In these instances, as he writes, "God may be the remote cause in some sense, but along with the creature, he is also the proximate cause of the act. What God does as part of the proximate cause differs from what his creature does, but their joint efforts produce the intended

---

are framed today are not how debates about free will were understood in previous generations. See "Freedom, Liberty and the Westminster Confession" at http://paulhelmsdeep.blogspot .com/2014/10/freedom-liberty-and-westminster.html. Jonathan Edwards (1703–58) may be the first theologian to conceive of free agency in what today we might call compatibilist terms in his magisterial work *Freedom of the Will*. Nonetheless, the Westminster Confession is far more akin to compatibilism than not, especially if compatibilism is defined simply as the thesis that human freedom is compatible with divine determinism.

end."[9] He cites as an example the inspiration of Scripture, in which God directly and immediately impresses his thoughts on the minds of the inspired writers, although they might not be aware of this. We should note, however, that God never acts as the proximate cause of evil.[10] The Bible always attributes the direct cause of evil to secondary agents.

Note also that the human side of the compatibilist equation speaks of choices made independently, and this is what gives them responsibility. We are creatures, distinct from the Creator. But unlike the independence of libertarianism, compatibilism shows that human choices are also dependent on God. Our actions are always a response to God's secret initiation, whether he acts remotely and indirectly or in some cases with direct proximate causal energy. Yet from our perspective, it is not always clear how God operates, nor does the Bible always tell us.

In a related vein, we can say that the human will is both active and passive. Jonathan Edwards, the great American theologian of the colonial era, makes this point as he speaks of saving grace in the life of the convert:

> In efficacious grace we are not merely passive, nor yet does God do some, and we do the rest. But God does all, and we do all. God produces all, and we act all. For that is what he produces, viz. our own acts. God is the only proper author and fountain; we only are the proper actors. We are in different respects, wholly passive and wholly active.[11]

Thus, God's decree and man's freely exercised will to choose are both necessary and sufficient causes of any human action.[12] From the human side of the equation, the confluence of various external influences (people, circumstances, etc.) and internal influences (beliefs,

9. John S. Feinberg, *No One Like Him* (Wheaton, IL: Crossway, 2001), 652.
10. Recall D. A. Carson's point in which God's relationship to good and evil is asymmetrical (see chapter 2).
11. Quoted in D. Martyn Lloyd-Jones, *The Puritans: Their Origins and Successors* (Carlisle, PA: Banner of Truth, 1987), 356.
12. See chapter 1 on necessary and sufficient conditions.

desires, etc.) that produce the most compelling motive is what serves as the sufficient cause for any choice to be made. While no single factor is necessary, the creation of the most compelling motive, no matter how that comes about, is both necessary and sufficient for a choice to occur along the human plane. When the human plane is linked with the divine plane, we have an adequate explanation for human freedom and responsibility.

Furthermore, God's saving, efficacious grace is alone sufficient to secure the remarkable transformation of sinners that the Bible calls *regeneration*. It is this work of irresistible grace that secures a new spiritual kind of freedom that previously such recipients did not know. It enables them to exercise faith and repentance freely as a result of God's foreordaining of their salvation.[13] We will explore this sort of freedom in later chapters.

A Model for Compatibilism

Contemplating the collusion of these various strands of the compatibilist framework is bewildering. God designed life and history like a vast tapestry. We typically live and view life as though we existed on the back side of that tapestry, where all we see are random ripples and knots and frayed sections of yarn with multiple colors all jumbled together and looking like an apocalyptic wasteland. When we are able to step away from the back side and turn to look at the front side, we encounter an amazing and cohesive piece of artistry that takes our breath away. The otherwise concealed handiwork of God's exquisitely designed decrees comes into full view.

If libertarianism were true, it would seem that the front side of the tapestry would be no different from the back side. There might be a discernible pattern, but only a hodgepodge of disparately linked patches desperately trying to make sense of the whole. Yet we know that if the complex unfolding of history teetered on the edge of the arbitrary and chaotic, then God's glory would be diminished. But the aesthetics of his glory prevails; and when we catch a glimpse of his

---

13. Paul Helm, "The Augustinian-Calvinist View," in *Divine Foreknowledge: Four Views*, ed. James K. Beilby and Paul R. Eddy (Downers Grove, IL: InterVarsity Press, 2001), 171.

masterpiece, it leaves us to ponder how his celestial decrees actually work in weaving all the earthbound strands of yarn together.

Some have supposed that God's causal relationship to human action is like a domino show in which an elaborate maze of precisely located dominoes is set up across a massive floor.[14] The dominoes represent individual people and the actions they perform. Once the first domino (Adam) is tipped over, a series of chain reactions begins. The motions connected to being tipped over represent acts of choosing. In this scenario God is the First Cause, the One who tips over the first domino—the first among constant trains of human acts and events. The simultaneous lines of dominoes continue to fall in an uninterrupted fashion until history comes to its end. Each line follows a succession of simple unidirectional causes and effects. The various sequences of human actions are preceded by immediate causes that lead to particular outcomes and then to further causes and outcomes.

Although such an analogy fits within a divinely deterministic worldview, it makes God far too remote and disconnected to people's lives. It is much more akin to the god of deism than to the God of the Bible. Furthermore, it belies a kind of causal pattern that is too mechanistic, making people appear as passive droids in a *Star Wars* film.[15] It is impersonal and doesn't allow for the dynamic and sometimes disordered interconnections marking the messiness that is life. It leans in a direction that denies God his transcendence and timeless (atemporal) relationship to his creation.[16] It doesn't look like the back side of history's tapestry. Anthony Hoekema has argued that our dependence on God's sovereignty speaks powerfully of our creatureliness. But if his sovereignty is emphasized at the expense

14. I am indebted to James N. Anderson for this illustration. See also J. P. Moreland and William Lane Craig, *Philosophical Foundations for a Christian Worldview* (Downers Grove, IL: InterVarsity Press, 2003), 273.

15. Some libertarians criticize compatibilism, saying that it treats humans as passive instrumental causes within the midst of a broader series of causes and effects (i.e., just one of the middle dominoes). Thus, they would have no control over their own actions because they were not the originating cause of them. See ibid., 275. But again, humans are both passive and active in the choices they make.

16. See Paul Helm, "Divine Timeless Eternity," in *God and Time: Four Views*, ed. Gregory E. Ganssle (Downers Grove, IL: InterVarsity Press, 2001), 28–60; Paul Helm, *Eternal God: A Study of God without Time* (Oxford: Oxford University Press, 1988).

of some kind of genuine human freedom and responsibility, then it denies our identity as authentic persons.[17] God's sovereignty and our personhood stand in dynamic, albeit compatible, tension.

Wayne Grudem has provided a more helpful model to understand the compatibilist relationship between divine determinism and human action. He compares God to the author of a great piece of fiction—not unlike a Shakespeare crafting the story of Macbeth.[18] In this case, God stands as the transcendent playwright, who pens the story of history and establishes all its human characters, good and bad. Each personality helps to shape the script along with all its moral and spiritual complexities, without which the story would have no substance or appeal. Grudem indicates in this model of providence that God is responsible for causing human actions to take place; yet humans are responsible as well. He writes, "God fully causes things in one way (as Creator), and we fully cause things in another way (as creatures)."[19]

A good story always has its protagonists and antagonists, its heroes and villains. Without the malignant stratagems of Sauron contrasted with the moral transcendence and determination of the lowly Frodo, Tolkien's *The Lord of the Rings* would fail to resonate with the marrow of our humanity. Such stories captivate our attention because of the clash of good and evil and the complexities of the conflict between the two. We want the hero to seize the day and want to see evil lying in ashes even though the story line is littered with tragedy along the way. If evil provided no foil for righteousness to prevail, life would sink into a hollow impassivity. This explains why the redemptive triumph of Christ over all diabolical powers becomes the greatest narrative of history.

Fiction imitates life, and thus God authored the real story to include evil and good, loss and redemption, tragedy and triumph. Without both polarizing elements, we never have the opportunity to appreciate the grandeur of the Creator's masterful and wise purposes in which the full panorama of his glory is put on display. God designs and determines

17. Anthony A. Hoekema, *Created in God's Image* (Grand Rapids: Eerdmans, 1986), 5–7.

18. Wayne Grudem, *Systematic Theology* (Grand Rapids: Zondervan, 1994), 321–22. John Frame borrows the Shakespeare analogy and develops it further in *The Doctrine of God*, 156–59.

19. Grudem, *Systematic Theology*, 322.

every intricate plot and subplot. As he tells the story, he serves as the prime executor of the action, but only as the author. The characters themselves act of their own accord, freely and responsibly. While the author of the story created the characters and set forth the trajectory of their lives, he does not live vicariously in the characters themselves. They exist independent of him and full of the vitality that he supplied to them.

Of course, the author-actor analogy is imperfect in many ways. The Bible does not give us anything like a model to explain the precise causal relationship between God's immutable decree and our freely and responsibly made choices. In either case, this analogy seeks to capture a more plausible glimpse of the mysterious relationship between the Creator and his creatures than other models do.

Compatibilist Freedom

Like libertarianism, a principal concern in compatibilism is to define the nature of human freedom. In what way does its concept of the liberty of the will differ from libertarianism? John Feinberg offers this distinction: "An action is free so long as there are antecedent conditions which decisively incline the [person's] will in one way or another without constraining it. To act without constraint means to act in accord with one's desires."[20] If our choices have any hint of being coerced or if the desires that appeal to us the most are thwarted by compelling reasons so that we don't act on those choices, then freedom is diminished or lost.

Coal miners in West Virginia in the early twentieth century often had no other jobs available to them. Those who descended into the bowels of the earth to extract the black chunks of carbon risked their lives every day, fearing shaft collapses, various kinds of gas explosions, and black-lung disease. West Virginia mine accidents claimed over thirty-two hundred lives in 1907 alone. Grimy-faced miners reluctantly endured these horrid conditions because it was the only way to feed their families.

Were they free to walk away?

Perhaps, and many did, but only if different circumstances prevailed. For most, constraining forces kept hordes of these coal vassals

20. Feinberg, *No One Like Him*, 290.

in the dirty, dark holes for their entire lives. Contrast this with those who have various reasons to love their jobs—professional athletes who sign multimillion-dollar contracts, surgeons who recover ill-fated lives, architects who design shiny edifices, and teachers who mold the futures of eager learners. We say that they are freer because they happily spring forward into their occupations with few constraints to discourage them.

Now, the sort of freedom described here applies only to *general* human actions of a morally inconsequential nature. In other words, what coffee cup will you choose as you open the cupboard—red or green? Such choices carry no moral significance and do not impact us one way or another in terms of our eternal destiny. But the Bible is concerned with a deeper and far more significant kind of freedom that is entirely *moral* and *spiritual* in nature. In this regard, humans suffer bondage of their wills due to enslavement to sin (John 8:34; 2 Peter 2:19). Sin constrains the will from choosing what is truly righteous, and yet many are unaware that such constraints exist because they freely choose to act in accordance with their sinful desires. The Son of God came to set people free from this spiritual bondage (John 8:36). The believer experiences the firstfruits of spiritual freedom in this life (see chapters 9 and 11), but the full consummation of such freedom will come only with our future glorification (see chapter 12).

The Decretive and Preceptive Wills of God

In the next two chapters, we will explore biblical examples of compatibilism. But before proceeding, it is vitally important to draw some distinctions in the will of God that will inform those investigations. Scripture indicates at least two senses in which the "will" of God is spoken. Consider first of all what theologians call God's *decretive* will. This is God's sovereign will whereby he ordains or decrees all events that transpire in space, time, and history, including all human actions, and ensures that they will certainly take place (chapter 3). God's decree is his blueprint for history. He doesn't usually tell us what he determines to happen, so sometimes this is called God's *secret will* (Deut. 29:29). Prophecy, however, is the unusual case in which God's decretive will is disclosed for us to see beforehand. Ephesians 1:11 speaks of God's decretive will when it says that he "works all things according to the counsel of his will."[21] In this passage, God labors ("works") to accomplish "all things" that transpire in creation. Nothing escapes his meticulous providential guidance. He does all this "according to the counsel of his will." This, of course, indicates his unswerving decree. It means that nothing can thwart God's decretive will, including human choices (Dan. 4:35).

Second, theologians speak in terms of God's *preceptive* will. This is the revealed will of God in Scripture that declares or instructs us in what God has established as righteous, wise, good, and true. Some call this God's *moral will, instructive will,* or *will of command.* For example, Ephesians 6:6 speaks of believers' "doing the will of God from the heart."[22] When we "do" the will of God, this obviously cannot refer to "doing" his decretive will. We have no providential power to execute God's plan for history. Paul talks about something that can be obeyed or disobeyed. When he adds "from the heart," this shows that the "will" spoken of here has a moral dimension. God is concerned that we do his will with the right motives. Thus, God's decretive will speaks of what *actually* happens, while his preceptive will speaks of what *ought* to happen.[23] In all that follows, we will see that these distinctions are important to make, but that they also serve to highlight a related matter.

Discerning God's Will

Believers often ask, "What is God's will for my life?" As they do so, they sometimes fail to draw these distinctions. Usually they have in mind something more akin to God's decretive will. *Should I marry Peter or John—or neither? Should I move to Detroit or stay in Dallas? Is*

---

21. Other passages indicating God's decretive will include Pss. 33:8–11; 103:19; Prov. 21:1; Isa. 14:24; 46:10; Jer. 50:45; Lam. 3:37–38; Dan. 4:17; Acts 2:23; 4:27–28; Rom. 1:10; 9:19; 1 Cor. 1:1; Eph. 1:5, 9; Phil. 2:13; Col. 1:19; James 1:18; Rev. 4:11.

22. Other passages indicating God's preceptive will include Ezra 10:11; Ps. 103:21; Isa. 65:12; Ezek. 18:23; Matt. 7:21; John 7:17; Acts 17:30; Rom. 12:2; 1 Thess. 4:3; 5:18; Heb. 10:36; 1 Peter 4:2; 1 John 2:17. For further discussion, see John Piper, "Are There Two Wills in God?," in *Still Sovereign*, ed. Thomas R. Schreiner and Bruce A. Ware (Grand Rapids: Baker, 2000), 107–31, also available at http://www.desiringgod.org/resource-library/articles/are-there-two-wills-in-god; and John M. Frame, *The Doctrine of God*, 531–42.

23. Paul Helm, *The Providence of God* (Downers Grove, IL: InterVarsity Press, 1994), 131.

this retail job right for me? The problem is that Christians are asking God to reveal what he has said is a secret.

When life perplexes us and we are not sure what God is doing, it produces a great deal of anxiety. We want to know his plans and whether they will turn out all right in the end. We wonder whether he has become distracted while our lives suddenly start to run off the rails. We ponder, "This doesn't make sense. I can't believe God would allow this to happen—there is no good purpose in it!" This is often the case when we've made every effort to obey the preceptive will of God and yet things go awry. Our efforts seem to go unnoticed by him and the situation only gets worse. We cry out with the psalmist Asaph:

> Will the Lord spurn forever,
>   and never again be favorable?
> Has his steadfast love forever ceased?
>   Are his promises at an end for all time?
> Has God forgotten to be gracious?
>   Has he in anger shut up his compassion? (Ps. 77:7–9)

We can't always be certain what God is doing. He doesn't reveal to us his sovereignly decreed plans for our personal lives. Nor has he given us a divining rod to discover it. Yet this gives us no reason to doubt him. In fact, it is a test of our faith to determine how much we will trust him (1 Peter 1:6–7). No matter what, our attention is always to be focused on what he has revealed to us as his preceptive will found in Scripture. It is the one secure source of truth for our lives when everything else seems unsettled and uncertain.

Psalm 37:4–5 provides a gateway into making sense of God's will. We read, "Delight yourself in the LORD, and he will give you the desires of your heart. Commit your way to the LORD; trust in him, and he will act." This reflects the wisdom literature found in Proverbs, and thus we find here not so much a strict promise but a truism.[24] Note its conditional nature. A believer cannot expect to find her heart's desires

---

24. Allen P. Ross, *A Commentary on the Psalms: Volume 1 (1–41)* (Grand Rapids: Kregel, 2011), 801.

fulfilled through answered prayer if she neglects to delight herself in the Lord. This means that her "delight is in the law of the LORD" (Ps. 1:2), with "the law" referring to God's moral revelation in Scripture.[25] Thus, not just any sort of desires will be fulfilled. If one delights and lives in the revealed preceptive will of God, then one's "desires" and "way" will be shaped by it. One finds that whatever desires she entertains, they will never conflict with God's righteous precepts.

The godly person will "commit" her hopes and dreams to the Lord; and as long as her plans don't violate any of his moral principles and she will "trust in him" to answer her petition, then "he will act."

Will he always act?

No, because remember, the statement is a truism, not an absolute promise. James instructs us not to be presumptuous. We "ought to say, 'If the Lord wills, we will live and do this or that'" (James 4:15). Nonetheless, if one meets the conditions of the passage, then she will not suffer disappointment in the Lord because she already delights in him. Perhaps the Lord will supply her with different desires conforming to his preceptive will and he will fulfill those in conformance to his decretive will. Our delight in God not only will shape our other desires, but will in fact become the desire that stands above all others. The bottom line is that discerning the will of God is surprisingly simple. When we meet the conditions of God's preceptive will, then we are free (!) to choose what we want. That sounds libertarian, but if you read on, you will soon discover that this is a compatibilist notion.[26]

Chapter Summary

A distinctly biblical form of compatibilism holds that there is a dual explanation for human acts of choosing. God determines the choices of every person, yet every person freely makes his or her own choices. People are free when they voluntarily choose what they most want to choose, as long as the choices are made in an unhindered way. In either case, what people actually choose, whether hindered

---

25. Ibid., 189.

26. On discerning God's will, see John MacArthur, *Found: God's Will* (Colorado Springs: David C. Cook, 2012); Kevin DeYoung, *Just Do Something* (Chicago: Moody, 2009); Garry Friesen, *Decision Making and the Will of God* (Colorado Springs: Multnomah, 2004).

or not, is determined by a matrix of decisive causes from both within and without. Human choices proceed from people's most compelling motives and desires, which in turn are conditioned on their base nature, whether good or evil. The more voluntary and unconstrained people's choices are, the more freedom and responsibility they have in making them.

God's relationship to human action is like Shakespeare's crafting the story of Macbeth. A good story always has its protagonists and antagonists, its heroes and villains. Without the malignant stratagems of Sauron contrasted with the moral transcendence and determination of the lowly Frodo, Tolkien's *The Lord of the Rings* would fail to resonate with the marrow of our humanity. Such stories captivate our attention because of the clash of good and evil and the complexities of the conflict between the two. If evil provided no foil for righteousness to prevail, life would sink into a hollow impassivity. This explains why the redemptive triumph of Christ over all diabolical powers becomes the greatest narrative of history.

Glossary

concurrence. The doctrine of God's providential action in the world whereby he is the *primary* but *remote cause* of all human actions. Likewise, humans are the *secondary* but *proximate cause* of their own actions.

decretive will. God's sovereign will whereby he ordains or decrees all events that transpire in space, time, and history, including all human actions. God ensures that his decrees will certainly take place. Sometimes this is called God's *secret will*, since he does not normally reveal what he intends to do.

general freedom. In *compatibilism*, the concept that humans have the freedom to choose what they most want to choose with regard to morally inconsequential actions, but that they remain in bondage to sin unless they are liberated by the work of *regeneration*. See also *moral/spiritual freedom*.

instructive will. See *preceptive will*.

moral/spiritual freedom. In *compatibilism*—which teaches that in their natural state human beings remain in bondage to their *sin* *nature*—the state of the sinner in which the work of *regeneration* liberates him or her from this bondage. See also *general freedom*.

moral will. See *preceptive will*.

preceptive will. God's revealed will in Scripture whereby he declares or instructs us what he has established as righteous, wise, good, and true. Some call this God's *moral will, instructive will*, or *will of command*.

primary cause. In *compatibilism*, God as the ultimate orchestrator of all human actions. His eternal decrees determine all that transpires in human history. See also *concurrence, secondary cause, proximate cause*, and *remote cause*.

proximate cause. In *compatibilism*, the immediate source of human choice; the near cause. While humans are the *secondary cause* of their own actions, they are also the immediate cause, acting in response to their most compelling motives and desires. See also *concurrence, primary cause*, and *remote cause*.

remote cause. In *compatibilism*, God as distant initiator of human actions, working through secondary means. While God is the *primary cause* of all human actions, he is not the *proximate cause* of those actions. In other words, he does not normally act directly upon humans, bypassing their freely made choices. See also *concurrence* and *secondary cause*.

secondary cause. In *compatibilism*, humans as the orchestrators of all their actions. God is the *primary cause* of all human actions, but he accomplishes his purposes through the means of secondary human agents. See also *concurrence, proximate cause*, and *remote cause*.

secret will. See *decretive will*.

sovereign will. See *decretive will*.

will of command. See *preceptive will*.

Study Questions

1. Place yourself in the "apple and grub worm pie" illustration. How would you choose? Would your choice be determined by prior causes? Would your choice be free? Explain your answers.

2. What is the dual explanation for human actions that biblical compatibilism embraces?

3. What is meant when the author says that the divine cause of human actions is (1) *primary* and (2) *remote*? Conversely, what is meant when the author says that the human cause of one's actions is (1) *secondary* and (2) *proximate*?

4. Give some examples of both *internal* and *external* causes affecting one's choices.

5. What does Jonathan Edwards mean when he says that the human will is both active and passive?

6. What is the "domino show" view of God's providential control, and why is it an inadequate model to describe God's sovereignty?

7. What is the "author-actor" view of God's providential control, and what benefits does this model have in describing God's sovereignty?

8. In compatibilism, in what sense are a person's actions free? How is one free and yet not free with regard to moral and spiritual choices?

9. How does the compatibilistic view of freedom of choice differ from the libertarian view?

10. What is the difference between God's decretive (sovereign) will and God's preceptive (moral) will?

11. How does Psalm 37:4–5 help us to discern God's will when making important decisions?

Resources for Further Study

D. A. Carson, *How Long, O Lord? Reflections on Suffering and Evil* (Grand Rapids: Baker, 2006). Chapters 11 and 12 provide a very insightful treatment of compatibilism.

Jonathan Edwards, *The Freedom of the Will*, vol. 1 of *The Works of Jonathan Edwards*, ed. Paul Ramsey (New Haven, CT: Yale University Press, 1957). The classic defense of compatibilism. Even though it is difficult reading, it rewards the diligent student.

John S. Feinberg, *No One Like Him* (Wheaton, IL: Crossway, 2001). Provides a thorough defense of compatibilism. See especially chapters 13 through 16. More philosophical.

John M. Frame, *The Doctrine of God* (Phillipsburg, NJ: P&R Publishing, 2002). Chapter 8 provides a good defense of compatibilism.

————. *Systematic Theology: An Introduction to Christian Belief* (Phillipsburg, NJ: P&R Publishing, 2013). Chapter 35 repeats the same basic material on compatibilism from *The Doctrine of God.*

James S. Spiegel, *The Benefits of Providence: A New Look at Divine Sovereignty* (Wheaton, IL: Crossway, 2005). Chapters 1 and 2 provide a good defense of compatibilism.

Sam Storms, "Jonathan Edwards on the Freedom of the Will," *Trinity Journal* 3, 2 (1982). One of the best explanations of Jonathan Edwards's classic work *Freedom of the Will.*

————. "The Will: Fettered Yet Free," in *A God Entranced Vision of All Things*, ed. John Piper and Justin Taylor (Wheaton, IL: Crossway, 2004). Some excellent insights on a compatibilist view of free agency.

Mark R. Talbot, "True Freedom: The Liberty That Scripture Portrays as Worth Having," in *Beyond the Bounds*, ed. John Piper, Justin Taylor, and Paul Kjoss Helseth (Wheaton, IL: Crossway, 2003). Some excellent insights on a compatibilist view of free agency.

Bruce A. Ware, "The Compatibility of Determinism and Human Freedom," in *Whomever He Wills: A Surprising Display of Sovereign Mercy*, ed. Matthew M. Barrett and Thomas J. Nettles (Cape Coral, FL: Founders Press, 2012). One of the best concise explanations of biblical compatibilism.

5

A Dual Explanation for Why Good Stuff Happens

In our criminal-justice system, a man is regarded as innocent unless proven guilty. This means that the prosecution bears the burden of proof to convict a man of a crime. A friend of mine was summoned to jury duty for a homicide trial in Los Angeles. In spite of the prosecution's best efforts to show otherwise, all the jurors thought the defendant was innocent except one—my friend. He was faced with a similar scenario to the one depicted in the classic 1957 film *Twelve Angry Men*. The film is also about a homicide trial, but in this case all but one jury member think the defendant is guilty. As the movie unfolds (spoiler alert!), the dissenting character (played by Henry Fonda) calmly, methodically, and relentlessly convinces the other jury members to change their minds. In the end, they pronounce the necessary unanimous "not guilty" verdict to acquit the defendant. My friend had the opposite task. He bore the burden of showing that the prosecution had a far stronger case than it had presented. One by one he convinced the other jurors that the defendant was guilty.

The notion of free will virtually accepted by default in the minds of most people, without much reflection, is that which resembles libertarianism. In many ways, compatibilists bear the burden of proof to show that this view of divine sovereignty and human action is correct. The notion of a dual explanation for human choices sounds like a nice theory, but where is the evidence? It might appear scant until a closer look at the prime depository of truth reveals otherwise.

The next two chapters will seek to demonstrate a positive case for compatibilism from the scriptural record.

Take note of the logic here. First, the broad survey of God's sovereignty in chapter 3 laid the groundwork for the divine side of the compatibilist equation. Chapter 4 mapped the parameters of compatibilism. In this chapter and the next, we will see how the divine and human sides of the equation are linked through the testimony of biblical examples.[1] Then in the following chapters, we will explore in greater detail the human side of the equation.

God Grants What He Commands

This chapter examines prevalent patterns of compatibilism in which a response of human obedience matches what God is already doing. God grants that which he commands. His sovereign decretive will matches his preceptive will, the moral instructions that are binding on his creatures. God does not determine the ends without also establishing the means.

Conforming to Holiness

An example of how God's two wills align in the outcome of human actions is shown by how he conforms his children to his own holiness. In Leviticus 20:7–8, we read: "Consecrate yourselves, therefore, and be holy, for I am the LORD your God. Keep my statutes and do them; I am the LORD who sanctifies you." God commands his people Israel to be holy because he himself is holy. This is a call to act responsibly. It assumes that the recipients have a moral obligation to exercise their wills in obedience. Yet within the same breath by which God issues this injunction, he states, "I am the LORD who sanctifies you [makes you holy]." Israel is to exercise her will to be holy, and yet it is still God who causes her to be holy.

This is a pattern that all believers need to absorb into their thinking. John MacArthur asks, "How do you overcome sin and live

---

1. Many of these examples are treated in D. A. Carson, *How Long, O Lord? Reflections on Suffering and Evil* (Grand Rapids: Baker, 2006), 183–88; D. A. Carson, *Divine Sovereignty and Human Responsibility: Biblical Perspectives in Tension* (Atlanta: John Knox: 1981), 9–38, 125–34. I am indebted to many of Carson's insights.

the Christian life? Is defeating sin something God does in you, or do you defeat it by obeying the commands of Scripture? In other words, is the Christian life an exercise in *passive* trust or *active* obedience?"[2] The answer is that both are true. As believers actively commit themselves to God's instruction for our obedience, we must in fact pray with confidence that God would grant that which he commands.[3] Praying in such a way should be a model for all petitionary prayer. As Jesus taught us, "Your will be done, on earth as it is in heaven" (Matt. 6:10).

Paul lays out this tension between passive trust and active obedience: "But by the grace of God I am what I am, and his grace toward me was not in vain. On the contrary, I worked harder than any of them, though it was not I, but the grace of God that is with me" (1 Cor. 15:10). The apostle embraces the responsibility and reality of his efforts to labor in ministry and obedience to God's call. Yet he also understands that it is not his own energy that empowers and motivates him, but the gracious action of God working in him: "For this I toil, struggling with all his energy that he powerfully works within me" (Col. 1:29; cf. Eph. 3:20).

This mind-set regarding the collusion of two actions—one human and one divine—is fueled by Paul's confidence that the reconciliation of the believer is accomplished by Christ's death, which results in our eventual glorification. Christ promises to "present" us one day as "holy and blameless and above reproach" in his very presence (Col. 1:22). And yet this promise, though certain, is predicated upon the fact that the believer must "continue in the faith, stable and steadfast, not shifting from the hope of the gospel that you heard" (v. 23). The ends are promised only by way of the prescribed means, and both the ends and the means are wholly directed by God.

This principle is magnified in Philippians 2:12–13: "Therefore, my beloved, as you have always obeyed, so now, not only as in my presence but much more in my absence, work out your own salvation

---

2. John MacArthur, "The Apparent Paradox of Sanctification," available at http://www.gty.org/blog/B140702 (emphasis in original).

3. Note the famous prayer of Augustine: "Grant what you command, and command what you will." *Confessions*, 10.29. This is how Solomon prayed at the dedication of the temple (compare 1 Kings 8:46–50 with vv. 57–58).

with fear and trembling, for it is God who works in you, both to will and to work for his good pleasure" (cf. Phil. 4:13; Heb. 13:20–21). Paul commands believers to "work out" their salvation, to labor hard "with fear and trembling" as blood, sweat, and tears roll down their weary bodies. But nothing of this intense work of sanctification is in vain, Paul stresses. To encourage our labor, he reminds us that it is simultaneously "God who works in you" (v. 13). The spiritual energy of sanctification that transpires "is discovered *not by God's grace trumping and erasing our effort but by fueling it.* . . . Human striving does not *compete* with but *completes* the sovereign will of God."[4] Without the prior "work" of God within, there is no "will" in us to "to work for his good pleasure." The New Living Translation captures Paul's sentiment well: "For God is working in you, giving you the desire to obey him and the power to do what pleases him."

The whole of the Christian life is a compatibilistic enterprise. Yet the important thing to note is that God is the lead actor in this unfolding drama. Although we seek to submit to the purposes of God, nonetheless it takes place only because his sovereign "will" works to accomplish "his good pleasure." Paul reiterates an earlier divine promise: "And I am sure of this, that he who began a good work in you will bring it to completion at the day of Jesus Christ" (Phil. 1:6). B. B. Warfield writes: "The Christian works out his own salvation under the energizing of God, to whose energizing is due every impulse to good that rises in him, every determination to good which he frames, every execution of a good purpose which he carries into effect."[5]

Four Models of Sanctification

This dual principle critically orients our perspective regarding sanctification. In examining how Christians commonly think about their growth in Christ, several models of sanctification are deficient.[6]

---

4. Dane Ortlund, *A New Inner Relish: Christian Motivation in the Thought of Jonathan Edwards* (Fearn, Scotland: Christian Focus, 2008), 117–18 (emphasis in original).

5. B. B. Warfield, "Working Out Salvation," in *Faith and Life* (Carlisle, PA: Banner of Truth, 1974), 312.

6. My first introduction to thinking about the following four models of sanctification came from Jerry Bridges, *The Crisis of Caring: Recovering the Meaning of True Fellowship* (Phillipsburg, NJ: Presbyterian and Reformed, 1985), 35–40.

First, sanctifying growth in holiness is not a matter of our working it out like a lonesome Texas Ranger pursuing a band of elusive Comanches across a barren prairie. We have no intrinsic power for Christlike growth on our own. We might call this *Me Alone* sanctification.

Second, it doesn't reflect the passive and powerless cliché "Let go and let God." We don't sit comfortably and drink our tea while God infuses us with a mystical holiness. Although it sounds pious, this *God Alone* model falls short as well.[7]

Third, others think sanctification is a cooperative effort whereby we do our part and God does his. God is our copilot, either making up for what we can't do on our own or supplying us with the necessary support to fly the plane of sanctification. This *God Plus Me* scenario might be mistaken as compatibilist, but don't be misled. This position is actually more in line with Arminianism. Sanctification in this case is synergistic.[8] God's grace is necessary for a believer to persevere in her faith, but that grace is not sufficient for perseverance. The believer must cooperate with that grace by the exercise of her free will. Without such diligence, she can fall away from the faith and be lost once again.

To be faithful to Scripture, however, we discover a wholly different model of sanctification. In this fourth model, we work 100 percent toward the progress of our sanctification while simultaneously trusting that God is 100 percent at work in us. We might call this the *All God and All Me* model of sanctification. The necessary trust in God's sufficient power to achieve Christlikeness is attended by a corresponding and necessary obedience that he demands from us (Eph. 1:18–19; 3:16–17). In the end, "sanctification is God's work,

---

7. Historically, this position is associated with what is called *Keswick theology*. For a critique, see Andrew David Naselli, "Keswick Theology: A Survey and Analysis of the Doctrine of Sanctification in the Early Keswick Movement," *Detroit Baptist Seminary Journal* 13 (2008): 17–67; Andrew David Naselli, *Let Go and Let God? A Survey and Analysis of Keswick Theology* (Bellingham, WA: Lexham Press, 2010).

8. The idea that God alone sanctifies could be termed *monergistic sanctification*. Likewise, the idea that it is a cooperative effort could be termed *synergistic sanctification*. Mike Riccardi clarifies these issues in the article "Sanctification: Monergistic or Synergistic?," available at http://thecripplegate.com/sanctification-monergistic-or-synergistic/.

but he performs it through the diligent self-discipline and righteous pursuits of his people, not in spite of them. God's sovereign work does not absolve believers from the need for obedience; it means their obedience is itself a Spirit-empowered work of God."[9] Thus, our final sanctification (Phil. 1:6) is assured.

Peter tells us that God's "divine power has granted to us all things that pertain to life and godliness" (2 Peter 1:3). He then goes on to say, "For this very reason, make every effort" to cultivate godly character (v. 5). The "reason" that we can cultivate the virtues to which Peter calls us has everything to do with the prior work of God granting us the power to do so. The "practice" of these godly virtues becomes the evidence of God's "calling and election" of us (v. 10). Furthermore, their cultivation gives us assurance that our "entrance into the eternal kingdom" will be "richly provided" for us (v. 11). No one will see heaven without achieving practical holiness (Heb. 12:14), but no one will see holiness without the sanctifying Spirit of Christ working his power in us (2:10–11). Only a compatibilist perspective clarifies the truth of sanctification that the Bible paints for us.[10]

Divine Security through Perseverance

In a vein that parallels sanctification, many believers are under the false illusion that they can lose their salvation, including self-conscious Arminians and those who think unwittingly in Arminian categories. The presuppositions that underlie this sort of thinking miss the truth that biblical compatibilism provides. Those who are skeptical about the eternality of salvation appeal to Scriptures that speak of the need to endure, continue, abide, persevere, and hold fast until the end.[11] To avoid apostatizing, "the only remedy is a constant perseverance in the faith, and continual growth to Christian Maturity."[12] If one doesn't maintain his cooperative efforts with God's grace, he will lose his

9. MacArthur, "The Apparent Paradox of Sanctification."

10. See Kevin DeYoung, *Hole in Our Holiness* (Wheaton, IL: Crossway, 2012), for a corrective to defective views of sanctification.

11. See, e.g., Matt. 24:13; John 8:31; 15:6; 1 Cor. 15:2; 2 Tim. 2:12; Heb. 3:6, 14; James 1:12; Rev. 3:10.

12. Grant R. Osborne, "Soteriology in the Epistle to the Hebrews," in *Grace Unlimited*, ed. Clark H. Pinnock (Minneapolis: Bethany House, 1975), 153.

salvation. But if we had no power to sufficiently secure our salvation in the first place, what makes us think we can maintain it?[13]

Again, Peter helps us out. He is emphatic that all believers have received an eternal "inheritance that is imperishable, undefiled, and unfading, kept in heaven" for us (1 Peter 1:4). The future hope of our salvation is secure.

How is this so?

Because "God's power" guards this inheritance (1 Peter 1:5). If Peter had stopped here, we would have a truncated view of our eternal security, and it might lead to a carelessness that takes this truth for granted. God certainly protects the salvation of all his children, but it doesn't happen strictly because this isolated statement says so. Rather, Peter indicates that this protection is secured through particular means, that is, "through faith" (v. 5). God ensures that everyone who is truly saved continues to be saved because his faith endures, perseveres, and holds fast until the end.

Such a faith is not generated by our own resources. It is a supernatural faith supplied by God. He decreed such faith in the lives of those whom he chose for salvation. Yet at the same time, his chosen ones actively exercise this enduring commitment, persevering in order to demonstrate that God is always at work in them. One can understand neither the doctrine of sanctification nor the doctrine of the eternal security and perseverance of the saints without this compatibilist perspective.

Rescue through Adherence to Divine Instructions

On numerous occasions, God commands others to act in accordance with what he has already promised to grant. As strange as it seems, God's sovereign (decretive) will appears dependent on the adherence of others to his instructive (preceptive) will. Yet the truth is quite the opposite. Adherence to God's instructions serves as an instrument in his hands. He requires compliance to his commands

---

13. Many inconsistent Arminians hold that believers *cannot* lose their salvation. Calvinists regard this as inconsistent because it suggests that some determinative force (generally God) prevents Christians from exercising their libertarian will to reject what they now no longer wish to hold to.

as the very *means* by which he accomplishes his goals. People are responsible to obey, but he also ensures that they will.

This pattern is reflected in Paul's shipwreck experience in Acts 27 while he is being led captive on a perilous voyage to Rome. The crew and passengers endure a tumultuous storm that assaults the Mediterranean Sea and tosses their little vessel to and fro while it struggles to navigate the tempest. In a moment of desperation when they all fear for their lives, Paul addresses the ship:

> Yet now I urge you to take heart, for there will be no loss of life among you, but only of the ship. For this very night there stood before me an angel of the God to whom I belong and whom I worship, and he said, "Do not be afraid, Paul; you must stand before Caesar. And behold, God has granted you all those who sail with you." So take heart, men, for I have faith in God that it will be exactly as I have been told. But we must run aground on some island. (Acts 27:22–26)

Paul assures his shipmates that God has "granted" (v. 24) the lives of everyone on board. His confidence is expressed in verse 25: "I have faith in God that it will be exactly as I have been told."

That might appear to be the end of the story. One could be a fatalist at this point and say, "It doesn't matter now what we do; God has promised the safety of our lives." Not so fast. Later, when the ship runs aground, threatening to break up the hull, a group of sailors panic and try to escape in a dinghy. Paul scolds the centurion, "Unless these men stay in the ship, you cannot be saved" (Acts 27:31). God's sovereign decree does not abrogate sound judgment, but it is in fact carried out by way of such exercises of practical wisdom. As long as everyone stays together, Paul promises, "not a hair is to perish from the head of any of you" (v. 34). The sea would claim no scalps as a result of two parallel realities: (1) God's sovereign decree and (2) commonsense choices dictated by divine instructions.

Confusing Divine Sovereignty with Fatalism

People often have a distorted view of God's sovereignty, one that leads to a fatalist outlook.[14] They think, "Well, if God has determined this to happen, then it doesn't matter what I do." This is not only sheer presumption; it simply isn't true. A soldier may pray for God's protection of his life, but that doesn't give him a blanket endorsement for imbibing large quantities of stupidity. He doesn't suddenly take off his bulletproof vest and quit donning his helmet. He doesn't stand up recklessly on top of his bunker in the midst of enemy fire. If God chooses to grant his request, it is likely never going to be in the absence of sound precautions.

Christians are in a never-ending battle to consistently devote themselves to the spiritual disciplines of the Christian life, such as Bible-reading, prayer, worship, evangelism, serving, and stewardship of their finances.[15] Neglecting these prescribed instruments for spiritual growth can frequently lead to unwise choices. At that point it is easy to blame God's sovereignty for the consequences that naturally follow such decisions. Of course, God is sovereign even in our foolishness, but this is no excuse for saying, "Oh, well! God is in control!" This is like the attitude of the careless and undisciplined soldier who bleeds to death from the bullet that hit his helmetless head: "Oh, well! God determined that I should die."

Christians who believe in God's unwavering sovereign decrees and take that as an excuse to avoid making wise, obedient choices need to understand compatibilism more than they think. Even though God is in control of our lives, we can look back and say that many of our choices were mistakes. They lacked wisdom, and we shouldn't have made them. It is neither wise nor responsible to take God's providential purposes for granted. Likewise, trying obsessively to figure them out is a useless exercise. Wisdom and responsibility lie in staying the course with simple faith and obedience. Our primary focus is to be concerned far more with God's instructive will than with his sovereign will.

But Christians distort God's sovereignty into another brand of fatalism. Prolonged trials and tribulations can lead to discouragement and a hopelessness that tests our trust in God's sovereign control. When

---

14. John Byl, *The Divine Challenge: On Matter, Mind, Math and Meaning* (Carlisle, PA: Banner of Truth, 2004), 223–24.

15. See Donald S. Whitney, *Spiritual Disciplines for the Christian Life* (Colorado Springs: NavPress, 2014).

the road that we plod along seems headed in only one dreadful direction with no possibility of changing course, it is easy to waffle. Christians can find themselves in these moments trading belief in a wise, loving, and sovereign God for a cold and impersonal fate that couldn't care less about their plight. The disconcerting reality about this switch in one's thinking is that it is God who has become the nebulous force of fate. This maneuver happens imperceptibly. Surely God would never allow such ongoing trials without answering our prayers for intervention or rewarding our obedience by altering our circumstances for the better!

After being on this dark highway for what seems like ages, downcast believers are tempted to stop praying, obeying, and pursuing wisdom to address whatever obstacles lie in their path. It is believed that exercising these disciplines has changed nothing, and so they are abandoned in a fit of frustration and despair. The believer gives up. God is perpetually silent. The good has only lost more ground while evil and calamity prevail. In this case, a fatalist god has usurped the biblical God. We need to shake our deluded selves loose from such nightmares.

In these moments, it is time to learn a lesson or two from the persistent widow in the parable that Jesus taught his disciples in Luke 18:1–8. Believers should never "lose heart" in praying (v. 1) and doing good (Gal. 6:9; 2 Thess. 3:13). Jesus calls us to persevere with our cries toward God (Luke 18:7) until we "wear [him] out" (v. 5 NASB). The question is whether the child of God has the persistent faith that will walk a hundred miles when at first he thought the journey was only one mile (v. 8). God usually brings prolonged trials to test this faith and see whether it will stand firm over the long haul (James 1:2–4; 1 Peter 1:6–7). Persistent prayer, faith, and obedience are the means that God uses to get us through trials and tribulations. They are part of the compatibilist plan.

God Elects to Salvation, and Sinners Convert

One obvious set of examples of compatibilism in Scripture concerns the doctrine of election.[16] Jesus gives us a dual explanation

---

16. See Steven J. Lawson, *Foundations of Grace: 1400 BC–AD 100*, A Long Line of

for conversion: "All that the Father gives me will come to me, and whoever comes to me I will never cast out" (John 6:37). The Father has given his Son a gift of people who will become his followers. How does Jesus receive this gift? Does the Father simply dump followers into his lap? No—they will "come" to him of their own accord even as the Father "draws" them (v. 44). The two actions work simultaneously: the Father's drawing is primary, and the followers' coming is secondary. It is the natural response to come when God silently woos the sinner to Christ. As sinners come, Jesus will never cast them out. Why? Because it is the Father's "will" that Jesus "lose nothing" (v. 39). This lays the foundation for the hope of every believer's assurance.

There are two reasons why sinners "come" to Christ. They come in response to both the *decretive* (sovereign) and the *preceptive* (instructive) wills of God. God doesn't choose people for salvation without those individuals' also exercising their wills to obey God's command to act in faith and repentance. God effectually calls them to salvation, and they in turn call on him for salvation (Joel 2:32).[17] Furthermore, no one can exercise faith and repentance in regard to that of which they are ignorant. Compatibilism therefore has important implications for the doctrine of election as well as evangelism.

Paul appeals to the human dimension of salvation in Romans 10:13: "Everyone who calls on the name of the Lord will be saved." This is a direct cause-effect relationship reflecting the human side of the compatibilist equation. Paul continues:

> How then will they call on him in whom they have not believed? And how are they to believe in him of whom they have never heard? And how are they to hear without someone preaching? And how are they to preach unless they are sent? As it is written, "How beautiful are the feet of those who preach the good news!" (Rom. 10:14–15)

Godly Men 1 (Orlando, FL: Reformation Trust, 2006), for an excellent treatment of the principal passages of Scripture dealing with God's election of sinners to salvation. See also Robert A. Peterson, *Election and Free Will: God's Gracious Choice and Our Responsibility* (Phillipsburg, NJ: P&R Publishing, 2007), for briefer treatments.

17. Carson, *Divine Sovereignty and Human Responsibility*, 15.

In order to believe the gospel, one must first hear it, which means that preachers must preach it, which means that they must be sent. Paul summarizes: "So faith comes from hearing, and hearing through the word of Christ" (v. 17). Salvation blossoms into reality only when God's preceptive and decretive wills are fully aligned.

We see this compatibilist pattern elsewhere. In Acts 13, the gospel had reached non-Jewish audiences, and many were converted. These Gentiles "began rejoicing and glorifying the word of the Lord, and as many as were appointed to eternal life believed" (v. 48). Note Luke's commentary. A certain number of these Gentiles were singled out and sovereignly "appointed" by God to receive eternal life.

Well, that's it, right? No need for evangelism? No need to preach the message? No need for a response to the gospel? No, no, no on all three counts. Upon hearing the message, they voluntarily exercised their wills and "believed." God appointed them to salvation, but they also heard the gospel and believed on Christ for salvation.

In Acts 16, Paul preached in the city of Philippi. Luke records: "A woman named Lydia . . . was listening; and the Lord opened her heart to respond to the things spoken by Paul" (v. 14 NASB). Note the critical components to her conversion. First, Paul preached. Second, Lydia listened. Third, "the Lord opened her heart." Fourth, she responded in faith. All necessary steps.

The only visible signs of her salvation experience, however, are that Paul preached, she listened, and then she responded. No indication exists that either Lydia or Paul was aware of God's invisible act of opening her heart. Yet without it, she would not have responded in faith. How many Christians can recall God's actively opening their hearts to salvation at the moment of their conversion? Not many. Yet the only way in which saving faith can be exercised is by the regenerative work of God through his Word and Spirit (John 3:3, 5; Titus 3:5; James 1:18).

Once again, there is a lesson for naive Calvinists who act as though God's sovereignty abrogated responsible obedience.[18] The excuses are manifold:

18. This is not classic Calvinism at all; rather, it is hyper-Calvinism.

If God has chosen people to salvation, then surely they will come. I don't need to bear witness to the gospel.

This job is a cesspool of temptations that I can't resist, but God controls all things, and that means that he wants me here.

God has promised to make me like Christ, so why weary myself to pursue the means of getting there?

These are cases of serious cognitive disconnect in which a distorted weight is laid on God's decretive will at the expense of his preceptive will. Compatibilism is a strong antidote to extremist and distorted forms of Calvinism. Believers can never excuse their inaction by mindless appeals to divine sovereignty.

Let me illustrate. The Durango and Silverton Narrow Gauge Railroad is a classic nineteenth-century steam train that runs back and forth between—yes, that's right—Durango and Silverton, Colorado. The railway runs through a clearly defined narrow path along the Animas River marked by deep canyon walls cut through the gorgeous San Juan Mountains. Its rail tracks are fixed with no divergent paths. When the train leaves Durango, its destination is always Silverton. It is absolutely decreed. But nobody with that knowledge assumes that because the destination is certain, all he has to do is to step on the train. The train will *never* end up in Silverton unless the engine works, water is in the boiler, coal is loaded in the tender box, and the engineer properly operates the train. The train's destination is certain as long as all the proper means for getting there are correctly functioning.

We have seen that the destinations God determines are fixed and certain. They will not deviate from the path he decreed. But in the instances of compatibilism that we have explored so far, God also does not depart from the established *means* he designed in order to achieve his *determined ends*. There are no excuses for slackers. Obedience to God's precepts revealed in Scripture is an integral part of the cause-effect pattern in these particular sovereign decrees.

This perspective drove many of the most important pioneers in modern missions. They also happened to be Calvinists. Notable are men such as John Eliot (1604–90), the first missionary to American Indians during the colonial era. David Brainerd (1718–47) later became a missionary to the Delaware Indians in New Jersey. His short life of constant suffering and labor was memorialized when his diary was published by Jonathan Edwards. The diary became a driving force for many subsequent missionary endeavors, including those of William Carey (1761–1834), who is often called "the father of modern missions." Carey uttered an iconic statement preached in a sermon urging others to consider missions: "Expect great things from God. Attempt great things for God." This aptly expresses the compatibilistic tension seen in Scripture.

Adoniram Judson (1788–1850) served as a missionary to Burma for forty years and was among the first missionaries in North America to travel overseas. Robert Morrison (1782–1834) was the first Protestant missionary to China and translated the first Bible into the Chinese language. Charles Simeon (1759–1836) was a British pastor well known for his expository preaching. His heart for missions led him to found the Church Missionary Society that has sent more than nine thousand missionaries around the world. Henry Martyn (1781–1812) was one of these missionaries. He was indefatigable in his short life of thirty-one years. When Martyn arrived in Calcutta in 1806, he said, "Now let me burn out for God!" He did so gloriously. David Livingstone (1813–73) was a national hero in Victorian England. The famous medical missionary to Africa was also an explorer who was searching for the origins of the Nile River. John G. Paton (1824–1907) brought the gospel to the cannibalistic tribes among the New Hebrides islands of the South Pacific. He faced constant threats of death, and some feared that he would be eaten. But Paton responded, "If I can but live and die serving and honoring the Lord Jesus, it will make no difference to me whether I am eaten by Cannibals or by worms."[19] Samuel Zwemer (1867–1952) was called "the apostle to Islam" and is the most effective missionary to Muslims to date. Although these men believed that God elects to salvation, they were not ignorant of the means he uses to accomplish his saving goals.[20]

---

19. John G. Paton, *John G. Paton: Missionary to the New Hebrides*, ed. James Paton (Carlisle, PA: Banner of Truth, 1965), 56.

20. We could also add Calvinistic preachers and evangelists used of God to see tens of thousands come to faith, such as William Tennent (1673–1746), Jonathan Edwards (1703–58),

The Revelation and Inspiration of Scripture

One interesting example in which the decretive and preceptive wills of God converge is the revelation and inspiration of Scripture. Scripture is the product of two sets of authors working in concert to produce a divinely inspired and authoritative set of documents communicating God's preceptive will. John MacArthur likes to address this topic by asking a question: "Who wrote the book of Romans, God or Paul?" The answer, of course, is that both did. All Scripture is God-breathed (2 Tim. 3:16). Paul declares, "For I would have you know, brothers, that the gospel that was preached by me is not man's gospel. For I did not receive it from any man, nor was I taught it, but I received it through a revelation of Jesus Christ" (Gal. 1:11–12).

Many suppose that if the Bible is inerrant, it must entail a dictation theory of inspiration.[21] If this were so, it would appear that the human authors mechanically cranked out the words of God in a form of automatic writing while their minds were distracted with other matters. Now, it is true that Paul likely received direct audible revelation from God at times, as did many other writers of Scripture.[22] Most of Paul's revelatory output, however, represents occasional letters he wrote under the inspiration of the Holy Spirit. John Frame defines the inspiration of Scripture as "a divine act that creates an identity between a divine word and a human word."[23] As Paul thought, God secretly inspired. Every word that Paul intended in the biblical letters sprang from his own mind, reflecting his own style, his own motives, and his own concerns. Yet all his intentions, thoughts, and concerns precisely mirrored those of God long before Paul put pen to paper.[24]

George Whitefield (1714–70), Howell Harris (1714–73), Daniel Rowland (1713–90), Asahel Nettleton (1783–1844), and Charles Spurgeon (1832–92).

21. Stephen J. Wellum, "The Importance of the Nature of Divine Sovereignty for Our View of Scripture," *Southern Baptist Journal of Theology* 4, 2 (Summer 2000): 81.

22. See Ex. 34:27; Jer. 30:2; 36:2; Rev. 1:19; 21:5.

23. John M. Frame, *The Doctrine of the Word of God* (Phillipsburg, NJ: P&R Publishing, 2010), 140. Frame endorses what is often called the *concursive* view of inspiration (i.e., corresponding to the broader doctrine of concurrence).

24. Some might argue that this would be true of anything that anybody wrote if compatibilism holds; therefore, it makes Scripture no more unique than any other human writing. Yet while God certainly stands behind all that is written from the perspective of his *decretive* will, Scripture alone contains his *preceptive* will for mankind—his precise and

Is it possible that Paul used libertarian free will to write that which was contrary to God's design? Absolutely not.

Paul was not free to write against what God intended, yet he freely wrote what he most wanted to write. God made sure that what Paul most wanted to write was *precisely* (i.e., every jot and tittle) what he himself wanted.[25] If one holds to libertarian freedom, it becomes very difficult to see how God guaranteed that the human authors of Scripture would write anything that corresponded to his desires. Maybe they just happened to write everything he intended, but this is so improbable as to render it virtually impossible.[26] Even if God strongly influenced them to write his divine precepts, they could have always resisted this influence, mixing it with their own contrary thoughts and words. Unless God causally determines the words of Scripture in some way, it seems that one is inevitably led to a defective view of Scripture's revelation, inspiration, and inerrancy and its infallible conveyance of divine truth.

In 1978 a group of distinguished evangelical scholars put together a critical document called the "Chicago Statement on Biblical Inerrancy." This statement remains perhaps the most important document on this subject in church history. Three sections in the middle of the document reflect a compatibilist understanding of Scripture. Articles 7, 8, and 9 make affirmations and denials that clarify how we should understand the doctrine of inspiration:

> Article VII. We affirm that inspiration was the work in which God by His Spirit, through human writers, gave us His Word. The origin of Scripture is divine. The mode of divine inspiration remains largely a mystery to us.
>
> We deny that inspiration can be reduced to human insight, or to heightened states of consciousness of any kind.

---

comprehensive instructions representing the fullness of spiritual truth. No other human writing is characterized by this infallible revelation and cannot be trusted in the same way that inspired Scripture can. God *ordains* all human writing, but he isn't the *author* of all human writing in the sense that it conveys his *own* thoughts, purposes, commands, and so on.

25. Bruce A. Ware, *God's Greater Glory: The Exalted God of Scripture and the Christian Faith* (Wheaton, IL: Crossway, 2004), 91.

26. Wellum, "Importance of Divine Sovereignty," 83–84.

Article VIII. We affirm that God in His Work of inspiration utilized the distinctive personalities and literary styles of the writers whom He had chosen and prepared.

We deny that God, in causing these writers to use the very words that He chose, overrode their personalities.

Article IX. We affirm that inspiration, though not conferring omniscience, guaranteed true and trustworthy utterance on all matters of which the Biblical authors were moved to speak and write.

We deny that the finitude or fallenness of these writers, by necessity or otherwise, introduced distortion or falsehood into God's Word.[27]

These statements demonstrate that Scripture is both divine and human, with the divine character serving as the driving force. Yet the divine nature of Scripture in no way abrogates the freely expressed and uniquely human quality of the immediate writers' specific words. Both authors express independent, yet unified intentions. The divine author acts invisibly and remotely, yet primarily. The human author acts visibly and immediately, yet secondarily. Both authors conspire to produce the divine Word that God determined humanity to hold in its hands. It is a compatibilistic work.

Chapter Summary

The Bible reveals prevalent patterns of compatibilism in which a response of human obedience matches what God is already doing. God's sovereign decretive will matches his preceptive will, the moral instructions that are binding on his creatures. God does not determine the ends without also establishing the means. This avoids fatalism, which says that if God determines what should happen, it doesn't matter what people do; they have no impact on the outcome of the future. The Bible teaches otherwise. For example, God determines to make his people holy, and yet they are commanded to be holy.

27. http://www.etsjets.org/files/documents/Chicago_Statement.pdf.

We also see that God elects sinners to salvation, but that they must repent and believe to be saved. Jesus gives us a dual explanation for conversion: "All that the Father gives me will come to me, and whoever comes to me I will never cast out" (John 6:37). The Father has given his Son a gift of people who will become his followers. How does Jesus receive this gift? They will "come" to him of their own accord even as the Father "draws" them (John 6:44). It is the natural response to come when God silently woos the sinner to Christ.

In another instance of compatibilism, we see that God determines every word of Scripture, yet men freely wrote the same words in accordance with their own intentions. The human authors were not free to write against what God intended, yet they freely wrote what they most intended to write. God made sure that what they most wanted to write was *precisely* what he himself wanted them to write.

Study Questions

1. In what way are Christians *active* and in what way are they *passive* in the outworking of holiness in their lives?

2. How do God's divine promises concerning our sanctification encourage us? Conversely, how can these same promises be taken for granted?

3. Describe the four different models of sanctification that the author considers. What are the strengths and weaknesses of each model?

4. According to 1 Peter 1:5, what is the relationship between "faith" and "God's power" in connection to salvation? Is one or the other indispensable to one's eternal security? Explain your answer.

5. What lessons can the believer learn from Paul's shipwreck experience in Acts 27? How does the believer balance the exercise of common sense and sound judgment with trust in God's sovereignty?

6. What is fatalism, and how do Christians sometimes confuse it with God's sovereignty? Can you provide an example of how Christians can think fatalistically?

7. Read John 6:37; Acts 13:48; and Acts 16:14. In what way does compatibilism help to explain how God elects sinners to salvation in these passages?

8. How does compatibilism correct faulty notions about divine election?
9. What does the dictation theory say about God's inspiration of Scripture?
10. What is the compatibilistic view of the inspiration of Scripture (sometimes called the *concursive* theory)?
11. How does libertarianism fail to make sense of how human writers were divinely inspired in the writing of Scripture?

Resources for Further Study

D. A. Carson, *How Long, O Lord? Reflections on Suffering and Evil* (Grand Rapids: Baker, 2006). Chapter 11 has a good survey of compatibilistic passages.

Kevin DeYoung, *Hole in Our Holiness* (Wheaton, IL: Crossway, 2012). An excellent corrective to defective views of sanctification.

Steven J. Lawson, *Foundations of Grace: 1400 BC–AD 100*, A Long Line of Godly Men 1 (Orlando, FL: Reformation Trust, 2006). Provides a very helpful and thorough examination of the principal passages of Scripture regarding divine election.

Robert A. Peterson, *Election and Free Will: God's Gracious Choice and Our Responsibility* (Phillipsburg, NJ: P&R Publishing, 2007). Good treatment of principal passages of Scripture on divine election.

Stephen J. Wellum, "The Importance of the Nature of Divine Sovereignty for Our View of Scripture," *Southern Baptist Journal of Theology* 4, 2 (Summer 2000). An excellent article on why a libertarian view of free will cannot make sense of the divine inspiration of Scripture, whereas compatibilism does.

6

A Dual Explanation for Why Bad Stuff Happens

There may be no more forlorn figure in the Bible than Judas. After A.D. 33, who dared to name his child *Judas*? It has become an eponym for treachery of the highest order. His name evokes the deepest scorn, and yet sometimes there resides a certain degree of sympathy for the sad plight of his life. Here is a man who had an unprecedented opportunity to sit and drink freely from the life-giving words that poured forth from the mouth of the Son of God. But in turn, Judas used his own mouth to silently betray his Master with a kiss. This was his divinely determined destiny, and he embraced it with both greed and regret. Yet what is most perplexing about the life of Judas is how God could take what was so wrong about the man to help advance what is so right—the death of "the Lamb of God, who takes away the sin of the world!" (John 1:29). History is replete with such complicated and disturbing episodes. They require deeper exploration.

In the previous chapter, we considered categories of compatibilism that harmonize God's decretive and preceptive wills. Now we consider passages of Scripture that highlight disharmony between God's two wills. The previous set of examples shows God as providentially superintending that which he commands. Here, however, we see him as superintending that which he *does not* command.[1] Paul Helm writes, "God controls all

---

1. Placing all instances of compatibilism into these two categories could appear artificial and forced. D. A. Carson warns against trying to filter God's will through rigid grids that miss the nuances of many passages that resist such efforts. See his *How Long, O Lord? Reflections on Suffering and Evil* (Grand Rapids: Baker, 2006), 196–200; *Divine Sovereignty and*

events and yet issues moral commands which are disobeyed in some of the very events which he controls."[2] This elicits talk of paradox in which "the breaking of his will [becomes] part of the fulfilling of his will."[3] In these instances, although human actions match precisely what God decrees, God's intentions and man's intentions are diametrically opposed.[4]

Contemplating the notion that God can and does decree things that he otherwise disapproves of is rather disconcerting. It does not fit our tidy picture of God. Nonetheless, it represents the prerogatives of God, and we must leave to him alone the unsearchable wisdom that he utilizes in choreographing such events. When alignment between God's wills is not forthcoming, we must not become dismayed, but rather acknowledge that in many instances in this world, God's wisdom is not ours. He does not ask us to approve of evil as it is acted out on the human stage, but he does ask us to trust him when his contrary designs for evil are deeper than we can fathom (Isa. 55:9; Rom. 11:33).

Good and Evil Intentions

One of the clearest examples of this category comes from the interactions of Joseph with his brothers, who years earlier sold him to Midianite slave traders (Gen. 37:25–36). Joseph has been made prime minister of Egypt, where he once was the slave that his brothers forced him to be. Now in God's providence, they meet again, and Joseph seeks to reconcile with them. In Genesis 45, he admits their egregious sin (v. 4), but he also notes their remorse: "And now do not be distressed or angry with yourselves because you sold me here, for God sent me before you to preserve life" (v. 5). In one breath he acknowledges that they sent him off to Egypt and in the next that "God sent" him. Just to be clear, verse 8 reiterates the fact: "So it was not you who sent me here, but God." Joseph attributes responsibility to their part in the matter while saying

---

Human Responsibility: Biblical Perspectives in Tension (Atlanta: John Knox: 1981), 212–14. Nonetheless, I find these categories useful, even if they do not fully capture the dynamics of God's actions in relation to man's.

2. Paul Helm, *The Providence of God* (Downers Grove, IL: InterVarsity Press, 1994), 133.

3. Ibid., 48.

4. Some say that God's will with respect to evil should be called his *permissive* will. But this is misleading, for it "suggest[s] that somehow God relinquishes control" over evil. John S. Feinberg, *No One Like Him* (Wheaton, IL: Crossway, 2001), 696.

that it parallels what God has already determined (cf. Ps. 105:17). At the time of the incident, neither Joseph nor his brothers had any idea what God chose to do behind the scenes, whereas God knew precisely how they would choose because he had determined the whole outcome.

The climactic statement is made in Genesis 50:20: "As for you, you meant evil against me, but God meant it for good." Carson observes concerning the seemingly ill-fated episode: "The events are presented neither as a wonderful plan of God that the evil brothers almost destroyed by their monstrous wickedness, nor as an evil act that God turned around by his timely intervention. Rather, it was simultaneously the product of two quite different intentionalities, human and divine, vile and good respectively."[5] Joseph's brothers made a choice and *meant* one thing and God made a choice and *meant* another. The two choices had opposite intentions but worked in harmony to achieve the same end.

Christians often say that God turns something bad into something good. This presupposes that the bad thing happened apart from the knowledge or purpose of God and that he must intervene after the fact to straighten things out. But Scripture paints a blunter picture than this.[6] God purposed the evil that Joseph endured but had a good end for it: the preservation of his family. Deeper still, Joseph's misfortune was the instrument by which God maintained all the promises he made to Abraham concerning the establishment of the great nation Israel, which would later facilitate the coming of the Messiah.

The surprising conflict between the two wills of God runs counter to the flow of our human reasoning. If God has some good intention, then should he not achieve that intention by means of circumstances that avoid all taint of evil? If God is going to get you from point A to *good* point C, then why does he have to take you through *bad* point B to get there? This doesn't seem particularly wise on his part. Instead of questioning God's wisdom, however, it is better to realize that often "God permits what He hates to achieve what He loves."[7]

5. D. A. Carson, "God, the Bible and Spiritual Warfare," *Journal of the Evangelical Theological Society* 42, 2 (June 1999): 262.

6. Carson, *Divine Sovereignty and Human Responsibility*, 10.

7. Joni Eareckson Tada and Steven Estes, *When God Weeps* (Grand Rapids: Zondervan, 1997), 84.

God drives us through the howling wind and the pounding hail for many reasons, all of which achieve a greater good.[8] Suffering evil may come to test our faith and serves to draw us closer to him. It forges godly character as nothing else does (1 Peter 1:6–7). Affliction provides us with an opportunity to be conduits of divine comfort to others when they suffer similar adversity (2 Cor. 1:3–7). It allows us a glimpse into the evil that Christ suffered on our behalf so that we may appreciate his sacrifice with greater depth. Persecution of believers also mirrors to others the suffering of Christ so that they can see the power of the gospel (Col. 1:24).[9] There are myriads of reasons why God purposes evil in order to achieve his good designs, and none of them detract from his wisdom.

God Purposes Evildoers to Go Their Own Way

Proverbs 16:4 proclaims, "The LORD has made everything for its own purpose, even the wicked for the day of evil" (NASB). We can never imagine how much evil God prevents in this world because it never transpires. There are times, however, when God removes his restraints and evil runs rampant. He allows a breach in the dam that holds back that body of putrid water ever ready to rush forward. The water may seem to lie calmly, but constant pressure below the surface presses against the dam of divine restraint. The sinful nature in mankind is always poised to break forth and wreak havoc. When it does, God permits evildoers to rush headlong into the natural course of their corruption until they reap what they sow.

The priestly sons of Eli represent a case in point. Here is a curious episode of God's decreeing that which defies his command. Eli reprimands his errant sons and their corrupt ways. "But they would not listen to the voice of their father, for it was the will of the LORD to put them to death" (1 Sam. 2:25; cf. Judg. 14:4). Instead of granting them repentance (Acts 5:31; 2 Tim. 2:25), God allows them to go their own way. They wouldn't listen because they were simply acting in accordance with God's sovereign desires. Later in 1 Samuel 2:35, God

---

8. Ibid., 97–125; James S. Spiegel, *The Benefits of Providence: A New Look at Divine Sovereignty* (Wheaton, IL: Crossway, 2005), 194–206.

9. John Piper, *Filling Up the Afflictions of Christ* (Wheaton, IL: Crossway, 2009), 21–24.

declares: "And I will raise up for myself a faithful priest, who shall do according to what is in my heart and in my mind." This indicates clearly that Eli's sons *did not* act in accordance with God's morally revealed desires. It is a case in which God's decretive will—desiring the death of Eli's sons—is at odds with his preceptive will—desiring that priests be faithful and obedient. God could have determined obedience to their father's demand (paralleling his own), but he did not. Judgment prevailed over mercy.

We see this same pattern in Romans 1. Here the phrase "God gave them up" occurs three times (vv. 24, 26, 28). It speaks of how God relents from his moral restraints and allows evildoers to follow the logical end of their sinful inclinations. He lets them pursue "the lusts of their hearts" (v. 24), their "dishonorable passions" (v. 26), and their "debased mind" (v. 28). God will hinder their evil desires no more, and this serves as a means of judgment. By being allowed to engage in the fullest expression of their rebellious hearts, these wicked people "are storing up wrath" for themselves "on the day of wrath when God's righteous judgment will be revealed" (2:5). What a dreadful day when individuals, communities, and even whole societies implode at the removal of God's hand.

In the meantime, we should never wonder why things are as bad as they are, but marvel at why they aren't worse. God's mercy abounds in this corrupted world. Yet when God does remove his restraints, let no one think he does so by planting temptation in the minds of well-intentioned people. This would contradict the fact that God tempts no one (James 1:13–15). Rather, temptation is already lurking below the surface in the sin nature of humanity, lying in wait to explode once the dam is breached. It appears dormant, but it always crouches like a lion in the shadows, awaiting the opportunity to fasten its ferocious teeth on its prey.

God's Instruments of Restraint

The restraining force of God is often mediated by way of external laws in civil societies (Rom. 13:1–4). When the threat of punishment for violation of moral codes is removed, so is the restraint of evil. Jan Gross has chronicled a brutal example during the occupation of Poland by the Nazis in World War II. Poland was rife with anti-Semitism, and the Nazi occupiers took advantage of this state of affairs. Jedwabne was a small village of sixteen hundred people in which half the residents were Jews. Nazi authorities assured the town's leaders that if the non-Jewish residents took matters into their own hands and eliminated the despised Jews, no repercussions would ensue.

The hatred that seethed below the surface and had been kept in check by the normal sanction of law was suddenly let loose in a fury of violence. Some eight hundred Jewish men, women, and children were rounded up and shot, beaten, bludgeoned, and burned to death by their non-Jewish neighbors. Only seven Jews escaped the mayhem. A glimpse of the unfettered evil of ordinary men's hearts was revealed on that tragic day in the summer of 1941.[10] "The heart is deceitful above all things, and desperately sick; who can understand it?" (Jer. 17:9). If it were not for the safe barriers of civil laws, penalties, and enforcers of peace and order placed all around us, similar anarchic episodes would play out in our midst every day.

God also restrains evil in the world through internal means. He has stamped the knowledge of moral virtue on the hearts of all people (Rom. 2:14–15). The human conscience compels us to experience guilt and shame when we violate the knowledge of moral good. Furthermore, it affirms our morally right choices. The God-given conscience implanted within has shaped the civil laws that govern societies.

Of course, the exercise of moral virtue in those who are unregenerate has tremendous value for the public welfare of societies; nevertheless, it falls short of the glory of God's righteous standard and can never justify sinners in his sight (Rom. 3:23–24). Thus, while it is important that we pursue public means of promoting civic virtue as Christians, it is far more important that we proclaim the gospel. The gospel is the most effective restraint of evil that the world has ever seen.

The Hardened Heart of Pharaoh

The exodus of the Israelites from Egyptian slavery is full of drama virtually unrivaled in history. Moses records for us a series

10. Jan T. Gross, *Neighbors* (New York: Penguin Books, 2002).

of devastating plagues that God executed on the Egyptians before Israel's deliverance. We read of the unfolding disaster in Exodus 4–14. Throughout these episodes of divine judgment, God commands Pharaoh no fewer than ten times to let his people go. Yet in chapter after chapter, Pharaoh's heart is hardened.[11] On eight occasions we read that Pharaoh hardened his own heart.[12] On nine occasions, however, we read that God hardened Pharaoh's heart.[13] No alternating pattern exists here, as if God hardened Pharaoh's heart at one moment and Pharaoh the next. This would suggest that his heart was hardened against his will when God acted, but fully in accord with his own will when he acted, which is nonsense. In every case, Pharaoh fully intended to harden his heart, yet at the same time this reflected the express purpose of God.[14]

A number of things are instructive. For example, God's sovereignty is clear as he orchestrates events according to his decreed plan. The incident puts to rest any doubts about the truth of Proverbs 21:1: "The king's heart is a stream of water in the hand of the LORD; he turns it wherever he will" (cf. Ps. 105:25). We read:

> Then the LORD said to Moses, "Rise up early in the morning and present yourself before Pharaoh and say to him, 'Thus says the LORD, the God of the Hebrews, "Let my people go, that they may serve me. For this time I will send all my plagues on you yourself, and on your servants and your people, so that you may know that there is none like me in all the earth. For by now I could have put out my hand and struck you and your people with pestilence, and you would have been cut off from the earth. But for this purpose I have raised you up, to

11. See G. K. Beale, "An Exegetical and Theological Consideration of the Hardening of Pharaoh's Heart in Exodus 4–14 and Romans 9," *Trinity Journal* 5, 2 (1984): 129–54. Also available at http://faculty.gordon.edu/hu/bi/ted_hildebrandt/otesources/02-exodus /text/articles/beale-hardening-tj.htm.

12. See Ex. 7:13, 22; 8:15, 19, 32; 9:7, 34–35.

13. See Ex. 4:21; 7:3; 9:12; 10:1, 20, 27; 11:10; 14:4, 8.

14. Note in Revelation 17:16 that the beast and the ten horns desire to eat the flesh of the harlot of Babylon and burn her with fire even as God incites "their hearts to carry out his purpose" (v. 17).

show you my power, so that my name may be proclaimed in all the earth. You are still exalting yourself against my people and will not let them go.'"" (Ex. 9:13–17)

God prolongs the plagues in order to humble Pharaoh with his unbridled lordship. The Almighty says, "I have raised you up" (Ex. 9:16), and have not cut you "off from the earth" (v. 15), "so that you may know that there is none like me in all the earth" (v. 14). In hardening Pharaoh's heart, God prevents his moral will from being obeyed. This reveals a greater sovereign purpose that is at odds with God's moral instructions. By determining Pharaoh's stubborn disobedience, God intends to put his glory on display while the Egyptian ruler appears to have no say in the matter (Rom. 9:17).[15] This is hard to square with any notion that Pharaoh had libertarian free will.

Yet in spite of God's unyielding decree, Pharaoh is held responsible for his actions. "At no time was Pharaoh's volition independent of [God's] influence when he hardened his heart."[16] Nonetheless, God attributes culpability to the stubborn ruler: "You are still exalting yourself against my people and will not let them go" (Ex. 9:17). This culpability is evident elsewhere. For example, in 5:2, Pharaoh spews forth in arrogance, "Who is the LORD, that I should obey his voice and let Israel go? I do not know the LORD, and moreover, I will not let Israel go." Moses warns the king in 8:29, "Let not Pharaoh cheat again by not letting the people go to sacrifice to the LORD." In 9:27, Pharaoh acknowledges, "This time I have sinned; the LORD is in the right, and I and my people are in the wrong." His confession here is shallow because in 9:34 we read that after another plague, "he sinned yet again and hardened his heart." The ruler acted of his own accord rooted in his own evil intentions. But then only two verses later, we read that God hardens Pharaoh once again (10:1).

What is the point? God's sovereign dictation of the heart abrogates neither man's freedom (i.e., voluntary actions) nor his responsibility.

Exodus 10:27 sheds further light on the compatibilist nature of these passages. "But the LORD hardened Pharaoh's heart, and he was

---

15. Beale, "Hardening," 150.
16. Ibid., 149.

not willing to let them go" (NASB). Here are two wills set side by side. God *willingly* hardens Pharaoh's heart while Pharaoh is simultaneously *unwilling* to let the people go.[17] Note carefully that God's will does not override the human will. The two wills spring forth from each individual and yet at the same time work in concert to achieve God's purpose. The goals of God are not in mortal combat with human goals. He does not wrestle with his creatures, trying to get them to act against their will. Rather, the human will acts in full complicity with the desires of one's heart, and therein resides culpability.

Jonah and the Sailors

In many passages God ordains the actions of evildoers and then holds them responsible for their sin.[18] Concerning Judas, Jesus said, "For the Son of Man goes as it has been determined, but woe to that man by whom he is betrayed!" (Luke 22:22). Consider the episode of the prophet Jonah. He flees from the command of God to preach to the city of Nineveh by taking passage aboard a ship bound in the opposite direction. The sailors learn of God's displeasure with the prophet as a storm nearly destroys them. Furthermore, Jonah commands them to throw him overboard so that God's anger will give way to calm seas (Jonah 1:10–12). They willingly obey (v. 15), even as Jonah 2:3 attributes this action to God. The sailors reluctantly commit this horrible deed while crying to God for mercy: "Therefore they called out to the LORD, 'O LORD, let us not perish for this man's life, and lay not on us innocent blood, for you, O LORD, have done as it pleased you'" (1:14).

They do not act in ignorance of God's control of the whole situation. Nonetheless, the knowledge that God uses their ethically questionable action for his purposes provides them with no excuse, and so they find themselves on the horns of a dilemma. They see damnable consequences no matter what they do. Scripture forbids doing evil that good may come (Rom. 3:8). God alone reserves the right to ordain evil actions because he always acts righteously and judges all things

17. Note that in Exodus 5:22, Moses says that God has "done evil" to his people, while in verse 23, he says that Pharaoh is the one who has "done evil" to God's people.
18. Jer. 25:9 (cf. v. 12); Ezek. 14:9–10; Matt. 18:7; Acts 2:23; 2 Thess. 2:11–12.

righteously.[19] For this reason, we can be sure in this particular case that God takes into account both the sailors' obedience to his directive and the subsequent remorse for their actions.

God Ordains Evil as Judgment

A number of compatibilist passages picture God as using evil rulers to execute judgment on others. Consider Isaiah 10:5–19, a passage that "throbs with tension."[20] Here Assyria is referred to as the rod of God's anger and the staff of his indignation firmly resting in his hands (v. 5). What is God's intention for this rod and staff? He says, "Against a godless nation I send him" (v. 6). That nation is Israel. If the Assyrians had the ability of contrary choice, then how could God possibly "send" them as his instruments of judgment?[21] The fact is that they were not free to act contrarily; they do precisely as God secretly commanded. The Assyrians will trample the Jews in the streets like mud (v. 6). Do they see themselves as fulfilling their role as judges?

Not at all.

Isaiah 10:7 clarifies: "But [Assyria] does not so intend, and his heart does not so think; but it is in his heart to destroy, and to cut off nations not a few." Assyria has no intention of being a righteous judge of peoples. Rather, the Assyrians intend to wallow in vile acts of violence. They are a wicked people with wicked imperial greed.

Now, once Assyria has finished its rampage, wreaking havoc on Jerusalem and its inhabitants, what is to be said? According to Isaiah 10:12, God declares that the nation will have "finished all *his* work." Okay, no problem, right? Assyria can go home now, job well done.

Not quite.

Isaiah responds with these shocking words in which he prophesies that God "will punish the speech of the arrogant heart of the king of Assyria and the boastful look in his eyes" (Isa. 10:12).

What? Isn't the king a tool of righteous judgment?

19. See Gen. 18:25; Ex. 34:6–7; Deut. 10:17–18; Pss. 9:4; 33:4–5; 96:13; Isa. 9:7; 11:3–4; Jer. 11:20; 1 Peter 2:23; Rev. 19:11.
20. Carson, *Divine Sovereignty and Human Responsibility*, 13.
21. Bruce A. Ware, *God's Greater Glory: The Exalted God of Scripture and the Christian Faith* (Wheaton, IL: Crossway, 2004), 88.

In God's eyes he is, but not in his own. In his heart he is a pompous dictator who desires to sweep up anyone who gets in his way of achieving super-villain status. So self-confident is he that he can't help but boast, "By the strength of *my* hand I have done it, and by *my* wisdom, for I have understanding" (Isa. 10:13). He envisions himself as merrily going about, plucking up eggs out of unattended birds' nests. No flap of a wing or scolding of a mother's beak can be heard to defend all this unguarded treasure (v. 14).

In his haughtiness, a sorry picture emerges of a ruler who has no concept of a sovereign God. The Almighty responds in Isaiah 10:15: "Shall the axe boast over him who hews with it, or the saw magnify itself against him who wields it? As if a rod should wield him who lifts it, or as if a staff should lift him who is not wood!" The king of Assyria thinks that no God exists but himself. Only a fool thinks he is the wielder when in fact he is the wielded. God uses him as a righteous judge, but that is not his own self-perception. Instead, God holds him responsible for his villainous intentions.

What is the ruler's punishment?

God "will send wasting sickness among his stout warriors" (Isa. 10:16). Israel will "burn and devour" him (v. 17), and God will draw his kingdom to a close "as when a sick man wastes away" (v. 18).

One is tempted to think that this whole episode represents unfair manipulation on God's part, using people to do his dirty work and then punishing them for it. But we tread on thin ice here. We can easily find ourselves in the midst of Isaiah 45:9: "Woe to him who strives with him who formed him, a pot among earthen pots! Does the clay say to him who forms it, 'What are you making?' or 'Your work has no handles'?" (cf. Jer. 18:6).

Paul makes the sober observation in Romans 9 that in the matter of election, God chooses to have mercy on whom he desires and conversely hardens whom he desires (v. 18). His decretive will is freely exercised in both cases. Paul takes up a dialogue with the obvious protester who regards this as capriciousness on God's part:

> You will say to me then, "Why does he still find fault? For who can resist his will?" But who are you, O man, to answer back

to God? Will what is molded say to its molder, "Why have you made me like this?" Has the potter no right over the clay, to make out of the same lump one vessel for honorable use and another for dishonorable use? (Rom. 9:19–21)

In such cases, we hold our hands over our mouths and marvel that God extends grace at all, since all deserve his wrath.

God to the Rescue

Second Kings 13 serves as another example of the common refrain: Israel rebels and God sends an evil ruler to punish her. This was the case after Jehoahaz became king of the northern tribes of Israel. Verse 3 reads: "And the anger of the LORD was kindled against Israel, and *he gave* them continually into the hand of Hazael king of Syria and into the hand of Ben-hadad the son of Hazael." This is a straightforward description of God's providential hand putting into the hands of others invisible instructions to carry out his just purpose.

Yet 2 Kings 13:4 adds a curious perspective in the aftermath of these repeated assaults on Israel: "Then Jehoahaz sought the favor of the LORD, and the LORD listened to him, for he saw the oppression of Israel, how the king of Syria oppressed them." The impression is given that God was somehow unaware of what the Syrian ruler was doing until Jehoahaz informed him. He "saw the oppression of Israel" as if he had previously been ignorant and had nothing to do with it. Also note that when the verse reads, "The king of Syria oppressed them," culpability is clearly placed on the ruler's shoulders, not God's.

Second Kings 13:3 frames the episode from the divine perspective, whereas verse 4 frames it from a human perspective. Jehoahaz is unaware that God has used the Syrians to judge his people. He pleads with God to come to the aid of a struggling ally as if he were a distant power from a foreign country. After being made aware of the crisis, the ally decides to act. Without the divine point of view in verse 3, we would miss a vital piece of the overall picture. Much of the Bible is framed like verse 4, describing a situation in which God appears to be just another participant in the unfolding events, acting and reacting as humans themselves do, except perhaps with greater authority and power.

If we view matters only from this truncated perspective, then we miss the fact that God is not like man. He is the Creator and Sustainer of the universe. Man is the creature and is very much distinct from the Creator. Nonetheless, the Creator condescends to the creature so that he often appears to be not unlike ourselves. Verse 4 of 2 Kings 13 indicates that God is *immanent*; he draws close to us and is concerned for our welfare. He thrusts himself right into the heart of our problems. He interacts back and forth with us as if close friends (Jer. 29:10–14). The author of the story is also an actor in the unfolding drama, and he necessarily relates to the other actors in a way that they can identify. Verse 3, however, reveals that God is also *transcendent*; he sits above the fray of the world, yet superintends all that takes place as the ubiquitous Overlord of history. He does not relinquish his status as the author.

Prayer and the Doctrine of Accommodation

These weaker, very finite, humanlike expressions of God's behavior represent what theologians call the doctrine of *accommodation*. Scripture often uses anthropomorphic language to describe God's interactions with his creatures. The word *anthropomorphic* combines the Greek words for *human* (*anthropos*) and *form* (*morphe*). It speaks of attributing human characteristics to God. In this regard, we see passages indicating that God changes his mind (Ex. 32:14), seems ignorant of what is going on (as with the Syrians), or regrets his actions (1 Sam. 15:11). Of course, God does not really change his mind (1 Sam. 15:29; Mal. 3:6; Heb. 13:8; James 1:17) or repent of his actions (Jer. 4:28) because he is not a man. John Calvin describes the matter this way:

> The mode of accommodation is for [God] to represent himself to us not as he is in himself, but as he seems to us. . . . Meanwhile neither God's plan nor his will is reversed, nor his volition altered; but what he had from eternity foreseen, approved, and

decreed, he pursues in uninterrupted tenor, however sudden the variation may appear in men's eyes.[22]

When "Jehoahaz sought the favor of the LORD" (2 Kings 13:4), he was assuming that prayer has the power to effect change in the situation he faced. But if God is sovereign, why pray at all?[23] If God's providential control of every event is certain, then prayer certainly doesn't change God's mind. In this regard, the doctrine of accommodation seems to affirm a hard form of determinism that is barely distinguishable from fatalism. The notion that God condescends to our way of understanding seems like a little joke that God plays with us—a bit of playacting to placate us. But compatibilism strikes a balance between two unbiblical positions. On the one hand, God decrees all that takes place, even though this does not equate to fatalism. Yet on the other hand, man has no power to thwart God's determined path for history even through prayer. So what gives?

Compatibilism reconciles the tension between the fact of God's unbending decree and the numerous commands that we should pray to effect change in our world. James teaches, "The prayer of a righteous person has great power as it is working" (James 5:16). God created the world in such a way that he determined that we would be his servants, his instruments of change. He rarely if ever accomplishes his goals apart from the human participants who carry out his plans. For believers, this means that we are servants for his good and righteous plans. The doctrine of accommodation coincides with the doctrine of compatibilism. When God does remarkable things in this world, it is precipitated by diligent, heartfelt, passionate prayer that appeals to a God of power and change.

Moses models this tension in Exodus 32.[24] When the prophet of God delayed his return from the mountain of Sinai, the Israelites

22. John Calvin, *Institutes of the Christian Religion*, ed. John T. McNeill, trans. Ford Lewis Battles (Philadelphia: Westminster, 1960), 1.1.17.13, 227. See also Helm, *The Providence of God*, 51–54.

23. See D. A. Carson, *A Call to Spiritual Reformation: Priorities from Paul and His Prayers* (Grand Rapids: Baker, 1992), 145–66; R. C. Sproul, *The Prayer of the Lord* (Orlando, FL: Reformation Trust, 2009), 113–24.

24. Carson, *How Long, O Lord?*, 209.

got a little too anxious and built for themselves a horrid idol—the golden calf. God informed Moses of their corruption. Then we read, "And the LORD said to Moses, 'I have seen this people, and behold, it is a stiff-necked people. Now therefore let me alone, that my wrath may burn hot against them and I may consume them, in order that I may make a great nation of you'" (Ex. 32:9–10). God's intention was not to inform Moses of a *real* change in plans. Rather, it was to incite Moses to pray as he had never prayed before. What is interesting is that when he prayed, he appealed primarily to God's everlasting promise to the patriarchs, to whom God had sworn to establish their descendants forever (v. 13).

The implication in Moses' prayer is this: is not God good for what he has unconditionally decreed? Of course, but part of his means of establishing his decree is to provoke his people to come alongside him and petition him to act in accordance with what he promises. Ironically, this appears as though God is moved to a place where he did not previously intend to go. Exodus 32:14 relates, "So the LORD *changed His mind* about the harm which He said He would do to His people" (NASB). Using the language of accommodation, this tells us that God had already planned to come to the rescue, but not without the faithful prayer of his servant Moses to summon him. Jehoahaz was the same sort of servant, praying the same sort of prayer. Furthermore, all believers are vital participants in God's plans, and the more fervently we pray and participate, the more certain we become that God acts in accordance with our obedience to him as well as his own sovereign decrees.[25]

Jesus exemplifies the tension between God's sovereign decree and the necessity of prayer in the advance of his decree. On the night of his public trials before the Sanhedrin, Jesus predicted that Peter would deny his Master three times before the dawn (Luke 22:34). In Luke 22:31–32 he says, "Simon, Simon, behold, Satan demanded to have you, that he might sift you like wheat, but I have prayed for you that your faith may not fail. And when you have turned again, strengthen

---

25. See Terrance L. Tiessen, *Providence & Prayer: How Does God Work in the World?* (Downers Grove, IL: InterVarsity Press, 2000), for a survey of how different theologies relate prayer to the providence of God. Tiessen himself advocates a modified Calvinist position.

your brothers." Several things stand out in Jesus' words. First, note that Satan has no independent control over Peter. He must be granted divine permission to "sift" him in the same way that he needed permission to sift Job. Second, the inevitability of Peter's denial is stated as though it were already a fact. Not only does God know what Peter will do, but the implication is that he has determined this course of events. Yet it is also clear that "when" the denials happen, afterward Peter will "have turned again" back to his devotion to Christ. This anticipation of restoration is reinforced by Jesus' commanding Peter to "strengthen your brothers" long before he turns back.

Even more interesting, however, is the fact that Jesus says, "I have prayed for you that your faith may not fail" (Luke 22:32). Part of the tension here is the thought of Peter's potential for failure even as Jesus expresses certainty about his friend's ultimate triumph. Yet part of what makes his success certain has to do with Jesus' intercessions on behalf of the faltering disciple. One might ask why Jesus must pray for what he knows will surely transpire, especially given the fact that he is party to the divine decrees that determine the future. What we see here is a different sort of accommodating activity of our Lord. Jesus humbly mimics a Moses or a Jehoahaz, modeling for his disciples how prayer is one of the strongest weapons in God's arsenal. By it, God's people vitally participate in the advance of his sovereign purposes. Therefore, let us not neglect the power of prayer.

God, Man, and Redemption

Compatibilism provides a crucial perspective in how it frames the historic episodes underlying God's plan of redemption. The pivotal event on which everything past and future hinges is the death and resurrection of the Son of God. The narrative of the Old Testament slowly pushes the flow of history to the apex of the cross. Messianic prophecy reveals this marquee event as a monument carved in stone before the foundation of the earth was laid (Gal. 4:4; 1 Peter 1:20). As with all other prophecy, God superintends its fulfillment through the agency of human actions. A vast and diverse matrix of decisions by multitudes of people had to converge for Jesus to die according to divine prophecy. Only a master author could write that kind of story.

The dual collusion of the divine and human intentions precisely comes together in the unfolding of Jesus' death, as two passages in the book of Acts make clear.[26] In Acts 2, Peter introduces Jesus as the crucified Messiah to his captive Jewish audience: "This Jesus, delivered up according to the definite plan and foreknowledge of God, you crucified and killed by the hands of lawless men" (v. 23). Peter minces no words as he gives the one event its twofold explanation. God predetermined it to happen according to his foreknowledge (i.e., his prophetic plan). Yet the lawless masses that Peter addresses are held responsible for putting Jesus to death. Both explanations accurately reflect the truth.

The second passage is from Acts 4:27–28, where we see an intriguing reflection of the Jerusalem church. The believers pray to God: "For truly in this city there were gathered together against your holy servant Jesus, whom you anointed, both Herod and Pontius Pilate, along with the Gentiles and the peoples of Israel, to do whatever your hand and your plan had predestined to take place." The point is clear. Each of the key instigators of Jesus' death is enlisted as a pawn in God's service. This in no way suggests that they are passive participants. This "was a wicked political conspiracy, a willful human corruption, the travesty of justice sacrificed on the altar of expediency."[27] All the conspirators make deliberate decisions as "willful killing agents" that lead to Jesus' death.[28] And all of them bear responsibility for those decisions. Nonetheless, they have fulfilled the prophetic role that God has assigned them. Carson explains:

> It will not do to analyze what happened as an instance where wicked agents performed an evil deed, and then God intervened to turn it into good, for in that case the cross itself becomes an afterthought in the mind of God, a mere reactive tactic. All of Scripture is against the notion. . . . But neither will it do to reduce the guilt of the conspirators because God remained

---

26. Thaddeus J. Williams, *Love, Freedom, and Evil: Does Authentic Love Require Free Will?* (New York: Rodopi, 2011), 89–93.

27. Carson, "God, the Bible and Spiritual Warfare," 263.

28. Williams, *Love, Freedom, and Evil*, 91.

in charge. If there is no guilt attaching to those who were immediately responsible for sending Jesus to the cross, why should one think that there is guilt attaching to any action performed under the sovereignty of God? And in that case, of course, we do not need any atonement for guilt: The cross is superfluous and useless.[29]

One pawn in the unfolding drama is Pilate, the Roman ruler charged with the task of deciding Jesus' fate. Pilate fears the Jewish authorities and has to walk a fine line between pleasing them and Rome. Pilate doesn't see Jesus as being guilty of anything that deserves death and prefers to release him. But while examining the suspected criminal, he is frustrated by Jesus' silence about his true identity:

> So Pilate said to him, "You will not speak to me? Do you not know that I have authority to release you and authority to crucify you?" Jesus answered him, "You would have no authority over me at all unless it had been given you from above. Therefore he who delivered me over to you has the greater sin." (John 19:10–11)

Jesus fears no man, least of all Pilate. Pilate's decision doesn't ultimately derive from his tortured deliberations, or the power vested in him by Rome, or the pressure bearing on him from the Jews. Of course, in one sense, all those things drive his decision, but only because God has decreed everything that transpires on that day so that Pilate is compelled to do what he does. He has no libertarian freedom to act otherwise and thus to scuttle God's plan of redemption.

The compatibilist Loraine Boettner made a list of all the nefarious actions that took place around the actual crucifixion itself. Each was prophesied in the Old Testament, and each involved minute and ordinary decisions of various individuals. In considering how the divine and human wills merged, Boettner explains, "Listen to the babble of hell around the cross, and tell us if those men were not free! Yet read

---

29. Carson, "God, the Bible and Spiritual Warfare," 263.

all the forecast and prophecy and record of the tragedy and tell us if every incident of it was not ordained of God!"[30]

Emphasizing the Divine and Human Sides of History

These last two chapters have provided representative biblical examples of this dual explanation for human actions. Many other examples could be cited. The common narrative of Scripture doesn't usually frame human actions within this compatibilist grid. Most examples of human action reflect only the visible and immediately perceivable human side of the compatibilist equation, as though God had no role in what takes place. But if we miss the divine role, it provokes a skewed and reductionist perspective.

On the other hand, sometimes Scripture mentions only the divine side of the equation. In those cases, we are tempted to forget that humans play a responsible role in freely exercising their wills to produce the outcomes of history. The temptation of eager but unthoughtful Calvinists is to regard these explicit passages of divine sovereignty as ruling out any human responsibility and freedom. This is equally misguided. Regardless of which side is emphasized, both are at work as history unfolds. The comprehensive picture that compatibilism provides helps us to set human freedom and responsibility within a larger context of God's sovereignty from which to make better sense of history. We next turn to a detailed examination of the human side of the equation.

Chapter Summary

Many passages of Scripture highlight disharmony between God's decretive and preceptive wills. In these cases, God providentially superintends that which he *does not* command. Although the evil choices that people make match precisely what God decrees, God's intentions and man's intentions are diametrically opposed. This is seen in the life of Joseph, whose brothers sold him into slavery while simultaneously God chose to do the same. What they intended for evil God intended for good.

---

30. Loraine Boettner, *The Reformed Doctrine of Predestination* (Philadelphia: Presbyterian and Reformed, 1932), 225–26.

God ordains the actions of evildoers and then holds them responsible for their sin. We read of devastating plagues that God executed on the Egyptians before Israel's deliverance. Throughout these episodes of divine judgment, God commands Pharaoh no fewer than ten times to let his people go. Yet in chapter after chapter, Pharaoh's heart is hardened. On eight occasions we read that Pharaoh hardened his own heart. On nine occasions, however, we read that God hardened Pharaoh's heart. In every case, Pharaoh fully intended to harden his heart, yet at the same time this reflected the express purpose of God. In spite of God's unyielding decree, Pharaoh is held responsible for his actions.

Elsewhere we see that God uses evil rulers to execute judgment on others. For example, this was the case when Hazael and Ben-hadad assaulted Israel at the instigation of God. He then used the prayers of King Jehoahaz to deliver his people from these evil warlords. The lesson is that prayer is one of the strongest weapons in God's arsenal. By it, God's people vitally participate in the advance of his sovereign purposes.

We also see the dual collusion of the divine and human intentions precisely come together in the unfolding of Jesus' death. God determined this most horrific of injustices in the world to come at the hands of evil men with evil intentions. All the instigators bear responsibility for their diabolical decisions. Nonetheless, they have fulfilled the prophetic role that God has assigned them.

Glossary

accommodation. A doctrine concerning God whereby he condescends to his creatures in such a way that he is able to communicate and interact with them on a level that they can relate to. God often appears to be a finite creature like us, even though he is the transcendent Creator of all. See also *anthropomorphic, immanence,* and *transcendence.*

anthropomorphic. Of or relating to attributing human characteristics to God. Combines the Greek word for *human* (*anthropos*) and *form* (*morphe*). Anthropomorphic language is used in the Bible. See also *accommodation.*

immanence. The attribute of God in which he draws near to his creatures even though he is distinct from his creation as the Creator. He makes his presence known by becoming directly involved in the lives of human beings. See also *transcendence*.

transcendence. The attribute of God as Creator indicating that he is wholly distinct from the creation and his creatures. He is above and beyond the created universe even though he interacts with it directly. See also *immanence*.

Study Questions

1. This chapter explores disharmony between God's decretive and preceptive wills. It also explores disharmony between divine and human intentions in the same acts. Explain what this means.

2. The story of Joseph's being sold into slavery by his brothers has a good ending, but it raises a question. Does God take such bad (evil) circumstances and turn them into something good only after the fact? Explain your answer.

3. What does the phrase "God gave them up" mean in Romans 1:24, 26, and 28?

4. In what ways does God restrain evil in the world?

5. Who was responsible for the hardening of Pharaoh's heart throughout Exodus 4–14? How is God free from culpability for Pharaoh's actions while Pharaoh maintains culpability?

6. Did God have reason to blame the sailors for throwing Jonah overboard from their ship? Explain your answer.

7. Consider Isaiah 10:5–19. Does God unfairly manipulate the Assyrians and their ruler in this passage while holding them responsible for what he absolutely determined that they would do? Explain your answer.

8. What is the doctrine of accommodation?

9. What lessons can we learn about prayer from the episodes of Jehoahaz in 2 Kings 13:3–4, Moses in Exodus 32:7–14, and Jesus in Luke 22:31–32?

10. Consider how many decisions and actions of a broad spectrum of people had to converge in order for Jesus to be tried and crucified. Explain what would happen if any one of these multiple parties

had libertarian free will. How does the plot to kill Jesus confirm the truth of compatibilism?

Resources for Further Study

D. A. Carson, *How Long, O Lord? Reflections on Suffering and Evil* (Grand Rapids: Baker, 2006). Chapter 11 has a good survey of compatibilistic passages.

Terrance L. Tiessen, *Providence & Prayer: How Does God Work in the World?* (Downers Grove, IL: InterVarsity Press, 2000). An excellent survey of how different views of divine sovereignty and human free agency affect one's view of prayer.

7

To Be Free or Not to Be Free

Consider again that the relationship between God's sovereignty and human choosing is like a tapestry. The artistry on the presentable side of the fabric represents the orderly pattern of God's providential designs for history, with every event crafted in exquisite detail and flowing seamlessly in and out of corresponding sections of the whole. Stepping back a little, we can see the work in its entire glory, with every scene fitting an overall pattern that is cohesive and beautifully rendered. The grand panorama extols the purposeful imagination, skill, and wisdom of the artist. Of course, this represents the divine side of the compatibilist tapestry that we explored in chapter 4.

The back side of the tapestry represents the strictly human dimension of the compatibilist world that we are considering. Here, things are not so beautiful and ordered. It is a bit chaotic with occasional hints of an overall pattern that seems to make sense, but never with any absolute certainty. In chapters 4, 5, and 6, we flipped back and forth between the front and the back of the tapestry to see that the disheveled back side did in fact correspond to the front side.

In the following chapters, I plan to focus the camera on the detailed warp and woof of the human side. My strategy is to start with the immediate act of choosing that lies on the surface of human actions and then uncover successive layers (like peeling an onion) of reasons why people make the choices they do. As we eventually uncover the core source of choosing, a discernible pattern will emerge that explains in what ways humans are both free and not so free.

Calvinists have been wont to reject the term *free will*—and for good reasons. But because the rejection of this term can be misleading, many harbor skepticism about Calvinistic claims. Namely, people understand that at some level we are free: we are independent and we make choices that proceed from our own power of choosing. Libertarians have seized on this self-evident truth but have provided a narrative of human freedom that is wanting. Calvinists speak of the human will as being in bondage, which is true in some respects but untrue in others. Given particular circumstances, the human will can be free and in bondage at the same time and in different ways. Eventually Christians will experience full freedom of the will, but the nature of this freedom needs careful explanation.

A biblical theology of the human act of choosing requires us to uncover all the causal connections between God, people, circumstances, and the unique workings of the human soul that generate our actions. As we have seen, God is the primary determiner of man's free actions, working through secondary human causes, such as our desires, beliefs, conscience, motives, and preferences, leading to the choices that we voluntarily make. These are internal factors that can be influenced by external circumstantial factors as well. Standing behind these internal and external factors, however, is a person's base nature, whether it is under the grip of sin's corruption or unsullied by such sin. Biblically speaking, man's nature is his fundamental moral and spiritual disposition. All of one's desires and motives with regard to moral and spiritual matters are dictated by this core nature. Thus, man is free to act only in accordance with his nature.

This overview of the human will speaks of two kinds of freedom—a *general* and *spiritual* freedom. First, we are free in a general sense when we are both able to act voluntarily and free from hindrances. Physical and natural constraints can hinder a person's ability to freely choose. Likewise, coercive constraints coming from the actions of other people can hinder the ability to choose. This general freedom largely concerns morally neutral matters. We are free to choose what communities we inhabit, what conversations we engage in, what colleges we attend, and what carpet colors we prefer. But to the extent that such choices involve ethical matters, then we venture into another realm.

Thus, we need to distinguish between a general freedom of will in ordinary matters and a specifically moral and spiritual freedom. The latter is not possible as long as one suffers from a moral and spiritual inability. The Bible teaches that the sin nature from which humans suffer constrains their ability to act with moral and spiritual freedom. Until we are free from sin, we are never truly free. Ultimate human freedom entails acting in an unhindered way in full adherence to God's revealed truth—his instructive will contained in the Scriptures. A glimpse of such freedom exists for the believer, who has been regenerated and given a new heart that enables him to obey God's Word with pure and righteous motives. Yet remaining sin still constrains this freedom. Comprehensive freedom unhindered by the ravages of sin is possible in the believer's life only when he or she experiences future glorification at the coming of Christ.

With these broad parameters set forth, I will now seek to unpack this pattern of cause-effect relationships that undergirds the choices we make. I will also explore a number of corollary matters that have implications for our understanding of the human will, its freedom, and its responsibility. To achieve all this, I will set forth for consideration a series of propositional statements about the nature of human choosing.

Our Will Is Free in That We Do What We Want to Do

This first proposition is straightforward enough. It states that all our choices are free when they are made voluntarily—that is, freely, willingly, or intentionally. Jonathan Edwards writes, "A man never, in any instance, wills anything contrary to his desires, or desires anything contrary to his will."[1] This concept of voluntary action is the only proper way to speak of free agency. In this regard, it is better to speak of *people* being free rather than the *will* being free—to speak of free agents, not free wills.

Edwards emphasized the fact that the will is not an independent faculty of a person. It is simply an act of the mind by which a person makes a choice.[2] The will is not some autonomous dictator that wields power to direct us; rather, we direct the will. The source of

1. Jonathan Edwards, *The Freedom of the Will*, vol. 1 of *The Works of Jonathan Edwards*, ed. Paul Ramsey (New Haven, CT: Yale University Press, 1957), 139.
2. Ibid., 137. See also Anthony A. Hoekema, *Created in God's Image* (Grand Rapids: Eerdmans, 1986), 227.

choosing lies elsewhere: namely, by way of the heart's affections and the mind's deliberations by which motives emerge to generate the willing of a choice.[3]

Often the Bible uses the word *heart* to speak of all the cognitive, emotive, and choosing activities that people engage in. Jerry Bridges explains:

> *Heart* in Scripture is used in various ways. Sometimes it means our reason or understanding, sometimes our affections and emotion, and sometimes our will. Generally it denotes the whole soul of man and all its faculties, not individually, but as they all work together in doing good or evil. The mind as it reasons, discerns, and judges; the emotions as they like or dislike; the conscience as it determines and warns; and the will as it chooses or refuses—are all together called the heart.[4]

Notice also that the proposition doesn't say that people are free to do *whatever* they want to do, but simply *what* they want to do. This distinguishes the proposition from how libertarians conceive of free will, in which alternative choices can be made with far greater ease. Any view of human freedom must understand the limitations on what a person can choose to do. Libertarians acknowledge many limitations, but they allow for a more expansive array of choices than what actual experience warrants. Namely, we decidedly never act against what we want (desire) to do in spite of what the libertarian claims is possible. Sometimes competing or conflicting alternatives present themselves for choosing, but in the end we choose the alternative that we desire the most, regardless of whether it appeals to us otherwise (see chapter 8).

Self-Interest

Another way of understanding the notion of voluntary action or what some call the *freedom of inclination* is that people always act

---

3. Allen C. Guelzo, "The Return of the Will: Jonathan Edwards and the Possibilities of Free Will," in *Edwards in Our Time*, ed. Sang Hyun Lee and Allen C. Guelzo (Grand Rapids: Eerdmans, 1999), 90.

4. Jerry Bridges, *The Pursuit of Holiness* (Colorado Springs: NavPress, 1978), 63–64.

in a way that corresponds with what they believe to be in their best interest. Jesus simplifies this axiom by saying, "For where your treasure is, there your heart will be also" (Matt. 6:21). Blaise Pascal put the matter differently:

> All men seek happiness. This is without exception. Whatever different means they employ, they all tend to this end. . . . The will never takes the least step but to this object. This is the motive of every action of every man, even of those who hang themselves.[5]

Self-interest is the base motive of all action even as it is conjoined with other motives that either taint it with vice or transform it into something virtuous.

This is evidenced by the last statement Pascal makes about suicide. Troubled people often say, "I hate myself," but such a statement is patently false. Ironically, it reveals self-love.

How so?

Perhaps the person fears that he or she has done something foolish, immoral, or embarrassing. Maybe the person's reputation has been irreparably tarnished or cherished expectations dashed. In the end, the desire to benefit from a good reputation or having expectations met has been curtailed by the person's own failure. Thus, the phrase "I hate myself" is often code for "I have failed" and "now I have to figure out how to restore myself to personal benefit." Others use it to garner attention and affirmation. It betrays a form of self-pity that is wholly self-centered. Nobody suffers from self-hatred. Even when people commit suicide, in some perverse way they think such an act will benefit them.

Biblically, it is appropriate to speak of a natural self-love (self-interest) that people have. This is assumed in the commands given in Scripture about loving your neighbor "as yourself."[6] In Ephesians 5:29, Paul comments that no one ever hates his "own flesh, but nourishes and cherishes it." In Philippians 2:4, he exhorts, "Let each of you look

5. Blaise Pascal, *Pascal's Pensées*, trans. W. F. Trotter (New York: E. P. Dutton, 1958), 113 (thought #425), quoted in John Piper, *Desiring God* (Sisters, OR: Multnomah, 1996), 16.
6. Lev. 19:18; Matt. 22:39; Rom. 13:9; Gal. 5:14; James 2:8.

not only to his own interests, but also to the interests of others." This assumes that people naturally think first of their own best interests. The command essentially reframes the Golden Rule: "So whatever you wish that others would do to you, do also to them" (Matt. 7:12).

Some raise objections at this point. Isn't self-interest sinful? Aren't Christians called to self-denial and taking up their cross? Doesn't Paul say that love "does not insist on its own way" (1 Cor. 13:5)? These biblical injunctions appear to be incompatible with self-interest or self-love. Consider Luke 14:26: "If anyone comes to me and does not hate his own father and mother and wife and children and brothers and sisters, yes, and *even his own life*, he cannot be my disciple."

Has Jesus contradicted this notion of self-love? Not at all.

He uses the word *hate* as hyperbole; otherwise, to hate family members would contradict other Scripture about loving others. Furthermore, we cannot assume that hating one's "life" is equal to hating one's "self." The idea is not to hate yourself but to hate the life you live if it is lived for anything other than Christ.

Consider Mark 8:34–35, where Jesus lays down the most notorious of these difficult demands:

> If anyone would come after me, let him deny himself and take up his cross and follow me. For whoever would save his life will lose it, but whoever loses his life for my sake and the gospel's will save it.

The fifth-century church father Augustine makes a perceptive comment on this passage: "If you love your soul, there is danger of its being destroyed. Therefore you may [must] not love it, since you do not want it to be destroyed. But in not wanting it to be destroyed you love it."[7] Jesus calls his followers to abandon all desolate and worthless pleasures of this earthly life. They pale in comparison to a life abandoned to him. The call is not to hate yourself, but to hate what can never bring you lasting, genuine joy, which is found only in following Christ at all costs.

7. Quoted in Piper, *Desiring God*, 203 (bracketed term added for clarity).

Self-love is a two-edged sword. In our depravity, it is used to gratify evil desires and corresponds to greed, covetousness, envy, jealousy, and so on. This is the sort of condition that Paul speaks of when he says that in the last days "people will be lovers of self" (2 Tim. 3:2). But in regenerated believers, self-love is restored to something truly virtuous. Genuine self-interest finds satisfaction in what brings glory to God and in that which interests him (Ps. 16:11). If acting in one's best interest seeks glory for oneself, then it is clearly sinful. The foundation for one's pursuit of happiness becomes the self, not God; and this is what is normally meant by *selfishness* or *self-centeredness*. But when one adheres to what God has established as good and right and true, then one truly acts in his best interest (i.e., out of love for himself).[8]

Note the important corollary. In one sense, all sin and temptation is the product of deception. As people engage in sinful choices and behaviors, they come to believe (i.e., perceive) that those choices are in their best interest when in fact they are not. Satan capitalized on this when he tempted Adam and Eve, as recorded in Genesis 3:1–7. He deceived them into thinking that the consequences for eating the forbidden fruit would not be death (v. 4) but spiritual and moral enlightenment (v. 5). They became convinced that he had their best interests in mind while God did not. This is the way of temptation. It compels us to choose what we think is best for us, and the nature of such self-interested concern means that we *always* choose what we *want* even if what we want will destroy us.

Hindrances to Freedom

Both libertarianism and compatibilism are concerned about anything that interferes with human freedom. Yet there is disagreement on what constitutes such hindrances. From a libertarian perspective, anything regarded as a sufficient antecedent cause for the choices we make impedes the freedom we have to make those choices. In compatibilism, however, it is not necessary causal conditions per se that prevent freedom, but rather the kinds of causes that one is talking

8. This is at the heart of John Piper's argument in *Desiring God*; see especially 15–23, 32–50, 277–86.

about. Physical restraints, natural inabilities, moral inabilities, coercion from others, and so on represent causes that restrict freedom. Other causes promote freedom, as we will see later.

Some level of agreement exists in several of these areas, however—but not without important differences. For example, all agree that one of the most powerful forces of obstruction to human freedom is constraining actions and circumstances. Extreme forms of constraint remove freedom altogether. If a Mack truck comes flying around the corner and throws you fifty feet across the street, you become a total victim of circumstances outside your control. You didn't make the choice to be a projectile, and thus you have no freedom in the matter whatsoever. Most absolute forms of constraint are physical in nature.

Lesser forms of constraint, such as coercion, are generally mental in nature. Coercion restricts the voluntary exercise of the will, usually through mental manipulation. It seeks to plant an intimidating obstacle within the mind so as to force a person to act against his or her wishes. The use of threat by powerful dictators such as North Korea's Kim Jong-un constrains the choices of the citizens of that oppressed nation. Billy the bully promises Johnny five shiny quarters if he pulls Sally's hair, but he promises five knuckles to the jaw if Johnny refuses. In either case, Johnny faces troubling consequences. He is persuaded even though he'd rather run away. Notice that coercion of this nature doesn't eliminate the ability to choose, but it certainly seeks to thwart our choices and the freedom we expect in making them.

Unfortunately, libertarians suggest that *any* persuasive force that invariably leads a person to a particular choice is constraining. But is all such persuasion constraining? Compatibilists argue, for example, that God acts on the minds of unbelievers in such a way that the truth of the gospel becomes compelling (attractive). The winsome nature of the truth changes their minds about that which they previously rejected. In other words, gospel persuasion does not force a person to act against his or her will, but transforms the person's desires so that new and opposite desires arise.

In fact, God acts in such a way that *none* of the recipients of his causal power feel coerced to act against their will. Pharaoh acted in full accordance with his hardened heart even though God stood behind it

(Ex. 10:27). In order to orchestrate the crucifixion of Christ, God had to manage the intricate matrix of choices by Herod, Pontius Pilate, the Jewish Sanhedrin, the Roman soldiers, and the hostile crowds in addition to the circumstances that conspired to effect the choices of all these people (Acts 4:27–28). Yet it cannot be argued that any of the individuals involved felt forced against their wills to act as they did. Rather, all the participants acted freely.

Natural and Moral Ability

Another area of disagreement concerns a distinction that compatibilists make between *natural ability* and *moral ability*.[9] In principle, compatibilists and libertarians agree on the question of natural ability. There are some things that we humans have no natural ability to do even though we might *want* to do them. All throughout history, we curious earthbound creatures have had a compulsion to fly. Before the Wright brothers finally succeeded in crafting an independent machine for flying, humans sought ways to fly as much as possible through the architecture of their own bodies and physical capabilities. Even with the aid of artificial devices, they continually failed, often dying in the process. Some will say, "Wait! Now we have wingsuits!" I reply that that's not flying; rather, that's falling dangerously, even if gracefully! There is simply no natural way for us to fly on our own, no matter how strong the desire may be.

In some cases, a person may have a natural ability to do something he wants to do but is restrained by external physical factors. A prisoner may want to see his wife and children, but his prison cell contains steel bars that he cannot break. Also, a person may have lost a natural ability. Consider someone such as Joni Eareckson Tada, who has blessed millions through her ministry to disabled people. She became a quadriplegic through a diving accident. As much as she may desire to escape her wheelchair to walk, she is physically unable.[10] Natural and physical inabilities hinder one's general freedom of choice in ordinary matters.

9. Edwards, *Freedom of the Will*, 156–66.
10. See Joni Eareckson Tada, *The God I Love* (Grand Rapids: Zondervan, 2003).

When it comes to spiritual and moral matters, however, we encounter a different sort of hindrance. There are actions that man has a natural ability to do but that, because he suffers from a moral inability, he cannot do. For example, people have a natural ability to exercise faith. People place their faith in all sorts of things. We trust that our cars will function safely at sixty-five miles an hour. We trust that the local bank will secure our money once it leaves our hands. Faith is a natural part of human behavior. Yet faith in Christ remains impossible so long as people remain in a state of spiritual inertness (i.e., "dead in . . . trespasses and sins," Eph. 2:1). They have no *moral* ability to exercise such faith. Furthermore, the Scripture indicates that spiritually dead people lack a desire to do so; they don't *want* to believe (John 10:26; Rom. 3:9–18). Their wills are bound by sin so that they *cannot* and *will not* believe on Christ for salvation.

This notion separates Calvinism from Arminianism. Arminians believe that we must be free from the shackles that sin places on the power of choosing; otherwise, it would be unfair for God to punish those who are unable to believe. But this perspective has already been shown to be wanting in chapter 2. Even though one is unable to pay a debt he owes, this inability doesn't exonerate him from his obligation. Sinners act intentionally when reaping the debt they incur before God, and we saw that responsibility is tied to our intentions. Furthermore, our consciences bear witness that our immoral actions are exercised in defiance of God's law written on human hearts (Rom. 2:14–15; cf. 1:32).

Assessing Prevenient Grace

Proponents of classical Arminianism don't deny the doctrine of depravity and its enslavement of the human will to sin.[11] But the practical force of depravity appears mitigated by introducing the

---

11. Roger Olson quotes extensively from the writings of Arminians, from Jacob Arminius in the sixteenth century down through the twentieth century, to indicate that they embrace original sin and total depravity in the same way that Luther and Calvin did. Olson, *Arminian Theology: Myths and Realities* (Downers Grove, IL: InterVarsity Press, 2006), 150; see ibid., 141–57.

doctrine of *prevenient grace* whereby God restores libertarian free will to all unbelievers.[12] Arminian theologian Roger Olson states:

> This common (not universal) Arminian doctrine of universal prevenient grace means that because of Jesus Christ and the Holy Spirit no human being is actually in a state of absolute darkness and depravity. Because of original sin, helplessness to do good is the natural state of humanity, but because of the work of Christ and the operation of the Holy Spirit universally no human being actually exists in that natural state.[13]

Olson denies that this mitigates the force of depravity. He asserts that this enabling grace is like the gift of special glasses to a blind man so that he can see better or hearing aids to a deaf woman so that she can hear better.[14] The restoration of free will then allows a person to cooperate with further effusions of God's grace (in this case, *saving grace*) whenever one encounters the gospel message. It enables a person to have a good will toward God. But free will also enables people to resist these further advances of grace. Of course, this seems odd, since they were not allowed to resist the first advance of prevenient grace.

Without quibbling about whether the doctrine of prevenient grace mitigates human depravity, we should note that different problems persist that undermine this whole narrative. For example, if prevenient grace pervades the whole of the human race so as to restore libertarian freedom, then under the definition of such freedom, humans have the theoretical potential through the force of their will to act contrary to any evil desire. Of course, the probability that anyone would resist every evil urge that occurred within him seems impossible. Nonetheless, libertarianism does make it possible to act so that moral alternatives always present themselves as live possibilities; otherwise, freedom is curtailed as well as responsibility. Libertarianism argues that culpability for our actions can come about *only* if we have the alternative of acting

---

12. Ibid., 76. Ironically, this bestowal of grace is poured out on all with irresistible force. Ibid., 66.

13. Ibid., 154.

14. Ibid.

otherwise (see chapter 2). God could never hold people accountable for their sin without their having the ability to act in a contrary fashion.

Thus, if Arminians are to be consistent with their libertarian principles, then there is always an outside chance that a person could choose what is morally right in every circumstance. If this were the case, what need would there be of further effusions of saving grace? Now, let us be clear: this would not entail a belief in autonomous works-righteousness that is commensurate with the heresy known as *Pelagianism*. The reason is that the restoration of this ability to make morally good choices is preceded by the fact that God's prevenient grace makes such choices possible in the first place. Pelagianism holds that man has the ability to do good apart from the necessity of any divine grace, and Arminians reject this notion vehemently.[15] I agree that there is no reason to equate Arminianism with Pelagianism.[16]

But another problem raises its ugly head. Consistent Arminians wish to affirm the depravity of man, and that in spite of prevenient grace man still appears to have some degree of bondage to sin. Roger Olson affirms together with the Arminian John Wesley that all men "are dead in sin by *nature* even if universal prevenient grace of God is working in them."[17] In other words, the special glasses and hearing aids, though helpful, still prevent one from seeing and hearing clearly. But if fallen human beings in the Arminians' anthropology are in some way hindered from freely exercising their wills to do what is good and God-pleasing before regeneration, then libertarian freedom cannot possibly exist for the unbeliever. According to libertarian tenets, if the sin nature of humans in any way hinders their ability to freely choose the good, then constraining forces are at work and humans are not free. At this point, the doctrine of depravity and the nature of libertarian freedom are in direct conflict with each other. Arminians cannot have it both ways. At best, this renders

15. Ibid., 142–43.
16. See R. C. Sproul, *Willing to Believe: The Controversy over Free Will* (Grand Rapids: Baker, 1997), 33–45, for a detailed assessment of Pelagianism. Others say that Arminianism is a form of semi-Pelagianism, while some Arminians claim the title of semi-Augustinianism. Assessing these claims is beyond the scope of this discussion.
17. Olson, *Arminian Theology*, 149.

Arminians' embrace of libertarianism a burden too great to bear and makes shipwreck of their view of human responsibility, depravity, and even the kind of grace necessary for salvation.[18] Something far more powerful must work within the human soul to extract sinners from their sinful bondage.

Having said all this, we should note that Calvinism concedes that unbelievers do have an ability to make certain morally upright decisions (Rom. 2:14–15) and that this is a result of a common grace bestowed on humanity (Matt. 7:11; Luke 6:33).[19] Man is never as evil as he could be. Such choices, however, fall entirely short of glorifying God (Rom. 3:23) and being pleasing in his sight (8:7–8) and therefore fail to meet the standard of true righteousness. To perform truly righteous deeds requires the outside actions of a sovereign God to causally and monergistically transform moral *inability* into a moral *ability*. This is the work of regeneration (John 3:3, 5; Titus 3:4–5). I will explore the will's bondage to sin and the work of regeneration in greater detail in chapter 9.

Our Will Is Not Free in That We Can Do Only What We Want to Do

Our second principal proposition states that man is never free to act against his will. Our choices have definite limitations. A woman may act against her conscience (1 Cor. 8:7; Titus 1:15), but she never violates what she wants to do. People do not have the power of contrary choice. They *always* choose *only* what they most *want* to do. If a person wanted to choose something other than what she did choose, then she would have alternative reasons for doing so. Given the same prior conditions, she would always make the same choice. This distinguishes compatibilist freedom from libertarian freedom, and it should be admitted that it is more restrictive.

18. For a further critique of prevenient grace, see Thomas R. Schreiner, "Does Scripture Teach Prevenient Grace in the Wesleyan Sense?," in *Still Sovereign*, ed. Thomas R. Schreiner and Bruce A. Ware (Grand Rapids: Baker, 2000), 229–46; and especially Matthew Barrett, *Salvation by Grace: A Case for Effectual Calling and Regeneration* (Phillipsburg, NJ: P&R Publishing, 2013), 207–81.

19. Wayne Grudem, *Systematic Theology* (Grand Rapids: Zondervan, 1994), 660–61.

Edward Smith was the captain of the *RMS Titanic*. On the night of April 14, 1912, he and his crew ignored six separate warnings that icebergs capable of sinking the passenger liner were within its path. The ship never reduced its speed or altered its course. By the time it steamed full ahead into the fateful mass of ice, it was too late to avoid catastrophe. The ship submersed violently down to the bottom of the sea, taking some fifteen hundred of its more than twenty-two hundred passengers to their watery deaths. We don't know why Captain Smith made the decision he did. We can only surmise that he thought he had good reasons. Perhaps he thought the *Titanic* was invincible. But we can be certain of this: if he thought the ship would sink under those conditions, he would have had reason to make a different choice (unless, of course, he harbored sinister desires).

Whatever reasons (causes) stand behind each choice that one makes, those reasons always lead *necessarily* to that specific choice. First, choices must have sufficient prior causes; otherwise, they risk being made randomly. Second, only one choice can arise from the matrix of causes that underlie that choice. The collusion of all specific prior causes can never result in multiple outcomes. That would result in an arbitrary, unpredictable, chaotic, and purposeless world. God is not the author of disorder. If the same precise circumstances in any given situation were repeated, the outcome would be the same. We might never uncover all or even any of the reasons that led to Captain Smith's fateful decision, but we can be certain that they existed and that they necessarily led to the choice he made. This necessary cause-effect principle whereby sufficient reasons always determine choices also indicates that people don't face alternative choices without any preference for one or the other.

Nonetheless, compatibilism doesn't say that alternative choices are impossible. Captain Smith could have ordered the *Titanic* to slow down or alter its course just as easily as leaving the ship to continue as it did. The point is, if he had a preference for that alternative decision, he would have also had alternative reasons for making it. This also assumes that he had the ability and the opportunity to make the other choice. Alternative outcomes can occur if favorable preconditions exist (1 Sam. 23:7–14; Matt. 11:20–24). Yes, he was free to make either choice, but he was not free to act against the reasons that led to the actual choice he made, including God's decree of that choice. Captain Smith made his choice freely, that is, voluntarily, but also necessarily as a result of the prior causes for his choice. The necessity and sufficiency of prior causes affirm determinism. The voluntary nature of his choice shows that freedom is compatible with determinism.

If humans were free to act contrary to the compelling reasons that underlie their decisions, then it would defeat personal responsibility. The only thing that little Jimmy can say when asked why he won't eat his broccoli is: "I don't know." Of course, we know why—he hates broccoli, and we are certain he knows that, too! He just hides behind an excuse, which becomes a way of avoiding responsibility. This means that other motives (causes) are at work when he sings out, "I don't know." But let us suppose that he really doesn't know why he won't eat the stuff. That is certainly possible. Nonetheless, his will is not a blank slate harboring independent autonomous power to act in any way it wants regardless of the forces swaying it one way or another. Jimmy has no power to cut himself loose from the decisive reasons that determine his choices.

Consider the pivotal event during the Protestant Reformation when Martin Luther stood before the Diet at Worms. Those stormy days in 1521 decided the future of the fledgling Protestant movement. Luther stood trembling as an avalanche of coercion sought to drive the recantation of his books and teachings. But the reluctant monk was not free to act against a far more compelling force than the power of the Holy Roman Empire. Therefore, he declared, "I am bound by the Scriptures I have quoted and my conscience is captive to the Word of God. I cannot and will not recant anything, since it is neither safe nor right to go against conscience. . . . I cannot do otherwise. Here I stand."[20] Luther was bound and free at the same time. He was inextricably bound by superior compelling forces that outweighed those of the human realm. Yet he freely abided by those compelling forces with headlong devotion. Luther did what he wanted to do, but could not do otherwise.

20. Martin Brecht, *Martin Luther: His Road to Reformation 1483–1521*, trans. James L. Schaaf (Philadelphia: Fortress Press, 1985), 460, 537.

So even the most expansive definition of the freedom of choice must recognize limitations. It is never true in any conception of free agency that humans are free to do *whatever* they want. Free agency should consider how actual experience reflects such notions but, more importantly, how Scripture informs the parameters of the human will. The essence of a compatibilist notion of freedom is that we are free to choose what we want when we have the ability to choose and when no physical or mental constraints are placed on what we choose. This also means that alternative choices can and do present themselves to us. Thus, *if* we have the desire to make a *different* choice, then we *will* make that choice. The question is: where do various desires come from? We answer that question next.

Chapter Summary

The act of choosing from the human side of the compatibilist equation can be conceived of as a series of concentric layers, like those of an onion. Each layer down moves closer to the heart of what drives human choosing. First, the outside layer represents the bare act of choosing in which people always choose what they *want* to choose. Furthermore, our choices always correspond to what we perceive to be in our best interest. Biblically, it is appropriate to speak of a natural self-love (self-interest) that people have. This is assumed in the commands Scripture gives about loving one's neighbor as oneself. But self-love is a two-edged sword. In our depravity, it is used to gratify evil desires. In regenerated believers, however, it is restored to something truly virtuous. Genuine self-interest finds satisfaction in what brings glory to God and in that which interests him.

Furthermore, humans are free to choose as long as natural inabilities, external circumstances, and moral constraints do not hinder their choices. In either case, given all the prior causal conditions that necessitate particular choices, no other choices can be made. People are not free to act against what they want to do.

Glossary

moral ability. In *compatibilism*, the ability of a regenerate person to conform to God's standard of righteousness. The unregenerate person has a moral inability to act in any God-pleasing manner. All moral actions of the unregenerate fall short of the standard of righteousness that God sets. See also *natural ability*.

natural ability. The ability that a person has or does not have to act in some way. People may have natural abilities that allow them to act in some way as well as disabilities that prevent them from acting in some way. Also, external natural restraints may hinder one from acting in some way. See also *moral ability*.

Pelagianism. A belief system derived from the teachings of the British monk Pelagius (c. 354–415). Pelagius taught that divine grace was not necessary for humans to achieve salvation. Rather, people are born morally neutral and with their *free will* are able to equally choose between sinful and righteous actions. Pelagianism is regarded as heretical by both Calvinists and Arminians.

prevenient grace. In *Arminianism*—which teaches that mankind is morally depraved due to our *sin nature* inherited from Adam, thus placing our wills in bondage to sin—the grace that God bestows on unbelievers that restores their *free will* (i.e., defined as *libertarianism*) and allows them to cooperate with or resist further effusions of God's grace.

self-interest. In *compatibilism*, the motivation that people have to always act in a way that they perceive will serve their own best interest or what will benefit them the most. Also termed *self-love*.

self-love. See *self-interest*.

Study Questions

1. The first proposition of compatibilist freedom simply states that people choose what they want to do and never choose contrary to their desires. Do you agree or disagree with this statement? Explain why.

2. Do people ever hate themselves? Or is the expression "I hate myself" a cover for self-love or self-interest? Explain your answer.

3. Read Mark 8:34–35. Is Jesus calling for people to hate themselves in this passage? If not, what does he mean?

4. In what way is self-love a "two-edged sword," according to the author?

5. Explain some of the different kinds of hindrances that can constrain one's freedom of choice. What is the difference between an absolute hindrance and those that have varying degrees of constraining power?

6. Explain the difference between *natural ability* and *moral ability*. Give examples of each.

7. Explain the Arminian doctrine of prevenient grace. What problems does this doctrine pose for a biblical view of one's freedom of choice?

8. A second proposition of compatibilism states that given a specific set of prior reasons (causes), only one choice (outcome) can transpire. Can you think of situations in which this might not be true? Make sure to scrutinize all the details of your example carefully.

9. If only one choice could be made, given all the preconditions for that choice, does this mean that we have no alternative options when making a choice? Explain your answer.

10. If people could act contrary (i.e., with libertarian freedom) to the reasons that determine their choices, how would this undermine their responsibility for those choices?

Resources for Further Study

Matthew Barrett, *Salvation by Grace: A Case for Effectual Calling and Regeneration* (Phillipsburg, NJ: P&R Publishing, 2013). Chapters 5 and 6 provide one of the most incisive critiques of Arminianism's doctrine of prevenient grace as well as its synergistic view of salvation.

John Piper, *Desiring God* (Sisters, OR: Multnomah, 1996). Demonstrates how a biblical view of self-interest is at the heart of what glorifies God.

Thomas R. Schreiner, "Does Scripture Teach Prevenient Grace in the Wesleyan Sense?," in *Still Sovereign*, ed. Thomas R. Schreiner and Bruce A. Ware (Grand Rapids: Baker, 2000), 229–46. A good critique of the Arminian doctrine of prevenient grace.

R. C. Sproul, *Willing to Believe: The Controversy over Free Will* (Grand Rapids: Baker, 1997). Chapter 1 provides a detailed assessment of Pelagianism.

8

Why We Do the Things We Do

What makes us choose one thing over another? Why do we care about some decisions and not others? Why are there so many competing choices? If you understand the world of marketing, you know that any good advertising campaign appeals to what people *want most*. A really successful advertising campaign will actually fabricate a desire so that people will suddenly want a product or service that they had previously never thought about. Marketing understands the fundamental nature of choosing. The best marketing strategy will enhance the desirability of a product or service so that you will *want* it *more* than the competition. Desires are the gatekeepers of our hearts that guard the way to our choosing.

In the previous chapter, we explored the first layer of human freedom in decision-making: that we are free to do what we want to do. Furthermore, so long as absolute constraints are absent, we *always* do what we want to do, which means that we are *not* free to do otherwise. These propositions seem so obvious that they almost appear trivial. Nonetheless, they represent the antithesis of libertarianism, which is more widely affirmed. But after probing common experience a little deeper, a biblical compatibilism makes far more sense of the data. Scripture affirms that the heart of our wanting and choosing in a particular direction stems from what we perceive to be in our best interest. This is the fountainhead from which all our desires spring forth. We will consider these desires in this chapter. They form the next layer down in the cause-effect paradigm of human choosing, as indicated by our next proposition.

What We Want to Do Is Always in Accordance with Our Desires

We choose what we want to choose; and what we want to choose arises from specific desires, motives, inclinations, passions, preferences, and so on. These are the immediate causes decisively directing the choices that a person wants to make.[1] Other matters can affect these internal dispositions, such as personality, core beliefs, and physical and mental states of being. If we suffer from poor health, physical ailments, exhaustion, emotional fatigue, and so forth, it directly affects our desires and motives for the choices we make. The endless combinations of these various mental and physical conditions stem from that most basic of motives—self-interest. We do what we think at the moment of choosing is the thing that will benefit us the most.

When it comes directly to moral choices, the one place where some of these desires and motives arise is the conscience. The conscience speaks of the divine stamp of morality placed within us and indicates our accountability to God and his law (Rom. 2:14–15). The conscience reveals to us the knowledge of right and wrong. Accordingly, many desires and motives can either be dictated by one's conscience or violate it. When functioning properly, it sends us signals that either affirm our morally right choices or shame us for morally wrong ones. Unfortunately, the conscience can be suppressed such that doing right is not so pressing and doing wrong is not so shaming (Rom. 1:32; 1 Tim. 4:1–3).

The apostle James connects specific actions that we choose to engage in to the internal desires that drive our choices, in this case sinful ones:

> What is the source of quarrels and conflicts among you? Is not the source your pleasures that wage war in your members? You lust and do not have; so you commit murder. You are envious and cannot obtain; so you fight and quarrel. You do not have because you do not ask. You ask and do not receive, because

1. Loraine Boettner, *The Reformed Doctrine of Predestination* (Philadelphia: Presbyterian and Reformed, 1932), 219.

you ask with wrong motives, so that you may spend it on your
pleasures. (James 4:1–3 NASB)

Evil desires produce envious expectations and lusts that are not met,
thus provoking choices that result in quarrels and conflicts and even
murder. Sometimes prayers demand resources to fulfill immoral
pleasures. Those prayers go unanswered because the motives are wrong.
Earlier, James warns: "But each person is tempted when he is lured
and enticed by his own desire. Then desire when it has conceived gives
birth to sin, and sin when it is fully grown brings forth death" (James
1:14–15). The apostle presumes that these immoral motives undergird
personal responsibility. Again, culpability for our actions stems from
the intentions behind our actual choices, not from the libertarian idea
that we could have chosen otherwise.

External Influences

Internal motives and desires are the engines that drive human
action. But these internal factors can be influenced by external factors
as well. Every situation has a unique set of circumstances that influence
one's choices. People influence us. Many fondly remember a coach or
a teacher who took time to pour his or her life into our own when no
one else did. The media influence us. People need to be informed about
the world they live in. Where do we get our news: CNN, Fox, Yahoo?
Culture influences us. Some consider the fads of popular fashion and
either imitate or repudiate them. Our upbringing influences us. How
often do we mold household rules after the ones that our parents
made? Our education influences us. Some have been shaped at Bob
Jones University and others at Cal Berkeley. At every turn, multiple
external factors weigh heavily on the way we think, what our hearts
crave, and the direction in which our choosing leans.

The extent to which these corroborating forces have compelling
value or constraining power determines the degree of causal force they
bring to bear. A captivating preacher has more power to persuade than
a boring one whose sermons you forget the moment you walk out the
church doors. But unless outside influences exert absolute constraints
on the person choosing, their power is limited. The preacher might

persuade a man to love his wife, but he cannot force him to do so. On the other hand, a preacher might not compel a heckler to leave the sanctuary during the sermon, but a 250-pound usher trained in martial arts could, by physically removing the man against his will.

Nonetheless, under most circumstances, the immediate causal power of choosing rests within the person choosing and not outside forces.[2] In the end, you cannot wholly praise or blame these external factors for the choices you make. All such influences are sifted and sorted and assessed by the complex counsels of the heart and mind. It is your own internal inclinations that are responsible for generating your actions. No option is selected that is disconnected from the desires that emanate from the heart's affections and the mind's intellectual deliberations. You take in the data of the external world. Then the heart latches on to what it sets its affections on (Matt. 6:21), while the mind cogitates and evaluates and eventually churns out sufficient reasons, either good or bad, for the choices it deems acceptable. This doesn't mean that every possible contributing cause or influence can be discerned, only that they reside somewhere among the brewing mixture of ingredients within.

We Always Do What We Most Want to Do

We come now to a related proposition that reflects one of the most crucial points in the compatibilist understanding of the human will. Jonathan Edwards argues, "The will is always determined by the strongest motive."[3] People often have what I term *conflicting desires* or, conversely, *competing desires*, but in the end the most persuasive or prevailing desire inevitably determines the choice that one makes. People do what they *most* want to do—that which appears at the moment to be in their best interest or to their greatest advantage.

Now, people often regret their choices later (as Judas did), but the moment of choosing can bring together a blend of all sorts of convoluted desires and mental states of various intensities and perceived importance. These, of course, are influenced by external circumstances as well. After evaluating this jumbled mix with a certain rigor (or

2. Jonathan Edwards, *The Freedom of the Will*, vol. 1 of *The Works of Jonathan Edwards*, ed. Paul Ramsey (New Haven, CT: Yale University Press, 1957), 163.
3. Ibid., 142.

lack thereof), a set of motives emerges that takes precedence at the moment of choosing. Sometimes we are quite conscious of our motives and they weigh heavily on our mental state. In most cases, we act almost instinctively—unaware of the reasons why we choose what we do. Nonetheless, decisive reasons do reside in our innermost mental disposition, and when we make the actual decision, these reasons always tip the balance in favor of one choice over another. Let us consider the nature of these differing types of desires.

Conflicting Desires

Conflicting desires usually correspond to situations in which external coercion influences you to make a choice that under normal circumstances you wouldn't make. We often wrestle with opposing desires that battle within.[4] Tom walks down the street and encounters a thug who demands all his money. He is not favorably inclined to obey such a directive and dismisses the miscreant. But suppose Tom meets the same villainous fellow again and this time he presents a loaded .45 to his head, threatening, "Give me all your money, or I'll blow your brains out!"

This is a bit of a game-changer. It produces a new motive that Tom didn't previously entertain. Under these new circumstances, he is faced with the dilemma of acting on one or the other of two conflicting motives. Like most other people, Tom would rather part with his money (reluctantly, of course) than part with his life. Tom's second choice is far less desirable—it holds little appeal to what he really wants. Nonetheless, it is the more compelling choice and represents what he in fact *wants* to do *most* under the circumstances even if it is extremely disagreeable to him.[5]

John Frame makes an important point:

> On the compatibilist view, then, we can say that in one sense we always act according to our strongest desire, and in another

4. Technically, conflicting desires also represent competing desires, and vice versa. Since I am seeking to distinguish the two types of desires, however, I am avoiding these nuances.

5. R. C. Sproul, *Willing to Believe: The Controversy over Free Will* (Grand Rapids: Baker, 1997), 156–57.

sense we do not. We always act according to our strongest desire in the here and now, according to our strongest desire in each concrete situation. We would always like to act according to our broader preferences, but we do not always do that. So, in a compatibilist concept of freedom, we are always free to follow our most immediate desires, but not always free to carry out our more general desires.[6]

Many conflicting desires involve no threat from outside forces; rather, they reflect intense battles within between opposing thoughts that seek mastery over our souls. Jesus declares, "No one can serve two masters, for either he will hate the one and love the other, or he will be devoted to the one and despise the other" (Matt. 6:24). These conflicts at their core are moral in nature. The conscience, like an unbending steel beam, often remains steadfast and firm in its declaration of what is right. But the heart has the capacity to overrule the conscience, dictating a path that is contrary to sound judgment; and the heart always prevails (v. 21).

How often do young women face unwanted pregnancies? A girl senses strongly that what is inside her womb is not an impersonal blob of tissue, but a living, developing human being. Yet she convinces herself that she is not prepared for the responsibility of having a child, and so she undergoes a torturous battle in her mind and heart over what to do. In the end, her heart gives way to the desire that she believes will yield the most beneficial result. If she decides to keep the baby, then the thought that she once considered aborting the precious child becomes repulsive.

But if she decides to abort, then she must go through an elaborate process of persuasive self-justification in order to suppress her conscience. She may be an expert who continues to suppress her conscience after the abortion takes place, making her decision seem all the more justifiable. But she may be an amateur in the art of suppression—something that all human beings should strive for. In that case, she will greatly suffer the pangs of guilt and shame in the aftermath of her decision.

6. John M. Frame, *The Doctrine of God* (Phillipsburg, NJ: P&R Publishing, 2002), 137.

Competing Desires

On the other hand, sometimes choices are difficult because of *competing desires*. These are not desires in conflict with (opposing) one another; rather, they are nearly equal in their positive or negative appeal. If competing desires center on negative appeal, then you are faced with choosing the lesser of two or more evils. Or suppose that you have received two college scholarships—one to Michigan and the other to Michigan State. Both universities have positive appeal, so which one shall you choose? The choice might be difficult and attended with uncertainty and trepidation. But you weigh the pros and cons and deliberate on them until reasons emerge for one or the other option. When the final verdict is in, the most persuasive reasons that produce the strongest desire will determine whether you will be a Wolverine or a Spartan. The prevailing motives for the decision that wins might slightly edge out the loser so that the difference is barely discernible or not even discernible at all.

Notice that our desires variously fluctuate between those attended with intensity and those that are marked by complacency. But in either case, the strongest desire wins the day. For example, when a decision is critical and the options have nearly identical value (whether negative or positive), it drives up the stress factor considerably. You don't want to make the wrong choice. And when the options are insignificant, you could just as easily flip a coin. *Which of my favorite cereals shall I eat this morning—Cap'n Crunch or Lucky Charms?* It might come down to which box is closest to your hand. But that in itself becomes the prevailing motive. Our choices at times might appear to be random, but they never are. In most cases, we rarely think about our motives. We don't have a running tab in the back of our minds that registers all the pros and cons before we make our choices.[7] We just choose and then maybe sort out the motives later if we have to.

The Complexities of Circumstances and Motives

Decision-making is often a multifaceted enterprise. The interplay between circumstances and motives can be complex and elusive. For

7. Sproul, *Willing to Believe*, 157.

example, if there are conflicting motives because coercion by another person is involved, the voluntary nature of the resulting choices is greatly diminished. Furthermore, if decisions shift from more coerced to more voluntary, the corresponding set of desires that vie for our attention also shift from more conflicting to more competing. Coercion corresponds to conflicting desires. Likewise, more freely made choices correspond to competing desires, so long as the competing desires have a positive appeal. When competing desires have a negative appeal, either choice seems to proceed from coercion. If you are on a deserted island starving to death and your choices of food are moldy bread and rotten fish, then both choices seem coerced. Any number of complex situations can make the interplay with motives very messy. Understanding this dizzying dynamic requires an extended illustration.

Suppose that Stephen wants his son Marcus to go outside and get some physical exercise, but Marcus would rather stay inside and play his favorite video game.[8] In this case, there is no conflicting desire for Marcus. He has a single-hearted desire directed toward playing the video game. Now, Stephen could physically remove Marcus from the house and lock the doors. The child might kick and scream, but to no avail—he would be powerless against a mightier force. In this case, coercion is stronger because of absolute constraint. Thus, we say that Marcus is being forced to go outside against his will. He literally has no choice in the matter. It is a fierce battle of wills between a father and his son, but the son suffers a knockout blow.

No doubt the incident provokes the boy's anger, and although he bears some culpability for this, his father bears more (Eph. 6:4). This demonstrates that when coercion is at work, the coercive agent has a greater degree of influence on the coerced person's choices as well as greater culpability for what the person chooses. Billy the bully bears greater culpability for coercing Johnny to pull Sally's hair than if Johnny pulled Sally's hair of his own accord.

Now, Stephen could take a different tack by threatening Marcus with punishment if he doesn't go outside and play. The boy goes will-

8. The proceeding discussion using this father-son illustration bears some similarity to John Feinberg's classroom illustration in *No One Like Him* (Wheaton, IL: Crossway, 2001), 638–39. But he does not employ the *conflicting/competing* terminology that I use here.

ingly but under duress (reluctantly). He would rather play his video game, but not at the risk of being punished. In this case, Stephen has now created circumstances in which a *conflicting desire* emerges for Marcus. Furthermore, coercion is still involved, but to a lesser degree, and thus Marcus can act more voluntarily. A battle of wills still exists, but with a difference. In the first scenario, Stephen provides no motive for Marcus to consider; he just forces his will over his son's will. In the second scenario, Stephen provides Marcus with an alternative motive to consider—avoiding punishment. Now Marcus has a choice, whereas in the first scenario he had no choice at all. As a result, Marcus's freedom is somewhat enhanced. Now, even if he remains stubborn and refuses to obey his dad, this merely indicates that the threat of punishment is not sufficient to motivate him to abandon his most compelling desire, which always determines one's choices. Video games have a powerful lure on the minds of young boys. Marcus is free to do only what he *wants* to do.

Notice how this is distinguished from libertarianism, in which freedom is simply reduced to having more than one choice. In compatibilism, freedom is secured when a person has the ability to choose an option that he is *desirous* of choosing, in which the degree of voluntariness in his choice is liberated from coercion. Paul wishes his friend Philemon to exercise his will freely (voluntarily) and not from compulsion as he considers the godly way to treat his runaway slave Onesimus (Philem. 14). Likewise, Peter instructs church elders to "shepherd the flock of God that is among you, exercising oversight, not under *compulsion*, but *willingly*" (1 Peter 5:2).

This was the heart of Paul when it came to the preaching of the gospel: "For if I preach the gospel, I have nothing to boast of, for I am under compulsion; for woe is me if I do not preach the gospel. For if I do this voluntarily, I have a reward; but if against my will, I have a stewardship entrusted to me" (1 Cor. 9:16–17 NASB). In this case, when Paul says that he preaches "under compulsion," he is not saying that he does so against his higher preferences. Otherwise, he would contradict what he says in the next sentence. Rather, Paul is saying that he preaches with a "necessity" (v. 16 ESV). In other words, he is a chosen vessel of God for the proclamation of the gospel. In this sense, he has no choice. Yet he preaches "voluntarily" without any notion that God has coerced him to act against his prevailing desires. On the other hand, if Paul were compelled to preach "against [his] will," he would still do so because he has "a stewardship entrusted" to him.

Libertarianism also sees freedom of choice as liberation from coercion; it happens to say, however, that *any* persuasive influence directing a choice to one particular end is seen as an act of coercion. It is not that libertarians deny that choices have reasons; rather, no reason can become more compelling for one choice over another. I might have a reason for choosing Lucky Charms, but I could have equally chosen Cap'n Crunch for another reason, and neither choice is allowed to be more compelling than the other. But when a choice loses its appeal and is no more preferable than another choice, it is difficult to see how freedom is enhanced. If libertarianism were true, many decisions we make would bear the risk of sucking the color out of life.

Now consider a third scenario. Suppose Stephen promises Marcus that he will purchase that new coveted video game for him if he goes outside to play. Suddenly a far more desirable motivation is produced that convinces the boy to obey. So his choice is even more voluntarily made because little or no coercion is involved. Note here how *conflicting desires* suddenly give way to *competing desires—do I play the video game I love now or wait for the new video game later?* But this is not so terrible because either choice has positive appeal.

Notice the difference in the dynamics between the second and third scenario. In the second scenario, Marcus is motivated by a negative consequence, which can produce feelings of resentment and the like. In the third scenario, he is motivated by a positive consequence, which tends to lead to more desirable feelings of joy, pleasure, and so forth and represents a more attractive motive. People are often motivated more readily by positive consequences than negative ones because more satisfaction or reward is derived from them.

But the situation in a case such as that of Stephen and Marcus is more complicated than that. Without derailing our train of thought, we must stop and consider two moral lessons to be learned here.

First, is not the promise of appealing gifts a way to spoil the boy? It might be easier to get him to obey, but it poses a greater threat of producing greed and avarice. Stephen has capitulated to appeasing Marcus's decidedly unvirtuous desires by granting him more of what Stephen wanted to curb in the first place. Biblical wisdom suggests that promising the boy more video games might not be in his best interest or in the interests of his parents. Expediency is no substitute for wisely instructing a child's heart in what is truly for his own good.

So what is the first lesson? For the Christian, proper motivation in decision-making should be rooted in glorifying God and not our self-glorifying appetites. Genuine happiness can never take root in the deception of self-glory (James 1:14–16).

This leads to a second biblical lesson. Although it is correct to say that Marcus's freedom is considerably enhanced in the third scenario, this doesn't mean that such freedom is beneficial. Most people are accustomed to thinking that freedom of choice is always a good thing, which explains why the term *free will* is almost universally regarded as a self-evident virtue. But when people freely make choices with unhindered abandon, throwing off all restraints, and those choices are motivated by evil desires, it is not a good thing (Gen. 6:5). Ironically, such freedom leads to bondage.

The world that God created is full of restraints that promote a righteous and beneficial order: a good conscience (Rom. 2:14–15), civil laws that incorporate threats for disobedience or rewards for obedience (Rom. 13:1–4),[9] and the supernatural checks of God (Rom. 1:24–28; 2 Thess. 2:6–7). Beneficial freedom is that which promotes unhindered adherence to God's moral (preceptive) will (John 8:32). This happens when, first of all, people are wholly free from the constraints of evil motivations compounded by evil circumstances. Second, their hearts must be filled with the strongest of desires to obey and enjoy all that God commands. Then true freedom—which is always spiritual in nature—not only is enhanced but brings about the best possible good for those who experience it (Gal. 5:1; Rom. 6:7, 18, 22). This sort of freedom will be explored in greater depth in chapters 9 through 12.

---

9. This assumes that the precepts as well as the sanctions of given laws are righteous and good.

To the Degree That We Act Voluntarily, We Are Liable for Our Actions

The examination of choices that lie along a spectrum between coercion and voluntariness leads to our next major proposition. Almost all human actions are voluntary, but some actions are more coerced than others, thereby mitigating their voluntariness. The more voluntary one's actions are, the more liability is attached to those actions, and vice versa. In 1 Corinthians 9:17, Paul directly connects the voluntary nature of his preaching to receiving a "reward." One's reward or punishment for his actions is tied to the voluntary nature of his choices, not whether he could have acted otherwise. Thus, if a compelling force causes a conflicting motive within a person to act in a way in which he would otherwise not act, then he is not as liable for the action. If one feels forced to act against what his conscience tells him is clearly wrong, then he is not held as liable for such an action because its voluntary nature has been hampered.

Freedom from coercion and the ability to act voluntarily and responsibly are reflected in most systems of jurisprudence in which just measures are used to assess guilt (blame) or innocence. Manslaughter is the killing of another *without* malice of intent, whereas murder is the killing of another *with* malice of intent. Voluntary manslaughter involves intentional killing, but mitigating factors make the intention less culpable. For example, a sudden provocation leads to a fight, resulting in the death of the provocateur. Involuntary manslaughter is accidental killing in which the death occurred without intention. For example, a person driving her vehicle hits and kills a pedestrian by accident. One is held less liable for something done *accidentally* or *reluctantly* under duress. Conversely, one is held more liable for an immoral action if done freely (more intentionally). In fact, what makes it immoral is directly connected to the intentions of the perpetrator (James 1:14–15).

Sam Storms relates a poignant illustration that highlights this proposition.[10] The story involves a pizza deliveryman named Brian

---

10. Sam C. Storms, "The Will: Fettered Yet Free," in *A God Entranced Vision of All Things*, ed. John Piper and Justin Taylor (Wheaton, IL: Crossway, 2004), 209.

Wells who robbed a bank while an explosive device was strapped to his body. He fled the scene with the bomb intact and was later apprehended by the police, with whom he pleaded for help. He claimed that he had been forced to rob the bank by the crime's real perpetrator, who forcibly placed the device on him and threatened to detonate it if he didn't comply.[11] If his confession was true, what other choice would he have? Under such circumstances, our justice system is obligated to exonerate the person of culpability for the crime even though he robbed the bank. The compelling motive to rob the bank is not rooted in some malintent but in the preservation of one's own life.

Under such circumstances, however, one would not be without an alternative choice. Technically, because of the absence of absolute constraint, Brian was not forced against his will to rob the bank; he robbed it willingly. The difference is that he also did it reluctantly under extreme duress. All things being equal, we can suppose that his conscience would not allow him to engage in such a criminal act. But the strongest of any motive or compelling desire within a person at any given moment is always the one that directly determines one's choice, in this case the coercive influence of the main perpetrator.

Yet Brian could have taken his chances and refused to commit the robbery. He could have said that he would rather die than cause distress to the bank and its customers and risk their deaths if the perpetrator detonated the bomb in the middle of the robbery. In this sense, he is free to act in a contrary manner, but *only if* corresponding contrary motives prevail. The point is that the will is the absolute servant of the motive that most powerfully influences it, and it never acts in a contrary manner.

People are also not considered liable for actions if other legitimate hindrances prevent them from acting responsibly. For example, Christians ought to attend church on Sunday (Heb. 10:25). But if they are sick and bedridden, we do not hold them liable; they have a *natural inability* to act otherwise. But if they don't go to church because they prefer to watch a football game, they are more liable because they

11. See http://www.nytimes.com/2003/09/01/us/bomb-kills-pizza-deliveryman-after -arrest-in-bank-robbery.html.

had a *natural ability* and a moral responsibility to do so. They were under no constraints to prevent them from acting responsibly.

Stephen Holmes provides a similar scenario.[12] He states that one would not be held liable for not saving a drowning victim if he is unable to swim. His natural inability prevents him from doing what is morally right. If he is able to swim and doesn't make the effort to save the drowning victim, however, he is held liable. In that case, he is held liable not because he is unable to swim but because he is "unable to care."[13]

These illustrations point out that moral liability rests not just with natural ability but also with one's intentions. The more voluntarily we act, the more intentionally we act. When the Bible pinpoints the source of our liability, it is concerned not with freedom of contrary choice, but with the state of our heart. Did it *please* us to act in a certain way? "I the LORD search the heart and test the mind, to give every man according to his ways, according to the fruit of his deeds" (Jer. 17:10). God is able to cut through our hypocrisy and self-deception by examining what lies within. "All the ways of a man are clean in his own sight, but the LORD weighs the *motives*" (Prov. 16:2 NASB; cf. 21:2).

When Samuel was instructed to select a king for Israel, he sought after a man who would be marketable to the masses, a man of exterior substance and appeal. But what sort of moral character would such a man have? God's criterion differs considerably from ours. "But the LORD said to Samuel, 'Do not look on his appearance or on the height of his stature, because I have rejected him. For the LORD sees not as man sees: man looks on the outward appearance, but the LORD looks on the heart'" (1 Sam. 16:7).

Moral Knowledge, the Conscience, and Liability

If the knowledge we have of the moral significance of actions for which we might be culpable is increased, then our liability is increased. Ignorance of right and wrong is taken into consideration

---

12. Stephen R. Holmes, "Strange Voices: Edwards on the Will," in *Listening to the Past: The Place of Tradition in Theology* (Grand Rapids: Baker Academic, 2002), 89.
13. Ibid.

as a plausible cause for decreased liability.[14] A six-month-old baby excited by her first visit to the grocery store can't possibly know that swiping that toothbrush off the rack and keeping it for herself is morally irresponsible. One cannot always plead ignorance, however, if conditions are such that one is culpable for his or her ignorance. For example, a student cannot escape blame for failing an exam when he was responsible for knowing the material.[15]

From a biblical perspective, moral culpability for our actions is tied to our obligations before God. James Spiegel writes:

> Our essential moral status before God as creatures is defined . . . by the most basic and extensive duties toward him. Simply put, we are morally indebted to God because he is our creator and sustainer, as he is of the rest of the universe. The psalmist writes, "The earth is the LORD's, and everything in it, the world and all who live in it" (Ps. 24:1). And God says to Job, "Who has a claim against me that I must pay? Everything under heaven belongs to me" (Job 41:11). God exercises absolute ownership over every one of his creatures.[16]

God mediates our responsibility to him through the moral knowledge that he has supplied to every person's conscience. The conscience informs us of the difference between moral right and wrong as a testimony to the divine Lawgiver. One's actions either agree with his conscience or violate it (Rom. 2:14–15). Furthermore, the law judges us whether we can act contrary to it or not (8:7). It does not respect contrary choice. If one's conscience is neglected, it becomes seared (1 Tim. 4:2). The more rebellious sinful man becomes, the more he suppresses and distorts his conscience. He feigns an ignorance of moral truth, acting as though he didn't know better. Of course, if humans had a genuine ignorance of right and wrong, then our consciences couldn't bind us to what we didn't know. Consequently, God would

---

14. Joseph Keim Campbell, *Free Will* (Malden, MA: Polity Press, 2011), 31.
15. Ibid., 33.
16. James S. Spiegel, *The Benefits of Providence: A New Look at Divine Sovereignty* (Wheaton, IL: Crossway, 2005), 72.

have no reason to hold us responsible for sin. The problem is, no matter how much the conscience may be suppressed, the knowledge of sin remains, and thus culpability remains (Rom. 1:32).

What We Want to Do Follows Predictable Patterns

Compatibilism affirms determinism, the idea that every choice has antecedent reasons that dictate what choices we make. Choosing is undergirded by a cause-effect relationship. The chain of deterministic causes moves from the human plane of internal desires and external circumstances to the divine realm of providence. This means that our choices are predictable to some degree, making them analogous to the laws of nature. In a biblical worldview, the laws of nature are the predictable cause-effect patterns by which God governs the world.[17] Physical processes in creation act in a necessary, consistent, predictable, and uniform manner under the providential hand of God. Under ordinary (normal) circumstances, the laws of nature function necessarily and exactly the same way in repeated situations, given all the same conditions. Other factors, including various forces and constraints, affect outcomes differently, but the same laws act consistently and predictably.

Each time Babe Ruth swung his massive fifty-four-ounce bat known as the War Club, the ball he hit acted predictably. If one could instantly determine the velocity and direction of the pitch, the velocity, angle, and position of the bat as it was swung, and so forth, one could position oneself in the stands to catch his home-run hits.

In similar ways, human behavior is predictable. This does not preclude the fact that human choices can proceed in countless directions. But to the extent that we can know the prior conditions—people's motives, personalities, patterns of previous behavior, and external circumstances influencing their desires—we can reasonably predict what people might do. Only one possible outcome will result, given all the preconditions affecting people's choices. Of course, it is impossible to know everything that is at work behind the scenes, so in a practical sense, many choices are hard to predict. Nonetheless, we

---

17. Again, this is the doctrine of concurrence. See Frame, *The Doctrine of God*, 287–88.

might say that human choices follow discernible patterns of human behavior.[18] Furthermore, unless God intervenes in an extraordinary way (miraculously), these patterns hold true as the means by which he normally governs human behavior.

Robin watches her one-year-old daughter, Julia, take her first confident steps in the front yard of their house. She has cherished her only child from the day she was born because for ten years Robin was unable to have children. Then suddenly little Julia walks out into the road as a motorcycle races down the lane. Can you predict Robin's actions? Will she not run with Olympic speed to retrieve her errant little girl? Now imagine that Robin is a different sort of mother, almost continuously high on methamphetamines. She has had several children whose fathers she doesn't even know. Some of her children have been taken away by child protective services because of abuse and neglect. What do you suppose Robin's reaction will be when Julia steps out into the road? Perhaps different? A little dazed? Slower, maybe?

If libertarianism holds true, then the choices in these different scenarios could almost never be predicted. Preceding factors don't have the power to decisively determine choices. In many cases, it might be possible to predict the outcomes, but because we can always choose contrary to any preceding influences, libertarianism says that we simply cannot know. But libertarianism fails to make sense of actual experience because we never make choices without sufficient prior reasons. When antecedent factors are understood, specific choices necessarily follow, just as Babe Ruth's home-run hits follow the laws of physics.

18. I avoid the phrase "*laws* of human behavior," since human behavior is not precisely quantifiable in the way that physical laws are (laws of motion, gravity, thermodynamics, etc.). John Feinberg writes, "More often than not, [antecedent conditions for a person's choices] are so complex that one could never write all the sentences needed to specify them. Moreover, there do not appear to be general laws covering actions so that one could say, 'in instances of type A an agent will always choose action x.'" "God Ordains All Things," in *Predestination and Free Will: Four Views of Divine Sovereignty and Human Freedom*, ed. David Basinger and Randall Basinger (Downers Grove, IL: InterVarsity Press, 1986), 23. This might seem to be an argument for libertarianism, but it merely says that knowing every possible antecedent causal condition for our choices is impossible.

Choices Have Consequences

Related to the predictability of choices is the matter of consequences as well. Choices have natural consequences. Walking out into a busy street can cause you to be run over. Whispering to someone across a stadium won't cause you to be heard. Eating a large deep-dish pizza from Gino's East in Chicago every day will increase your chances of obesity. Choices have moral consequences as well. Much of the book of Proverbs details the moral consequences of one's actions. Consider the following examples:

> Wealth gained hastily will dwindle,
>> but whoever gathers little by little will increase it. (Prov. 13:11)

> A hot-tempered man stirs up strife,
>> but he who is slow to anger quiets contention. (Prov. 15:18)

> A joyful heart is good medicine,
>> but a crushed spirit dries up the bones. (Prov. 17:22)

We do not expect God to intervene miraculously to prevent the consequences of our actions. Randy Alcorn writes:

> If God disarmed every shooter and prevented every drunk driver from crashing, this world would not be a real world in which people make consequential choices. It would not be a world of character development and faith building. It would not be a world where families put their arms around one another to face life's difficulties. It would be a world where people went blithely along with their lives, content to do evil and put up with it, feeling no need to turn to God, no incentive to consider the gospel and prepare for eternity. In such a world, people would die without a sense of need, only to find themselves in Hell.[19]

19. Randy Alcorn, *If God Is Good: Faith in the Midst of Suffering and Evil* (Colorado Springs: Multnomah, 2009), 252.

God designed human choosing to bear consequences as a means to inform the conscience so that we are either affirmed in our wise choices or warned that our foolish ones are without excuse (Rom. 2:14–15). Consequences can move us closer toward God or further away from him.

God's Sovereignty and Predictability

In all this we must remember that both the laws of nature and the predictable patterns of human behavior simply describe the proximate (immediate) secondary cause-effect relationships that we see in the world. In both cases, God is the primary (remote) cause working through secondary means (i.e., natural laws and human nature). God could ordain any variety of outcomes that transpire in the natural world and the human plane of that world. But if he ordained something different to occur, then the preceding conditions would be different as well. Unless he chooses to intervene supernaturally by means of his *extraordinary* (special) providence, the outcomes of every natural event and every human choice follow the pattern of his *ordinary* (general) predictable providence.

If God had determined that Al Gore should have been elected during the 2000 U.S. presidential race instead of George Bush, then the election-machine "chad" fiasco in Florida would have favored him. Thus, the model of divine sovereignty that compatibilism affirms never asserts that only one possible outcome for history can transpire. Yes, God has ordained the only outcome that *does* transpire, but we cannot say that what he ordained is somehow *absolutely* necessary.[20] God's deterministic sovereignty does not amount to fatalism. He can choose to act in any manner he desires so long as it is not logically contradictory, such as making square circles or violating the perfections of his divine character. Thus, we can speak of possible alternative choices that present themselves from a human perspective. We face forks in the road and don't always know which path we *should* choose or *will* choose. But once the choice is made, it can be

---

20. Robert Kane, *A Contemporary Introduction to Free Will* (New York: Oxford University Press, 2005), 6.

traced to whatever causes arose to determine that choice, including what God saw fit.

We view life almost exclusively from our own vantage point. We generally never think about the invisible hand of divine providence unless God gives us discernible clues along the way. A few years ago, my family experienced an unexpected crisis requiring a financial outlay that we didn't have. We prayed about the matter for some days. Then a completely unexpected sum of money from an anonymous source arrived in the mail that exactly met our need. God's hand was invisible but nonetheless quite discernible.

It is easy to dismiss God as the primary cause of natural and human events. When Babe Ruth hits a baseball, it is easy to think that the only factors determining the event are his bat, his swing, the pitcher, his throw, the ball, and the laws of physics. This thinking easily leads to a deistic view of God—the idea that God created the world and set its laws in motion but subsequently remains a passive observer of what takes place. In a deistic worldview, physical matter and the laws of nature take on a self-determining power wholly independent of the Creator. But the Bible teaches that God sustains all aspects of creation.[21] Thus, when a person breathes, it is not the result of *self-determining* functions of the body (Acts 17:25). When a person makes a choice, his action appears to be self-caused because he is not usually conscious of any prior divine cause.

For some, it is easier to see God's hand in the providential sustaining of the world (who controls the weather?) but much less so in our own actions. The immediate perception of our thoughts, deliberations, and motives that lead to our choices seems disconnected from God. We do in fact function as creatures distinct from the Creator. We have self-awareness and personal identities that are independent from others and from God. Even though God causally controls all things, we are not fictitious extensions of his imagination.[22] We are real and distinct people, making real choices. God doesn't make them for us, and thus we retain full responsibility for those choices. It is no wonder

21. Job 38–41; Col. 1:16–17; Heb. 1:2–3; see also Neh. 9:6; 2 Peter 3:7.
22. This is the point at which the "author-actor" model of divine sovereignty and human action described in chapter 4 breaks down.

that we are tempted to affirm a human autonomy more commensurate with libertarianism. But only compatibilism maintains the balanced perspective between God's absolute sovereignty on the one hand and the full integrity of human identity, freedom, and responsibility on the other.

Chapter Summary

While chapter 7 focused on the bare act of choosing, this chapter focuses on the second layer down in the unfolding analysis of choosing—our internal dispositions. What people want to choose arises from specific desires, motives, inclinations, passions, preferences, and so on. These are the immediate causes decisively directing the choices that a person wants to make. Furthermore, these internal factors can be influenced by external factors as well, such as other people, media, upbringing, education, and culture. People often have *conflicting desires* or, conversely, *competing desires*, but in the end the most persuasive or prevailing desire inevitably determines the choices that one makes.

Conflicting desires usually correspond to situations in which external coercion influences us to make choices that under normal circumstances we wouldn't make. We often wrestle with opposing desires that battle within. On the other hand, sometimes choices are difficult because of competing desires. These are not desires in conflict with (opposing) one another; rather, they are nearly equal in their positive or negative appeal, and it becomes difficult to choose one or the other. Yet when all is said and done, the strongest motive that is produced by the matrix of internal and external factors is what determines one's choices. Furthermore, the more voluntary one's actions, the more culpability one incurs for those actions. Some actions are more coerced than others, thereby mitigating their voluntariness, and thus one's culpability.

Glossary

competing desires. Apposite (but not opposing) desires that are nearly equal in their positive or negative appeal, making it difficult to act on one or the other. For example, which favorite cereal shall

I choose—Lucky Charms or Cap'n Crunch? See also *conflicting desires*.

conflicting desires. Opposing desires that battle with each other. Usually the conflicting desires arise in situations in which external coercion influences someone toward choices that under normal circumstances the person wouldn't make. For example, a person might not normally give all his money to a stranger. But he might if the stranger held a gun to his head. The second scenario produces a conflicting desire. One doesn't want to part with his money, but neither does he want to part with his life. See also *competing desires*.

conscience. The human faculty that reveals to us the knowledge of moral right and wrong. God stamped his moral law on the conscience of every human being, and this serves to indicate our accountability before him. The moral signals that the conscience provides can be heeded or suppressed.

extraordinary providence. Rare instances in which God's superintendence of events involves miracles or supernatural occurrences (e.g., Jesus' turning water into wine). See also *ordinary providence*.

ordinary providence. Everyday instances in which God's superintendence of events involves predictable patterns that are normally identified in scientific parlance as laws of nature. See also *extraordinary providence*.

Study Questions

1. What are some of the various mental and physical conditions that might influence the choices we make?
2. What is the conscience, and how does it affect our choices?
3. What are some of the external factors (i.e., things outside ourselves) that influence our choices? Can these external factors override internal factors? Explain your answer.
4. Various internal and external factors influence many and varied desires within that lead to possible choices. With a multitude of desires within, what determines the choice that a person ends up making?

5. Explain the difference between what the author calls *conflicting* and *competing desires*.

6. Do people choose to do things that are disagreeable to them? Why or why not?

7. Consider the illustration of Stephen and his son Marcus. How do the actions of another affect our moral responsibility? Can we blame others for the choices we make? What determines who is culpable for a sinful choice that one party makes when other parties are involved?

8. How do negative consequences versus positive consequences work to motivate the choices that people make? Is the use of positive consequences a better or more effective motivator than negative consequences? Explain your answer.

9. Again consider the illustration of Stephen and Marcus. Is increased freedom of choice always beneficial? Explain your answer. Why are restraints to freedom often beneficial?

10. How does coercion affect both the voluntary nature of our choices and the liability we have in making them? How does the bank-robbery illustration enhance our understanding of moral liability?

11. How does natural ability or inability affect our moral liability?

12. How does the moral knowledge that God supplies to us through our consciences affect our moral liability?

13. In what way do our choices follow predictable patterns? Furthermore, how does God's sovereign determination affect the predictability of the choices that people make?

Resources for Further Study

Stephen R. Holmes, "Strange Voices: Edwards on the Will," in *Listening to the Past: The Place of Tradition in Theology* (Grand Rapids: Baker Academic, 2002). This chapter contains some good insights into Jonathan Edwards's view of human responsibility in light of compatibilist freedom.

Sam C. Storms, "The Will: Fettered Yet Free," in *A God Entranced Vision of All Things*, ed. John Piper and Justin Taylor (Wheaton, IL: Crossway, 2004). A good treatment of human responsibility in light of one's view of free agency.

9

A Tale of Two Natures

The metamorphosis of a monarch butterfly is one of the most remarkable transformations of life to life witnessed in God's creation.[1] It begins when the caterpillar slinks around the garden, feasting on milkweed leaves until it gets so plump that it appears ready to burst at any moment. In the process of stuffing itself, it wiggles its way out of (molts) its old skin (exoskeleton) multiple times. Finally, at the peak of the larva stage, the caterpillar deftly attaches itself to a sturdy stick, dangling its body headfirst toward the ground as it enters pupation. To engage in such acrobatics, it fastens a silken loop onto the ready twig and grabs it tightly with the hooklike cremaster protruding from its tail. Once securely fastened, the caterpillar then splits through its skin for one last time. What painstakingly emerges is the chrysalis. The creature twists and gyrates until the old skin crunches up like a dirty sock and falls away. The chrysalis slowly forms into a jade-colored vase that contains what remains of the caterpillar.

What happens next is part of the mystery of creation.

The caterpillar tissue dissolves into a nebulous goo that is miraculously reformed into the strange new components of the butterfly. In this seemingly comatose state, a head, a thorax, an abdomen, and a delicate set of wings are secretly under construction. As the monarch nears its rebirth, the chrysalis turns increasingly transparent while inside the wonderful colors of the butterfly turn increasingly vibrant for the curious observer. Then in the dawn of a new day, the fresh

1. Daniel Devine, "Inexplicable Insect Metamorphosis," *Creation* 29, 3 (June 2007): 31–33.

winged creature emerges, looking nothing like the loathsome worm it once was. Even though we know that some continuity exists between the old and the new, the nature of the caterpillar gives way to the nature of a butterfly.

This metamorphic miracle is not too unlike the rebirth of the old human nature into the new. Regeneration is the topic of exploration in this chapter and those that follow. In order to take this journey, let us get our bearings once again.

We have considered the human side of the compatibilist equation from the perspective of peeling away concentric layers—like peeling an onion. The outside layer represents the bare act of choosing. This act is characterized by the fact that people always choose what they want to choose. But what people want to choose is determined by the next layer down—the strongest desires of the heart and mind, the mission-control center of our humanity (Prov. 4:23). The will is simply a servant of the directives that issue forth from command central, even as people and circumstances influence our internal desires and intellectual deliberations. We have conflicting and competing desires that battle within, but in the end the most compelling desire, whether it is appealing or not, determines the choice we make. Furthermore, that desire corresponds to what we perceive to be in our best interest.

But a third layer rests below this confluence of different factors. This core layer speaks of the fundamental disposition of our hearts and minds—our base nature. We speak of *human nature* to indicate that people act with certain proclivities that characterize the uniqueness of being human. This certainly includes our natural physical characteristics and capacities, but we are really concerned about the metaphysical nature of humanity—our souls. From a biblical perspective, our soulish nature represents our basic moral and spiritual orientation. On the human side of the compatibilist equation, it is the forger of human action, the underlying source of one's desires, motives, passions, and affections by which choices are generated—in particular, moral and spiritual choices.

The Bible speaks of people as being either dead in sins (Eph. 2:1) or alive in Christ (v. 5). Either we are corrupted as a result of the sin nature that we inherited from Adam (Rom. 5:12, 17–19) or we possess a redeemed nature due to the regenerative work of the Holy

Spirit (Titus 3:5). Each nature determines the sorts of desires that emerge in the heart and mind. This core of human choosing narrows our focus strictly on moral and spiritual actions. General actions of a morally neutral disposition (e.g., *what coffee cup shall I use?*) concern us very little at this point. See fig. 9.1.

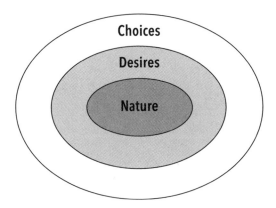

Fig. 9.1. The Human Side of the Compatibilist Equation

Choices—We choose what we *want* to choose, and we can do no other.

Desires—What we want to choose corresponds to our strongest desire, which in turn corresponds to what we perceive to be in our best interest.

Nature—The moral dimension of our desires and choices is dictated by our nature, whether we are dead in sins (Eph. 2:1) or have been made alive in Christ (v. 5).

The Human Side of the Compatibilist Equation

Furthermore, the Bible itself spends little time focusing on the largely inconsequential reality of general actions, but it exerts a great deal of energy in expounding on moral and spiritual actions. God is concerned that the desires of our hearts be guided by his instructive will so that we make righteous decisions. He is less concerned about whether we choose Michigan or Michigan State than he is about our being conformed to the instruction of his Word. But how this righteous conformance is achieved takes us into the inner sanctum of our nature. Let us now consider the next set of propositions in this chain of causal factors.

Our Desires Are Always in Compliance with Our Nature

A marlin is designed to roam the seas. Its body is configured to take in oxygen through a set of gills. Its fins make it suitable for gliding through the water as a master swimmer. The marlin's gills are worthless in the open air. Its fins don't allow it to soar through the skies as a falcon's wings do. Its nature is not that of a bird but of a fish. Its nature restricts its freedom, confining it to a particular domain—the watery realm of the ocean.

In an analogous way, the nature of the human soul is restrictive as well. It permits us to act in only certain ways that we cannot escape unless our nature undergoes a transformation. We are always subject to our nature. Our freedom is determined by it, yet we are inextricably bound to it. We are free and in bondage at the same time. We act necessarily and voluntarily in accordance with our nature but never contrary to it. An apple tree loves to produce apples and necessarily does so, but it is never free to produce oranges. Likewise, as moral agents we are restricted in what we *want* to do and what we are *able* to do.

Even God himself is confined by his nature. God has no capacity to sin. His nature is wholly righteous and good. Thus, all his desires, intentions, and purposes arise from his nature, and he can never act contrary to it. He is never free to sin. The Father could never hate the Son, and the Son could never hate the Father. Furthermore, God acts necessarily in accordance with his nature, and yet this in no way mitigates his freedom. He freely and perfectly loves the Son because it is what he wants to do. He has no *ability* to love the Son less, nor would he ever *want* to. God doesn't have libertarian freedom, and perhaps more importantly, he doesn't grant some indispensable attribute to his creatures that he himself cannot possess.

The Sin Nature

When it comes to human nature, Scripture defines its normal disposition as being "dead" in "trespasses and sins" (Eph. 2:1, 5). Humans suffer from a condition in which nothing spiritual adheres to the walls of their souls. They are bare and lifeless panels, devoid of spiritual substance and purpose. Although people are alive and passionately pursue this quest or that dream, their state of existence is that of spiritual zombies. To be "spiritual" means to possess the Holy Spirit, and the "natural [unspiritual] person" lives without his presence (1 Cor. 2:14–15; cf. Rom. 8:9). This describes all unbelievers. As a result, the proclivity toward corrupted thoughts, desires, motives, and affections has been the default setting for the human soul ever since Adam thrust us under this curse (Rom. 5:12, 17–19). The prophet Isaiah declares: "The earth lies defiled under its inhabitants; for they have transgressed the laws, violated the statutes, broken the everlasting covenant" (Isa. 24:5).

Paul catalogues this paralyzing condition in Romans 3:10–18, in which he declares that not a single unregenerate person is "righteous" (v. 10) or capable of grasping spiritual truth (v. 11). No one naturally seeks after God in any effective, life-transforming way (v. 11). Whatever good that people do is not really good (v. 12). People may go through various contortions, feverishly exerting themselves toward achieving moral nirvana—but it all fails. It never even begins to approach the heights of the standard of God's glorious holiness (v. 23). In his corrupted state, the natural man exhibits no fear of God, no reverence for the majesty of his being (v. 18).

Elsewhere, Paul says that to be devoid of the Spirit is to be controlled by the "flesh," a term that he uses to indicate human nature as it is enslaved to sin (Rom. 8:5–8; cf. 6:16, 19). This echoes the unambiguous teaching of Jesus: "Truly, truly, I say to you, everyone who commits sin is a slave to sin" (John 8:34). There is no freedom for the sinner. The apostle Peter says that false teachers promise freedom while "they themselves are slaves of corruption." It is the blind leading the blind because Peter indicates that the lot of all humanity is to be overcome by sin, for which there is no natural escape (2 Peter 2:19).

The basic orientation of the sinner's mind is one of hostility toward God, according to Romans 8:7. There, Paul tells us that such a mind "does not [i.e., is unwilling to] submit to God's law; indeed, it cannot" (cf. 1 Cor. 2:14). Unregenerate souls never *want* to "please God" (Rom. 8:8; cf. 2 Thess. 2:10) because their defective and corrupted nature is in a state of perennial malfunction. They suffer not only from cognitive faculties that are innately suited to spiritual futility, intellectual blindness, and ignorance but also from a hardness of heart toward anything remotely spiritual (Eph. 4:17–18). The unregenerate cherishes his sin more than the truth.[2]

All of this sounds dreadful, but only because we have a relentless capacity for applying a heavy veneer of self-deception over the reality of our true condition. Humans naturally elevate themselves while severely devaluing the standard of righteousness that is set by the unbridled magnificence of God's moral perfections.

Drowning or Already Drowned?

Most Christians who might be unwittingly influenced by a libertarian perspective think man's sinful nature falls short of these dire descriptions.[3] They treat the natural state of the unregenerate person not as spiritual death, but rather as spiritual weakness or sickness. With some help from the divine Physician, their spiritual immune system will kick in and dispense with the disease that sin has reaped within as they turn to Christ.[4] The sin nature of the unbeliever is likened to the situation of people stranded in the ocean, struggling to swim. Without a lifesaver, they will drown in their sins. But if the line is thrown out to them and they freely choose to take hold of it and hang on tight, then they can make their way to safe harbor and into the arms of Christ.

If the unbeliever is spiritually dead, however, then he has neither ability nor inclination to reach out for saving help. Rather, he is like a lifeless body that slowly descends into the watery abyss. Unless the Captain of our souls dons the swimwear of our humanity and dives in after us, we have no hope. In order for us to experience rescue, the Holy Spirit must draw us upward and resuscitate our breathless state, filling our lungs with the oxygen of new life.

2. Matthew Barrett, *Salvation by Grace: A Case for Effectual Calling and Regeneration* (Phillipsburg, NJ: P&R Publishing, 2013), 65.

3. It should be noted that Arminianism maintains a robust view of human depravity, but its view of prevenient grace mitigates the effects of depravity. Many Christians unaccustomed to the nuances of Arminian theology often entertain a deficient view of the sinfulness of human sin.

4. Here the appeal is made to passages such as Matthew 9:12.

Jesus' teaching illuminates the problem by showing how the state of one's nature determines the sorts of desires and subsequent choices that are possible:

> Either make the tree good and its fruit good, or make the tree bad and its fruit bad, for the tree is known by its fruit. You brood of vipers! How can you speak good, when you are evil? For out of the abundance of the heart the mouth speaks. The good person out of his good treasure brings forth good, and the evil person out of his evil treasure brings forth evil. (Matt. 12:33–35)

Jesus uses two metaphors to describe two different natures that inhabit the souls of men. A bad tree represents the sin nature. It is corrupted and capable of producing only poisonous fruit. If the tree is transformed into a good tree, this represents regeneration, the implanting of a new nature into the soul of man.[5] This good nature produces an edible fruit that is good and righteous.

It is impossible for trees to produce fruit that is contrary to their nature (cf. Luke 6:45). Jesus explains the metaphor by saying that the mouth speaks out only what the heart is filled with. If a heart is saturated by an evil nature, then the mouth chooses to speak evil. It cannot speak otherwise because the heart is corrupted. He expands on this thought later in Matthew 15:19: "For out of the heart come evil thoughts, murder, adultery, sexual immorality, theft, false witness, slander." Likewise, Jesus speaks of the nature of man as a treasure chest. If the chest is full of gold, silver, and precious jewels, then it will not produce rusty old metal and worthless rocks.

These metaphors reiterate the Old Testament teaching on the subject. The prophet Jeremiah asks rhetorically: "Can the Ethiopian change his skin or the leopard his spots? Then also you can do good who are accustomed to do evil" (Jer. 13:23; cf. 17:9). David likewise quotes on old proverb that is equally forthright: "Out of the wicked comes wickedness" (1 Sam. 24:13). Isaiah informs us that lies are

---

5. Anthony A. Hoekema, *Saved by Grace* (Grand Rapids: Eerdmans, 1989), 96.

conceived in and uttered from the heart (Isa. 59:13). The nature of man determines the desires of the heart and the intellectual deliberations of the mind, which in turn determine the sorts of spiritual and moral choices that one is willing and able to make.

The Essence of the Sinful Nature

We have considered the proposition that people always do what they *want* to do. This means that they do whatever they perceive to be in their best interest. At the heart of one's sinful nature, such interests are corrupted and deceiving—even subtly so for many. The unregenerate person's self-interest is nothing less than self-centeredness that seeks personal glory. Self-glory is marked by self-absorption, self-importance, self-gratification, self-justification, and ultimately self-exaltation. It demands that "I" be the center of all (2 Tim. 3:2–5).

Kelly Kapic observes, "Sin creates a perversion in our creaturely self-centeredness so that we assume that not only are we the center of our own world, but we are indeed the center of everyone else's world."[6] Kapic doesn't deny an appropriate and essential sort of self-interest, but only when viewed properly as creatures of a God who is *the* center. He states:

> We are noble and glorious creatures, made in His image, but we are only part of this creation; we are not its sum and total. While it is true that we are inescapably the center of our own worlds, this is a far cry from saying we are the center of *the* world. Only the Triune Creator is rightly understood as the center of *the* universe.[7]

Even the good deeds performed by unredeemed creatures don't have the glory of God at the core. In one way or another, those enslaved by a sin nature have some self-glorifying end to every work of their hands.[8] That may not be apparent to external observers, nor even to

6. Kelly Kapic, "The Egocentric Predicament," *Tabletalk* 36, 3 (March 2012): 21.

7. Ibid. (emphasis in original).

8. Robert A. Peterson, *Election and Free Will: God's Gracious Choice and Our Responsibility* (Phillipsburg, NJ: P&R Publishing, 2007), 129.

the person who does such good deeds. There are many self-effacing philanthropists whose humility appears striking. But if their self-effacement isn't rooted in a broken and contrite heart before a holy God (Ps. 51:17; Isa. 57:15), then it is nothing more than a misty mirage. If they see no guilt before God's just bar (Isa. 6:5) and haven't pursued his offer of pardon of which they are ill-deserving, then their humility masks conceit. Without perceiving that Christ alone is the only hope of salvation (John 6:68), then even the humblest of the earth's creatures are depending on their own goodness to uphold them (Luke 18:9).

Jonathan Edwards argues that genuine morality is rooted in love for God. In his work *The Nature of True Virtue*, he writes, "Unless we will be atheists, we must allow that true virtue does primarily and most essentially consist in a supreme love to God; and that where this is wanting, there can be no true virtue."[9] The apostle John argues that we can neither love God nor love others in any genuine sense unless we have first experienced the salvific love of God (1 John 4:7–8, 10, 19; 5:2). No doubt unbelievers can exhibit tender, passionate, and beneficial acts of love and kindness, since they are created in God's image. But no matter how loving humans can be, without a vital, affectionate union with God through Christ, all the best of their otherwise admirable virtues ring hollow.

Unbelievers fall entirely short of God's glory (Rom. 3:23). The roots of such virtues are embedded in a corrupted nature that is alien to the pursuit of loving God and glorifying him. Unless such amiable sinners are supplied with a new nature, they can't see their moral poverty and spiritual need (John 3:3), nor would they desire to remedy it through God's only provision—the redemption of his Son. What is desperately required is the work of regeneration.

Regeneration Renews the Nature So That Sinners Convert

Miracles in creation represent physical acts of God's *extraordinary providence*. In the same way, regeneration represents a spiritual act of

---

9. Jonathan Edwards, *Ethical Writings*, vol. 8 of *The Works of Jonathan Edwards*, ed. Paul Ramsey (New Haven, CT: Yale University Press, 1989), 554.

God's *extraordinary providence* in human beings that initiates their salvation. God causes the natures of those whom he chooses to undergo a metamorphic rebirth. Jesus said to Nicodemus, "Truly, truly, I say to you, unless one is born again he cannot see the kingdom of God" (John 3:3). In order for someone to "see" and thus understand the gospel message of God's kingdom, a prior condition must be met (note the word *unless*). That condition is experiencing the second birth. It is impossible for anyone to grasp the truth of the gospel unless his heart and mind have first been transformed with a new life (Ezek. 36:26–27)—a new state of being that sees what couldn't be apprehended before because the sin nature blinded the person to it.

Jesus continues: "Unless one is born of water and the Spirit, he cannot enter the kingdom of God" (John 3:5). Sinners must first experience the cleansing water of the Holy Spirit before they can be saved. He must drench their corrupted natures with its purifying power. This is "the washing of regeneration and renewal of the Holy Spirit" that Paul speaks of in Titus 3:5. Unless a person undergoes this regenerative process, that person cannot "enter into the kingdom of God." *Enter* carries the idea that a person must exercise faith, having the ability and willingness to trust in Christ for salvation.

This explains why Calvinists have consistently proclaimed that regeneration precedes faith (conversion).[10] Unfortunately, many reverse this order. They suppose that exercising faith and repentance causes one to be born again. But no one can cause his or her own birth (John 1:12–13).[11] The Greek verb for *born* (*gennao*) occurs eight times in John 3:3–8, and each time it is passive. This means that the new birth is accomplished by the power of the Holy Spirit and not something that a person does for himself.

Paul's theology of the new life in Ephesians 2 makes this clear. In verse 5 he says, "Even when we were dead in our trespasses, [he] made us alive together with Christ—by grace you have been saved." The point at which unbelievers are "made alive" is when they "were dead," not when they exercised faith. A few verses later, Paul declares,

10. John Murray, *Redemption Accomplished and Applied* (Grand Rapids: Eerdmans, 1955), 103. See Barrett, *Salvation by Grace*, for an extensive defense of this position.
11. Murray, *Redemption Accomplished and Applied*, 99.

"For by grace you have been saved through faith. And this is not your own doing; it is the gift of God" (v. 8). The pronoun "this" in the second part of the verse refers to the first part of the verse. Accordingly, "grace," "saved," and "faith" are all part of the "gift of God."[12] So it is impossible to exercise saving faith unless God grants it as part of the gift of receiving new life (cf. Phil. 1:29).

None of these redemptive realities proceed from our own wills. It is impossible for spiritually dead people to engage in an action that is as full of spiritual life and power as exercising saving faith. God's choosing of people to salvation "depends not on human will or exertion, but on God, who has mercy" (Rom. 9:16). This does not mean that our will is not involved later. But Paul's point is that the exercise of faith doesn't incite God to act with grace and save us. Rather, it is his grace that incites us to act in faith whereby we willingly receive the benefits of salvation. Augustine's comment on Romans 9:16 is insightful: "The sentence . . . cannot be taken to mean simply that we cannot attain what we wish without the aid of God, but rather that without his calling we cannot even will."[13] God does not supply help to weak wills. Rather, he rescues them from their comatose state. He does not exert a powerful influence by which our free wills are given opportunity to either accept or reject his offer of salvation. Rather, he supplies the very willing itself that was previously nonexistent. God's efficacious call creates *ex nihilo* an efficacious willing in the sinner that is sudden and freely exercised.

The apostle John put the equation this way: "But to all who did receive him, who believed in his name, he gave the right to become children of God, who were born, not of blood nor of the will of the flesh nor of the will of man, but of God" (John 1:12–13). Believing in his name is preceded by the spiritual birthing that God alone achieves. The apostle Peter indicates that it is the great and merciful

12. The pronoun "this" is neuter; therefore, it can't refer to "grace" or "faith," since both are feminine nouns. Nor can it refer to "have been saved" because it is a masculine participle. Thus, it is best to see the pronoun as referring to the whole of the previous clause, as most scholars agree. See Harold W. Hoehner, *Ephesians: An Exegetical Commentary* (Grand Rapids: Baker, 2002), 343.

13. "To Simplician—on Various Questions," trans. John H. S. Burleigh, in *Augustine: Earlier Writings*, Library of Christian Classics (London: SCM Press, 1953), 395.

God who "has caused us to be born again" (1 Peter 1:3; cf. James 1:18). The sinner is wholly passive in this powerful work. It is nothing less than the raising up of the spiritually dead, who pass into new life (1 John 3:14).

The heart of the naturally disposed sinful person remains indifferent at best to God's offer of salvation. Others throw up their steely walls of resistance with an open recalcitrance. But when God calls his chosen ones to himself (John 6:44, 65), it is all a work of sweet, irresistible grace,[14] melting hearts with a divine love never encountered before. Far from coercively circumventing our hearts in determining our salvation, God's grace infuses them with the pleasant aroma of new affections.[15] Timothy George comments, "Christ does not rudely bludgeon his way into the human heart. He does not abrogate our creaturely freedom. No, he beckons and woos, he pleads and pursues, he waits and wins."[16] At the right moment, former rebels freely come drinking life from the well of their new benevolent Master. The Lover of our souls makes us headlong lovers of himself.

This transformative energy that saves is entirely engulfed within the grip of grace alone. "If grace is not necessary, sufficient, and efficacious" in the rescue of human souls, then "God is robbed of his glory and man is given the credit in salvation."[17] Grace cannot bear the weight of its meaning if humans have anything to do with God's dispensing of its riches. It must work without anything to encumber it. Sinners can do nothing to cooperate with it, provoke it, invite it, energize it, or merit it by their own good-naturedly efforts, which of course they don't have. True grace drives every one of its recipients to their lowly knees so that no one can boast in procuring salvation. All boasting and humble rejoicing can be properly directed only to the author of salvation (1 Cor. 1:29–31).

14. *Irresistible grace* is represented by the *I* in the traditional Calvinistic acronym *TULIP*. See David N. Steele, Curtis C. Thomas, and S. Lance Quinn, *The Five Points of Calvinism* (Phillipsburg, NJ: P&R Publishing, 2004), 52–64.

15. Thaddeus J. Williams, *Love, Freedom, and Evil: Does Authentic Love Require Free Will?* (New York: Rodopi, 2011), 127–28, 130.

16. Timothy George, *Amazing Grace: God's Pursuit, Our Response* (Wheaton, IL: Crossway, 2011), 86–87.

17. Barrett, *Salvation by Grace*, 9.

J. C. Ryle aptly describes the changes brought about by regeneration in its recipients:

> This change of heart in a true Christian is so complete that no word could be chosen more fitting to express it than that word "regeneration" or new birth. Doubtless it is no outward, bodily alteration, but undoubtedly it is an entire alteration of the inner man. It adds no new faculties to a man's mind, but it certainly gives an entirely new bent and bias to all his old ones. His will is so new, his taste so new, his opinions so new, his views of sin, the world, the Bible, and Christ so new, that he is to all intents and purposes a new man. The change seems to bring a new being into existence. It may well be called being *born again*.[18]

Regeneration and Conversion

Regeneration and conversion represent the two sides of the compatibilist equation. Regeneration reflects God's sovereign work whereby he chooses and calls sinners to salvation, whereas conversion reflects the sinner's subsequent response to this transformative work by choosing Christ for salvation. But the order is critical. Each event in the chain necessarily follows what precedes it. First, God must sovereignly choose (Eph. 1:4). Second, he regenerates the sinful natures of the elect with new natures. Meanwhile, they remain passively unaware of the Spirit's inner working (John 3:8).[19] Third, their new natures suddenly generate unprecedented desires that didn't exist before. Fourth, these new desires determine the active response of faith and repentance.

It is important to note that both the divine and human components to salvation are necessary. The reception of salvation is conditioned on faith, to be sure (2 Chron. 7:14; Matt. 16:24–25; Rom. 10:9–10), but

---

18. J. C. Ryle, *Regeneration* (Fearn, Scotland: Christian Focus, 2003), 14.
19. Many Reformed theologians would insert the effectual call either before or after regeneration. See Murray, *Redemption Accomplished and Applied*, 85–87. I believe there is little distinction between the two. See Hoekema, *Saved by Grace*, 106. The effectual call can be likened to Christ's calling Lazarus from the dead, which, of course, initiates renewed life in him.

the reception of a faith that saves is conditioned solely on the electing and regenerating work of God. Matthew Barrett explains:

> Prior to effectual calling and regeneration, the will of man is in bondage to sin. Therefore, the will is not active, but passive, that is, passive toward the things of God. If it were active, then synergism would follow. However, in monergism, the will is completely and totally passive, having no bearing on God's sovereign choice. The will only becomes active *as a result of* and *consequence of* regeneration.[20]

This no doubt is the position taken in the Westminster Confession of Faith in the section "Of Effectual Calling" (10.1). The divines indicate that God transforms sinners whom he predestined for salvation. Those who were in a "state of sin and death" have their minds enlightened and are given new hearts. Subsequently, God's inner work involves "renewing their wills, and, by his almighty power, determining them to that which is good, and effectually drawing them to Jesus Christ: yet so, as they come most freely, being made willing by his grace."

Again, synergism is a cooperative work of both God and man, whereas monergism is a work of God alone. Compatibilism must not be confused with synergism. Nonetheless, man's freely exercised choice in faith and repentance follows from the prior causal work of divine regeneration and effectual calling.

Dane Ortlund points to how Jonathan Edwards's theology "lofts high human responsibility alongside divine sovereignty." He quotes from a sermon of Edwards entitled "Glorying in the Savior," in which the colonial pastor

> describes Christians as those who "have subjected themselves to him and chosen him for their king; such as have indeed given themselves to him; such as have admitted Christ into the heart and placed him upon the throne there; such as have been begotten by the Spirit of Christ, been born of God, and

20. Barrett, *Salvation by Grace*, 189 (emphasis in original).

been made partakers of Christ's nature and temper." Though he begins by using active verbs to indicate the human role in conversion ("subjected themselves . . . chosen him . . . given themselves . . . admitted Christ"), he concludes by using passive verbs to indicate God's ultimacy ("been begotten . . . been born of God . . . been made partakers").[21]

Note the characteristics of the desires that result from the new birth. First, the freshly born spiritual babe exercises repentance from sin, which proceeds from the motive of remorse before a holy God. The sinner suddenly sees his helpless state and experiences a heartbreaking contrition because he has offended God and incurred his wrath. He falls humbly before his Judge and pleads for his merciful pardon.

Second, saving faith proceeds from the desire that Christ provokes by his wondrous work of redemption. The sinner has an epiphany of the glory and beauty of Christ and the grace of forgiveness that he furnishes through his death and resurrection. His renewed affections are attracted to this portrait of Christ, and he entrusts his life to his new Lord and Savior. The ugly truth of one's sin is met by the beauty of grace.

It is easy to assume that God's role in the causal chain leading to salvation is strictly external and disconnected except for decreeing what happens. In other ways, however, his work is internal, since it involves the reception of the divine presence within the regenerated person. The Holy Spirit indwells the regenerated individual and unites him or her to the person of Christ in a spiritual union (Rom. 8:9–11; 1 Cor. 12:13). Thus, new life involves the very life of God as he intimately makes his presence felt within and new babes begin living for his glory. He engages us in a direct and personal way, not as some remote deity who may or may not make time for us. The regenerate have unhindered access to the very throne of God (Heb. 4:16).

This astounding work of gospel transformation in the souls of desperate sinners is reflected in the words of Augustus Toplady's great hymn of the faith, *Rock of Ages*:

21. Dane Ortlund, *A New Inner Relish: Christian Motivation in the Thought of Jonathan Edwards* (Fearn, Scotland: Christian Focus, 2008), 116–17.

Nothing in my hand I bring,
Simply to thy cross I cling;
Naked, come to thee for dress;
Helpless, look to thee for grace;
Foul, I to the Fountain fly;
Wash me, Savior, or I die.

Chapter Summary

The primary concern up to this point has been a general freedom of choice that is of a morally inconsequential nature. What sort of cereal will you choose for breakfast—Cap'n Crunch or Lucky Charms? But the final layer down in the analysis of choosing focuses on specifically moral and spiritual choices. The core of human choosing corresponds to one's very nature. The Bible teaches that a person's nature either is dead and corrupted due to sin or has been made alive and renewed by the power of the Holy Spirit. Therefore, moral and spiritual desires, and thus one's choices, are dictated by one's nature.

Jesus uses two metaphors to describe two different natures that inhabit the souls of men. A bad tree represents the sin nature. It is corrupted and capable of producing only poisonous fruit. If the tree is transformed into a good tree, this represents regeneration, the implanting of a new nature into the soul of man. This good nature produces an edible fruit that is good and righteous. This means that the unregenerated nature of the unbeliever is morally incapable of making God-pleasing choices. Without exercising faith and repentance, one cannot be saved. But faith doesn't incite God to act with grace and save us. Rather, it is his grace that incites us to act in faith whereby we willingly receive the benefits of salvation.

The heart of the naturally disposed sinful person remains indifferent at best to God's offer of salvation. But when God calls his chosen ones to himself, it is all a work of sweet, irresistible grace, melting hearts with a divine love never encountered before. Thus, far from coercively circumventing our hearts in determining our salvation, God's grace infuses them with the pleasant aroma of new affections. In all this, regeneration and conversion represent the two sides of the compatibilist equation.

Glossary

conversion. The voluntary act of repenting from sin and exercising faith in Christ for salvation, neither of which is possible unless one has experienced the prior gracious work of *regeneration* by the power of the Holy Spirit.

irresistible grace. Is represented by the *I* in the traditional Calvinistic acronym *TULIP*. It refers to the grace of God as it draws sinners to Christ through the work of *regeneration* so that they come to him irresistibly. It is a gracious work because without it no one is willing or able to come to Christ on his or her own. See also *Calvinism*.

new nature. See *regeneration*.

regeneration. The extraordinary work of the Holy Spirit whereby he causes a *new nature* to arise in the souls of those whom God chooses to redeem. This new nature is inhabited by the Spirit, who works to transform unregenerate people. It is marked by the implantation of spiritual life where none existed before and generates godly desires and a *moral ability* to make choices that are truly God-pleasing. *Conversion* (i.e., the exercise of faith and repentance) and subsequent sanctifying actions in the regenerate person are not possible apart from this preceding gracious work of God.

sin nature. The corrupted nature that all people are born with that has a propensity for sin. The core moral and spiritual condition of all human beings is to be dead in sin. Their wills are in bondage to sin, and they are unable to perform God-pleasing actions apart from the work of *regeneration*. See also *old self*.

Study Questions

1. When the Bible speaks of the importance of our choices, its primary focus is on the moral and spiritual dimension of those choices. What lies at the core of these choices?

2. Read Romans 3:10–18. How does this passage describe the condition of humanity? Consider as many aspects of this condition as possible.

3. Read Matthew 12:33–35. What metaphors does Jesus use to describe two different kinds of human beings? How do these metaphors enhance our understanding of the two types of natures that they describe?

4. How does the sin nature corrupt the notion of "self-interest" that lies at the heart of all choices made by humans?

5. What is at the heart of the many benevolent deeds that unbelievers perform? Why do these deeds fail to meet the standard of righteousness that God demands of us?

6. What does the Bible mean by the idea of *regeneration*?

7. Why does biblical compatibilism (i.e., Calvinism) argue that regeneration precedes faith in the matter of salvation? What passages of Scripture does the author supply in support of this view?

8. What does it mean to say that divine saving grace is (1) necessary, (2) sufficient, and (3) efficacious?

9. What is the difference between *regeneration* and *conversion*? Explain how terms such as *monergism* and *synergism* as well as an active and passive will correspond to the work of regeneration and conversion.

10. Describe the new desires that result in the person who has been regenerated and what sorts of actions they produce.

11. In what way is God's work in the salvation of sinners external, and in what way is it internal?

Resources for Further Study

Matthew Barrett, *Salvation by Grace: A Case for Effectual Calling and Regeneration* (Phillipsburg, NJ: P&R Publishing, 2013). An excellent treatment of regeneration, irresistible grace, and effectual calling.

John Murray, *Redemption Accomplished and Applied* (Grand Rapids: Eerdmans, 1955). A classic Calvinist treatment of the work of redemption and how regeneration fits into its outworking in the life of the believer.

Dane Ortlund, *A New Inner Relish: Christian Motivation in the Thought of Jonathan Edwards* (Fearn, Scotland: Christian Focus, 2008). An engaging treatment of how Jonathan Edwards viewed the importance of proper motivation in the life of the believer.

John Piper, *Finally Alive* (Fearn, Scotland: Christian Focus, 2009). A thorough biblical and practical examination of the doctrine of regeneration.

10

Exploring Corridors

The matter of regeneration and conversion raises a number of important questions that are difficult to avoid if we are to grasp the full implications of God's sovereignty and the human response to his saving work in our lives. Therefore, in this chapter I will explore some side corridors along this portion of the compatibilist structure. I will consider why some people respond differently to the gospel and the implications of this phenomenon for understanding God's grace and his glory in salvation. Then I will consider whether the Holy Spirit's work in regeneration acts directly on the sinner's soul while bypassing human means. Finally, I will look at the thorny question of God's desires in the salvation of humanity. Does God want all people to be saved or only a few?

Why Some Believe and Some Don't

We begin by asking an important question. Why is it that some people believe in Christ and others do not? Imagine the perfect scenario: Jesus is standing in a boat along the shores of Galilee, preaching to thousands. His message is flawless (as it must be). His persuasive tone avoids manipulation on the one hand and sheer intellectualism on the other. His message targets the necessary cognitive information that the mind needs as well as a tender appeal to the heart's affections. He preaches with the passion and appeal that only Jesus could summon. What's more, he accompanies his message by performing undeniable miracles before the awestruck crowds.

Under such circumstances, would we not expect everyone hearing his gospel presentation to be immediately struck by its power and truth and thus believe? What causes one to believe and another to scoff? Can we say that the believer was smarter than the scoffer? Did he understand the message better? Was the believer more morally attuned to the message? Was he more sensitive to his sin and need for salvation? Did the scoffer lack something that the believer had? If one rejects the need for regeneration as a necessary prerequisite for belief and answers yes to these questions, then insurmountable problems arise. Unless choices are arbitrary—a problem that libertarianism faces—then one could believe only for virtuous reasons and another reject for carnal reasons. This amounts to salvation by works-righteousness, faith being a product of a righteous disposition.[1] Saving faith is attributed to something inherent in the person and not in the grace of God.

Libertarians may be quick to dismiss this line of reasoning, since they reject the notion that sufficient reasons exist to determine our choices. But this raises problems as well. Suppose a woman named Sarah heard Jesus' message and believed. Her belief could not be attributed to decisively virtuous reasons; otherwise, she would not be free. This means that at best she could believe with only a modicum of devotion. In order for Sarah's choice to be free and meaningful, she must reserve a degree of indifference as to reasons why she places her faith in Christ. If libertarianism held true, then no believer in Christ could be fully sold out to the Lord and Savior without sacrificing his or her freedom. This simply doesn't comport with reality or the Word of God.

But the Arminian brand of libertarianism would reject these conclusions as well. In the classical Arminian view of salvation, God's universal prevenient grace is necessary in order for salvation to become a reality for the sinner. This prevenient grace opens up the door for further displays of saving grace, yet this saving grace is said to be resistible.[2] The sinner needs this grace, which is full of divine conviction, enlightenment, and power, in order to exercise faith and repentance. Nonetheless, if one is unable to reject it and act contrary to it, then salvation is not a free decision. Thus, no matter how persuasive

1. R. C. Sproul, *Willing to Believe: The Controversy over Free Will* (Grand Rapids: Baker, 1997), 26.

2. Roger Olson, *Arminian Theology: Myths and Realities* (Downers Grove, IL: InterVarsity Press, 2006), 131.

and powerful God's calling and extension of saving grace toward the sinner is, the power of salvation ultimately rests in the hands of humanity, not God. One can pray for the salvation of others (Rom. 10:1) with the earnestness of an Elijah (James 5:17), but God's power can extend only so far before it meets the almighty will of man, to which it must yield.

Consider the futility of the libertarian model of prayer. Suppose you note that Sarah has heard the gospel that Christ preached and you desire her salvation. How do you pray to God? Do you ask God to intervene and save her? This isn't appropriate because you would be asking God to violate her free will. Do you ask God to use all his powers of persuasion to convince her of her need to believe? Perhaps, but in order to temper this request, you would have to pray that God would not put too much pressure on her because then she might feel coerced to act against her will. Your prayer would have to ask God to strike a balance between gentle and heavy-handed persuasion. If God honored the libertarian freedom of his creatures, then he could not guarantee that any of our petitions involving human choices could be answered.[3]

But is this what we believe about prayer?

In contrast, consider what J. I. Packer writes:

> You pray for the conversion of others. In what terms, now, do you intercede for them? Do you limit yourself to asking that God will bring them to a point where they can save themselves, independently of Him? I do not think you do. I think that what you do is to pray in categorical terms that God will, quite simply and decisively, save them: that He will open the eyes of their understanding, soften their hard hearts, renew their natures, and move their wills to receive the Savior. You ask God to work in them everything necessary for their salvation. You would not dream of making it a point in your prayer that you are not asking God actually to bring them to faith, because you recognize that that is something He cannot do. Nothing

---

3. John S. Feinberg, *No One Like Him* (Wheaton, IL: Crossway, 2001), 705–6.

of the sort! When you pray for unconverted people, you do so on the assumption that it is in God's power to bring them to faith. You entreat Him to do that very thing, and your confidence in asking rests upon the certainty that He is able to do what you ask. And indeed He is: this conviction, which animates your intercessions, is God's own truth, written on your heart by the Holy Spirit.[4]

Compatibilism finds no conflict with Sarah's exercise of faith. If what the Bible says about regeneration and grace is true, then one person *is* more inclined to believe than another. Sarah believes not because of something that emerged from within herself, but because the Holy Spirit had prepared her for the positive reception of the gospel. The Spirit implanted new life in Sarah. This is the only explanation for why she or anyone else could believe and others disbelieve, unless one adopts a theology of salvation claiming that only morally and intellectually superior people inherit salvation.

Jesus teaches that his sheep hear only his voice and not the voice of another. He calls them by name, and they follow because they know him (John 10:3–5, 14, 16). Conversely, he declares in John 8:47 that those who are not of God cannot hear his words of truth; they can make no sense of his preaching (v. 43) because they do not have a God-regenerated nature that is inclined to do so (cf. 12:37–40). Thus, only those who have been "appointed to eternal life" and renewed by the power of the Spirit "believe" (Acts 13:48) because God has "granted" such faith (Phil. 1:29).

But we need to consider another angle. Revelation 20:11–15 describes the judgment at the "great white throne." One reason that unbelievers are cast into the lake of fire is that their names were not found in the book of life (v. 15; cf. 17:8; 21:27). In other words, they were not chosen by God. Yet no one will stand before God, saying, "God, you have no right to cast me into the fiery abyss. I was not chosen, so I had no choice in the matter."

---

4. J. I. Packer, *Evangelism and the Sovereignty of God* (Downers Grove, IL: InterVarsity Press, 1991), 15.

Consider two facts. First, God retained the right "before the foundation of the world" not to choose some names to appear in the book of life (Rev. 13:8). Second, the people whose names are missing from the book are not judged on that basis; rather, they are judged "according to what they had done" (20:12–13). So there is a dual explanation for why people go into eternal perdition. One has to do with God's freedom not to extend his gracious electing hand to sinners. The other has to do with sinners' freely exercising their wills to engage in deeds worthy of eternal judgment.[5] This underscores that God is active in the election of sinners to salvation, but passive in the reprobation of others to eternal perdition.[6]

God's Glory in Salvation

Other disconcerting problems remain for libertarianism. In its account of free will, God's overtures of grace are largely defeated. As much energy as God exerts in trying to persuade his creatures to take hold of the amazing gift of eternal life, frankly he has failed. His desires for salvation are largely thwarted, since only a small fraction of people cooperate with his grace. Most remain unconvinced of his plan of redemption. They are indifferent at best. Many more look at the offer of gospel reconciliation with disdain.

Thus, libertarianism must concede that the dismal results of God's efforts in achieving his desires for man's salvation have become an utter blight on his glory. We might say that Satan has done a better job of convincing people to take his various highways to hell. Why is God unable to counter Satan's deceptions with convincing defeaters? If our wills are so neutrally disposed and not naturally inclined one way or the other, why is it that Satan has gained far more adherents for his dark kingdom than God has for the kingdom of light? We would expect at least a 50–50 split. Under the oppressive weight of libertarianism, a God with such few successes is a God whose majesty has been crushed.

Thankfully, the truth is quite to the contrary. The reception of grace is not controlled by the whims of humans before a helpless

---

5. Robert A. Peterson, *Election and Free Will: God's Gracious Choice and Our Responsibility* (Phillipsburg, NJ: P&R Publishing, 2007), 141.
6. Ibid., 142.

God. The glory of salvation does not lie in man's freedom to choose but in God's freedom to bestow such a prized gift on so few ill-deserving objects of his redemptive affection (Matt. 7:13–14). The value of precious commodities such as gold, fine diamonds, and pearls lies in the rarity of their existence. What distinguishes masters such as Michelangelo and Rembrandt is revealed in the narrow sphere of artistic genius they occupy that others never come near to reaching.

God's grace is too often taken for granted and treated as if it were dispersed like the sand along the world's seashores. This renders grace as banal, of no estimable worth. But saving grace is an extremely rare and priceless jewel cherished by the privileged few who receive it. It occupies an exclusive domain in its power to save, and it can suffer spoilage only if anything is added to it. For this reason, grace *alone* allows salvation to shout to God's glory *alone*.

Regeneration Employs Human Means

To be sure, God's grace operates alone; nonetheless, it uses other external and human means to draw us to Christ. Principally, God causes us to experience the new birth by the preaching and reception of his Word. James tells us that "of his own will he brought us forth by the word of truth" (James 1:18; cf. 1 Peter 1:23). The phrase "brought us forth" means "gave us birth." The Spirit applies the Word to the stony heart and blinded mind of the sinner. Cold, solid rock becomes warm, pliable tissue, and darkened knowledge gives way to enlightenment. Paul tells the Romans how eager he is to "preach the gospel" to them (Rom. 1:15). Why? Because he is "not ashamed of the gospel, for it is the power of God for salvation to everyone who believes" (v. 16; cf. 2 Thess. 2:14). In this remarkable work, the Holy Spirit serves as the *efficient* cause of regeneration, whereas the Word serves as the *instrumental* cause.[7]

Elsewhere, Paul makes it clear that "faith comes from hearing, and hearing through the word of Christ" (Rom. 10:17). Thus, part of the external factors undergirding the human choices that lead to salvation involves the sending of preachers (vv. 14–15) who faithfully

---

7. Matthew Barrett, *Salvation by Grace: A Case for Effectual Calling and Regeneration* (Phillipsburg, NJ: P&R Publishing, 2013), 131.

communicate "the word of Christ." We might also add the importance of prayer (v. 1). God mightily uses the prayers of the saints (Rev. 8:3–4) to accomplish his sovereign purposes as well. Again, this is reminiscent of the laws of physics behind Babe Ruth's home-run hits. God no more zaps people with salvation than baseballs fly into stadium seats when no bat is swung. He uses both internal and external means that become necessary components in the process of spiritual renewal. The Holy Spirit does his *supernatural* regenerating work on the inside even as earnest prayer and the faithful preaching of the Word do their *natural* work on the outside (albeit empowered by the Spirit).

This is what we see in the conversion of Lydia as Paul was preaching to a crowd of women in Philippi. Luke writes, "A woman named Lydia . . . was listening; and the Lord opened her heart to respond to the things spoken by Paul" (Acts 16:14 NASB). Note the two compatibilist events taking place. First, Paul responsibly preaches the Word with a desire to be faithful, yet God takes that Word and invests it with power toward the one who listens. Second, as Lydia willingly hears and positively responds in faith to the preaching, God all the while opens her heart. Without the human components of Paul's preaching and Lydia's listening and believing, no salvation takes place. Likewise, without the divine component sovereignly utilizing the human components to achieve God's purpose, salvation remains impossible. God sovereignly elects to salvation, but preachers are responsible to preach, and sinners are responsible to believe.

Later, when Paul struggled to see converts in the city of Corinth, something remarkable happened. "And the Lord said to Paul one night in a vision, 'Do not be afraid, but go on speaking and do not be silent, for I am with you, and no one will attack you to harm you, for I have many in this city who are my people'" (Acts 18:9–10). God had people whom he had specifically chosen for salvation residing in the city. Did Paul know who these people were? No. Why didn't he just ask God to reveal their names? That way, he wouldn't have to worry about being molested while he wasted his energy broadcasting the gospel to others who weren't going to believe anyway. Or, better yet, why didn't God just bring them all at once, as he had brought the animals to Noah to place in the ark?

The reason is simple—it is not God's method for evangelism. Paul must take on the responsibility of preaching day in and day out, toiling until people were converted. He did so for a year and a half (Acts 18:11), and God was faithful to his promise.

William Carey is known as the father of modern missions. He developed the first well-conceived strategic plan to reach lost souls among heathen nations since the Reformation. Carey presented his plan before a group of ministers in Northampton, England, in 1787. After Carey made his proposal, John Ryland Sr., taken aback by such a bold and unprecedented initiative, stood and said to Carey, "Young man, sit down. When God pleases to convert the heathen, he will do it without your aid or mine."[8] Such hyper-Calvinism was popular at the time and demonstrates a position akin to hard determinism that borders on fatalism. This is an unfortunate distortion of Calvinism, and compatibilism in particular.

Although hyper-Calvinism has largely been a minority position in church history, the sort of thinking it engenders is often unwittingly expressed by irresponsible Christians. The Calvinist preacher Charles Spurgeon captures the problem with his usual wit:

> The lazy-bones of our orthodox churches cry, "God will do his own work"; and then they look out the softest pillow they can find, and put it under their heads, and say, "The eternal purposes will be carried out: God will be glorified." That is all very fine talk, but it can be used with the most mischievous design. You can make opium out of it, which will lull you into a deep and dreadful slumber and prevent your being any kind of use at all.[9]

The Reception and Proclamation of the Gospel

Compatibilism prevents common mistakes in thinking about the reception as well as the proclamation of the gospel. For example,

8. Timothy George, *Faithful Witness: The Life and Times of William Carey* (Worchester, PA: Christian History Institute, 1998), 53.

9. Charles Haddon Spurgeon, *Metropolitan Tabernacle Pulpit*, 30:630, quoted in Timothy George, *Amazing Grace: God's Pursuit, Our Response* (Wheaton, IL: Crossway, 2011), 113–14.

a person might say to himself, "If God sovereignly chooses people for salvation, then I need not worry about hearing and believing the gospel. Furthermore, if God is sovereign, then I have no hope of getting to heaven—certainly he won't choose me!" J. I. Packer explains, "The Bible never says that sinners miss heaven because they are not elect, but because they 'neglect the great salvation' [Heb. 2:3], and because they will not repent and believe."[10] God's sovereignty never excuses human responsibility. Rather, God exercises his sovereignty in human affairs precisely through the express intentions and actions of his creatures.

On the other side of the fence, compatibilism prevents believers from making two critical mistakes in their evangelism. First, it prevents us from presuming on God's sovereignty to see that people come to salvation, as we have already seen (Rom. 10:14–15). Second, it prevents the mistake of using manipulative methodologies to get people to make a "decision" for Christ. The worst sort of evangelism employs subtle and sometimes not-so-subtle means of coercion. In this case, a "decision" can be mistaken for a choice that flows out of a new nature, when in fact the old nature has simply been deceived or coerced into making a superficial choice. Of course, the choice is real and is willingly made, but only in accordance with the person's unregenerated state. Time inevitably demonstrates that no spiritual fruit is produced because no spiritual nature can be found in such false converts.

For those whose evangelistic impulse is rooted in libertarian notions, salvation relies too much on human means. Here is the irony—while libertarianism charges that divine determinism equates to coercion, it is in fact libertarian methods of evangelism that lead to coercion. Since God limits his persuasive power to avoid forced conversions, eager preachers are all too happy to make up the difference. This often translates into manipulative preaching, emotional pleas, altar calls, sinner's prayers, and altered messages crafted to be more palatable to so-called seekers. In the end, the landscape of Christianity becomes littered with false conversions.

As the parable of the sower makes clear (Luke 8:11–15), many people "believe" in Jesus for all the wrong reasons. Some believe with

10. Packer, *Evangelism and the Sovereignty of God*, 105.

the hope that he will fix their broken marriage or friendships. Maybe he will reward their faith with a more satisfying life—increasing their riches or reputations or general happiness. Some look to Christ to provide a better example of morality than the world promotes. Many people want Jesus to love them just as they are so that their self-esteem can receive a boost. Many Jews in Jesus' day believed in him because they wanted a renegade warrior to relieve them from Roman oppression. All these motives for belief proceed from deceptive and corrupted desires. False motives invite a false gospel promoting a false Jesus who holds out a false hope embraced by a false faith.

To avoid deceiving and manipulating people into an illusory kingdom of God, lured in by erroneous messages, our evangelism must reflect the true gospel. Packer writes that the message must be delivered "with exact and studious faithfulness, adding nothing, altering nothing, and omitting nothing."[11] We must accurately handle the Word of truth by careful study (2 Tim. 2:15) and proclaim the whole purpose that it reveals (Acts 20:27).

But this doesn't mean that we should suppose that the normal instrument used by the Spirit to draw sinners to Christ is dull, lifeless words tossed about by preachers addicted to apathy. While the preacher avoids artificial devices to bring about conversions, neither does he draw sinners to Christ by blandly delivering bare propositions of truth, no matter how accurate they are. The preacher must be prepared by the Spirit and infused with his powerful unction. Charles Spurgeon exhorted his students:

> Gospel truth is diametrically opposed to fallen nature: and if I have not a power much stronger than that which lies in moral suasion, or in my own explanations and arguments, I have undertaken a task in which I am sure of defeat. . . . Except the Lord endow us with power from on high, our labor must be in vain, and our hopes must end in disappointment.[12]

---

11. Ibid., 43.
12. C. H. Spurgeon, *An All-Round Ministry* (Carlisle, PA: Banner of Truth, 1960), 322.

The ordinary physics of preaching encompasses a delivery of the Word that not only is faithful to the truth, but also passionately invites, implores, and persuades with all Spirit-drenched diligence until people believe. We need accurate gospel-focused and Spirit-anointed preaching.[13] These represent the normal means that God uses to draw sinners to himself. In and of themselves, they aren't manipulative tactics. Nonetheless, this doesn't mean that it is the preacher's responsibility to save. Only God saves.

Furthermore, it is every believer's obligation to bear witness at every opportunity regardless of the response (1 Peter 3:15). Yes, God predestines sinners to salvation, but *no one* who names the name of Christ has a reason or a right to neglect evangelism (Matt. 28:18–20). Without it, no one will be saved. Compatibilism assures us of that.

God's Desires for Mankind's Salvation

A rather thorny and difficult question arises in light of these issues. If God elects only some to salvation, does this mean that he doesn't desire others to be saved? We must understand what is meant by God's *desire*. God's *decretive* (sovereign) will can refer to his desires, yet his *preceptive* (instructive) will can also refer to his desires. Furthermore, in the mystery of God's providence, he has often decreed what he otherwise does not desire. In one sense, God did not desire that his Son be murdered on a cruel cross, since murder violates his express precepts (Ex. 20:13). In another sense, God wanted Christ to undergo murder because it achieved his greater and more benevolent purpose (Acts 2:23; 4:27–28).[14]

In a similar vein, God sovereignly decrees with certainty and therefore desires that only some will be saved (Eph. 1:4–5). Yet the Bible also makes it clear that God desires *all* men to repent (2 Peter 3:9) and to be saved (1 Tim. 2:4).[15] God has a salvific love for all people (John 3:16), and yet he reserves a special love only for the elect (Eph.

13. See Tony Sargent, *The Sacred Anointing: The Preaching of Dr. Martyn Lloyd-Jones* (Wheaton, IL: Crossway, 1994).

14. Feinberg, *No One Like Him*, 697.

15. John Piper, "Are There Two Wills in God?," in *Still Sovereign*, ed. Thomas R. Schreiner and Bruce A. Ware (Grand Rapids: Baker, 2000), 107–31, also available at http://www.desiringgod.org/resource-library/articles/are-there-two-wills-in-god; John M. Frame, *The Doctrine of God* (Phillipsburg, NJ: P&R Publishing, 2002), 534–38.

3:14–19).[16] Nonetheless, the gospel is to be freely offered to all people without exception. Paul calls out to the Athenians, proclaiming that God "commands all people everywhere to repent" (Acts 17:30). This reflects God's preceptive will: that which he commands and deems to be in the best interests of all mankind.

God calls out to his beloved people Israel: "Oh that they had such a mind as this always, to fear me and to keep all my commandments, that it might go well with them and with their descendants forever!" (Deut. 5:29). God would have this lost world conform to what is the highest good and the most noble of truths (Isa. 45:22). He takes no sinister pleasure in those who reject the truth and die in their sins only to suffer eternal perdition (Ezek. 18:23, 31–32; 33:11; 2 Peter 3:9).

The preceptive will of God represents an ideal state of affairs.[17] All things being equal, it would seem best that all of humanity should embrace the divine imperatives of salvation. Nonetheless, this is not the case. Jesus proclaims, "Enter by the narrow gate. For the gate is wide and the way is easy that leads to destruction, and those who enter by it are many. For the gate is narrow and the way is hard that leads to life, and those who find it are few" (Matt. 7:13–14). Although God delights in the salvation of men, we don't know why he has decreed it for only some. John Murray writes, "This is indeed mysterious, and why he has not brought to pass, in the exercise of his omnipotent power and grace, what is his ardent pleasure [i.e., preceptive will] lies hid in the sovereign counsel of his [decretive] will."[18] Regardless, our mandate is to express the love of Christ to a lost and dying world, because God loves that world, too (Luke 6:35). We plead for their salvation and leave it to God to dispense his electing grace.

Chapter Summary

Regeneration and conversion raise a number of issues that are important for grasping the full implications of God's sovereignty and

---

16. See D. A. Carson, *The Difficult Doctrine of the Love of God* (Wheaton, IL: Crossway, 2000), 16–21.

17. Frame, *The Doctrine of God*, 538.

18. John Murray, "The Free Offer of the Gospel," in *Collected Writings of John Murray* (Carlisle, PA: Banner of Truth, 1982), 4:131 (bracketed material added for clarity).

the human response to his saving work in the believer's life. First, why do some people believe on Christ and others do not? One cannot conclude that some believe Christ for virtuous reasons and others reject Christ for carnal reasons; otherwise, merit is attributed to the believer that necessitated his response. The appeal to libertarian free will does not help. The glory of salvation does not lie in man's freedom to choose but in God's freedom to bestow such a prized gift on so few ill-deserving objects of his redemptive affection. The value of precious commodities such as gold, fine diamonds, and pearls lies in their rarity. God's saving grace is likewise a rare jewel.

Second, if salvation is by grace, the one who believes requires a prior work of efficacious and irresistible divine enablement. Nonetheless, God never zaps people with salvation. The Word of God must be faithfully preached. It must be clearly heard, and the recipients must repent and believe. The Holy Spirit does his *supernatural* regenerating work on the inside even as earnest prayer and the faithful preaching of the Word do their *natural* work on the outside (albeit empowered by the Spirit).

Third, God desires that all men be saved as a reflection of his preceptive (moral) will. God would have this lost world conform to what is the highest good and the most noble of truths. He takes no sinister pleasure in those who reject the truth and die in their sins only to suffer eternal perdition. And although God delights in the salvation of his creatures, we don't know why he has decreed it for only a few.

Study Questions

1. When the gospel is clearly, powerfully, and lovingly proclaimed, why do some believe and some not believe? What conditions must exist in order for a person to believe on Christ for salvation? Do these conditions lie within the recipient of the gospel message? Why or why not?

2. Under the libertarian notion of free will, why does prayer for the salvation of unbelievers risk becoming futile?

3. Why is it that no unbeliever will stand before God in judgment and say: "God, you have no right to cast me into the fiery abyss. I was not chosen, so I had no choice in the matter"?

4. Why does the libertarian notion of free will make God appear to have failed in his efforts to see sinners come to salvation? Do you believe that this assessment about libertarianism is accurate?

5. Is the glory of salvation diminished even though so few experience it? Explain your answer.

6. What are some of the human means that God uses to bring about salvation? Consider your own testimony. What natural and human instruments did God use to bring about your conversion?

7. Explain why the following statements are false, and provide a correct perspective for them. First: "If God sovereignly chooses people for salvation, then I need not worry about hearing and believing the gospel." Second: "If God is sovereign, then I have no hope of getting to heaven—certainly he won't choose me!"

8. Why is Christianity today littered with false conversions? What methods of evangelism contribute to this problem?

9. What should faithful evangelism look like? How is evangelistic success measured?

10. Explain how God desires all people to be saved in one sense, and yet in another sense he desires that only a few people be saved. How do you explain the difference in these two desires?

11. How should believers respond to the fact that God chooses only a few to salvation?

Resources for Further Study

D. A. Carson, *The Difficult Doctrine of the Love of God* (Wheaton, IL: Crossway, 2000). An insightful examination of the different ways in which the Bible speaks of God's love for humanity.

J. I. Packer, *Evangelism and the Sovereignty of God* (Downers Grove, IL: InterVarsity Press, 1991). A classic work on various issues of evangelism in light of God's sovereignty and human responsibility.

11

Navigating the New Nature

Some years ago, I was privileged to help conduct a weekly chapel service at a rescue mission in the impoverished city of Patterson, New Jersey. Often the services were uneventful. Success was measured by how few of the men were distracted or slept during the services. But occasionally, surprising things took place. One such instance involved the life of a young African American, fresh off the streets and into the shelter where he could find a hot meal and a comfortable bed. At the first chapel service he attended, no unusual preaching transpired, no apparent unction of the Holy Spirit was present; nonetheless, he was transfixed by the message of salvation. He came to my colleague and me immediately afterward and confessed a palpable concern for his soul. He desperately pleaded, "What must I do to be saved?" We were happy to guide him to Christ.

For the next several weeks, a glorious transformation pervaded his life, marked by an insatiable hunger for the Word. But then trouble came—various kinds of assaults from different quarters. He was suddenly bombarded by members of different cult groups questioning his newfound faith. This led to unnerving questions that dampened his excitement and fueled confusion. Then he disappeared. I figured that he had slid back into the streets as another casualty in the war between gospel truth and the pull of a diabolical underworld of crime, drugs, and all manner of relentless temptations hostile to a homeless man with a fragile Christian faith.

But after several weeks, as we came to conduct our usual services, there he was. What we saw shocked us. He had bandages about his head and body. He was severely bruised and battered, but ironically his smile belied his horrible condition, for which he expressed no concern. All he wanted was to relay the new revelations that he was gleaning from the Word of God. I wondered aloud, "What gives?" How could he talk excitedly about his growing faith and ignore my obvious dismay? I pressed him to explain, and he did.

While he was walking among the busy corridors of the benumbed cityscape, a dark van had pulled up alongside him. Before he had time to consider what was happening, a group of young white thugs leaped out from the back of the vehicle with racial epithets recoiling off the cold storefronts as they proceeded to pummel him. He spent a number of days in the hospital recovering while clinging tightly to his Bible. I asked him whether he harbored bitterness toward his aggressors. With a quiet and sober dismissal, he said, "No . . . I forgive them as Christ forgave me." Then he hurriedly shifted back to his fresh insights from Scripture with the wonder of a country boy at his first carnival.

My friend's experience has three remarkable features worthy of mention. First, his conversion was far from some forced profession of faith that opponents of Calvinism insinuate must be the case if God determines salvation. He freely embraced Christ with headlong joy and devotion. Second, the unfavorable conditions under which he experienced new life in Christ make the narrative of his conversion both unique and surprising. Third, his life is proof that the work of regeneration does not suddenly cast aside all troubles and temptations, but in fact invites them with increased vigor. In the end, however, his newfound freedom in Christ secured a hope undeterred by the assaults of the enemy and the remains of the old sinful self.

These distinguishing marks of one man's spiritual transformation exemplify the next set of propositions drawing us deeper into our tour of the new nature. A biblical theology of the new life helps to make sense of many truths regarding both conversion and sanctification. Compatibilism is an important key to unlock these truths.

Regeneration Is Not an Act of Divine Coercion

A common charge leveled by libertarians is that if God sovereignly elects sinners to salvation, then it must be an act of coercion. If a person couldn't equally choose to reject the grace that leads to salvation as well as accept it, then one's free will would be curtailed. Steve Lemke claims that in the Calvinist doctrine of irresistible grace, God "is forcing one to change one's mind against one's will."[1] In this thinking, if a person has been chosen by God for salvation, then it is all settled—the person has no choice in the matter. The person would have to become a follower of Christ whether he or she liked it or not.

This represents muddled thinking not only about divine sovereignty, but also about the nature of choosing. No one ever becomes a Christian if he or she does not *want* to become a Christian. And certainly no one is ever dragged into the kingdom kicking and screaming. After canvassing the Bible's teaching on the sin nature, it is clear that unbelievers do resist the gospel or reject it outright. Many believers testify to such resistance right up until the time of their conversion and may even use this well-worn language to describe their entrance through the kingdom doorway.

C. S. Lewis pondered his conversion: "Who can duly adore that Love which will open the high gates to a prodigal who is brought kicking, struggling, resentful, and darting his eyes in every direction for a chance of escape?" After wrestling vigorously with objections to the Christian faith, one night, alone in his room, Lewis "gave in, and admitted that God was God, and knelt and prayed: perhaps that night, the most dejected and reluctant convert in all of England."[2] But did the Oxford don really become a Christian against his will? Was he somehow forced into the kingdom of God when in fact he wanted nothing to do with it at all?

Of course not. Something had to change.

What was once unmitigated resistance in the unbeliever gives way to full acceptance. Indifference gives way to deep interest. Hatred is transformed into unbridled affection. Before embracing genuine faith, many stubborn, arrogant, hateful rejecters of Christ appear as impossible candidates for God's gracious work of regeneration. But at

---

1. Steve W. Lemke, "A Biblical and Theological Critique of Irresistible Grace," in *Whosoever Will: A Biblical-Theological Critique of Five-Point Calvinism*, ed. David L. Allen and Steve W. Lemke (Nashville: B&H Publishing Group, 2010), 114.

2. C. S. Lewis, *Surprised by Joy: The Shape of My Early Life* (New York: Harcourt Brace & Company, 1956), 228–29.

the point of one's realization that they've truly believed on Christ, there are no longer any of the old obstinate desires. What sinners find is that God's grace is *irresistible* in the very best sense of that term.[3] People truly believe in Christ because they *want* to believe, and they do so freely (voluntarily), without coercion. The grace that marks regeneration transforms the desires of recalcitrant sinners so that coming to Christ for salvation becomes the most appealing and compelling choice they could make—it is in their own best interest. Dane Ortlund describes this change as a "motivational metamorphosis."[4] The believer is given a new nature that produces new motivations marked by a deep-seated affection for Christ and the things of God.

Consider the testimony of Paul: "Formerly I was a blasphemer, persecutor, and insolent opponent. But I received mercy because I had acted ignorantly in unbelief, and the grace of our Lord overflowed for me with the faith and love that are in Christ Jesus" (1 Tim. 1:13–14). Paul describes an orientation in his previous life as one directly opposed to God and his purposes. There is no indication that Paul planned to deviate from that path until he was suddenly shown mercy. The grace of Christ shone abundantly on him. This doesn't sound like someone who was compelled to act against his will, even though he was so adamantly opposed to the gospel. Paul's testimony demonstrates that it is the kindness of God that leads one to repentance (Rom. 2:4) and his cords of love that draw sinners to himself (Hos. 11:4). The metamorphic energy inherent in the Spirit's work of regeneration breeds affectionate change in hardened sinners that is stunning. God's electing and renewing work is a labor of love, not a dictatorial subterfuge hijacking our freedom.

---

3. Many Arminians cite texts to show that God's grace can be resisted (e.g., Pss. 78:10; 81:11–13; Matt. 23:37; Acts 7:51). These texts, and many others like them, represent the *general outward call* to faith and repentance (i.e., the free offer of the gospel) proffered indiscriminately to all, which is clearly resisted and rejected more times than not. These texts should be distinguished from texts that indicate the *effectual internal call* to the elect that coincides with the work of regeneration (e.g., Rom. 8:30; Eph. 4:4; 2 Tim. 1:9; 1 Peter 2:9; Rev. 17:14). See Matthew Barrett, *Salvation by Grace: A Case for Effectual Calling and Regeneration* (Phillipsburg, NJ: P&R Publishing, 2013), 84, 87–88, 120–21, 266–67. What distinguishes the two is that the Holy Spirit accompanies the preaching of the Word, causing it to become "effectual" for the elect. Ibid., 132–33.

4. Dane Ortlund, *A New Inner Relish: Christian Motivation in the Thought of Jonathan Edwards* (Fearn, Scotland: Christian Focus, 2008), 107.

It is important to note a corollary truth. Just as saving belief is voluntarily exercised, so also is unbelief. God never forces the unregenerate to act with unbelief or prevents a person from believing against his will. The unbeliever doesn't believe on Christ because he doesn't *want* to believe. In fact, he willingly acts against his conscience, which tells him that the consequences of unbelief and continued rejection of God result in death (Rom. 1:32). No one will stand before God in judgment and plead innocence because he wanted to believe but God wouldn't allow him to do so. Furthermore, although Romans 3:10–18 indicates that one is *unable* to choose salvation, the person doesn't do so for lack of want or desire. This is why Jesus can say that he will not reject anyone who comes to him (John 6:37). And this admonition in no way contradicts what he says later, that no one *can* come to him unless the Father draws him (v. 44). Jesus espouses compatibilism.

If divine coercion were a factor in unbelief, then one's liability would be lessened, and blame would seemingly rest with God. It would suggest that God somehow causes one to violate one's conscience and well-intentioned desires. James addresses this issue:

> Let no one say when he is tempted, "I am being tempted by God," for God cannot be tempted with evil, and he himself tempts no one. But each person is tempted when he is lured and enticed by his own desire. Then desire when it has conceived gives birth to sin, and sin when it is fully grown brings forth death. (James 1:13–15)

Even though God is responsible for decreeing the actions of mankind, he never tempts people to act sinfully (James 1:13). Rather, people are morally responsible for their actions because they act voluntarily (vv. 14–15) in accordance with their own evil desires. We might add that they also act in violation of God's express commands written on the heart (Rom. 2:14–15). Thus, divine judgment is justified because all unbelievers have knowledge that their rebellion is against God's good and just commands and they rebel in full compliance with their own uncoerced intentions.

The Work of Regeneration Is Surprising and Often Imperceptible

Since the work of regeneration operates apart from divine coercion, it casts an aura of mystery on the process. God's hand in transforming the sinner into a new person is an invisible work. Jesus declares, "The wind blows where it wishes, and you hear its sound, but you do not know where it comes from or where it goes. So it is with everyone who is born of the Spirit" (John 3:8). If you've ever sat before a campfire on a cool evening, you are made aware of the truth of Jesus' metaphor. It doesn't matter what side of the fire you decide to sit on, you never know where the wind will blow the smoke. Likewise, you never know whom the Spirit may draw into God's kingdom.

When I was in seminary, I conducted a yearlong evangelistic Bible study. I had two consistent attendees who couldn't have been more different. George was polite, serious, honest, curious, and a diligent learner. He always asked questions about the Bible. He had a profound awareness of his own sin and shortcomings. At one point he confessed his failures to me with tears pooling in his eyes. I thought George made a prime candidate for the Holy Spirit's work, yet he could never bring himself to see his need to trust Christ.

On the other hand, Mark was boisterous, scatterbrained, facetious, and always in trouble with his family and the law. Sometimes he would make light of my faith—never in a malicious way, but as though all this Christian stuff were merely trivial with no need for serious pursuit. It amazed me that he came to my Bible study as often as he did. I thought that if anyone was clowning his way to hell, he was. But a year after I graduated from seminary, I got a call from Mark. The tone of his voice was markedly different—focused, determined, and exuberant. He had given his life over to Christ and begun to experience radical changes. I was flabbergasted. How could this be?

Not only are we surprised by whom God chooses for salvation, but we are surprised by the paths people take when they come to Christ. Stephen Smallman has written a fascinating and instructive book on regeneration and conversion called *Beginnings.*[5] He demonstrates

5. Stephen Smallman, *Beginnings: Understanding How We Experience the New Birth*

that everyone's experience of the new birth is different. Some have a tendency to think that the relationship between regeneration and conversion is always the same. A person is convicted and convinced by the Holy Spirit of his need of salvation, resulting in an immediate and dramatic conversion.

Smallman remarks that the model for such conversion stories tends to be the apostle Paul, who was suddenly blinded by a light from Christ, fell on his knees, and gave himself over to his new Lord (Acts 9:1–19).[6] Christians are often asked, "When did you trust Christ?" We are encouraged to remember the day and hour. But many people cannot pinpoint the moment they experienced conversion. All they can say is: "At some time in my past I didn't believe, and now I do."

The apostle John had a radically different story from the apostle Paul. Out of all the occurrences of the word *believe* in the New Testament, John's Gospel uses two-thirds of them. This explains why many refer to the book as "The Gospel of Belief." He makes a clear purpose statement in John 20:31: "But these are written so that you may believe that Jesus is the Christ, the Son of God, and that by believing you may have life in his name." In the course of writing his Gospel, John reflects on his own life, placing his own moment of belief in the context of his narrative. He does so in the same chapter that contains his purpose statement. John, like the other disciples, didn't have a clear understanding of Jesus' mission, especially the need for him to be crucified and rise again. Even though Jesus explained these things to the Twelve, they all missed the significance.

After Jesus was crucified, Peter and John remained together. Mary Magdalene reported the empty tomb to them on Sunday morning, and they both quickly made their way to the gravesite. Impetuous Peter burst into the empty tomb, while John stood apprehensively outside (John 20:4–6). Finally, after Peter examined the graveclothes, John stepped inside the tomb. He writes these words of himself: "Then the other disciple, who had reached the tomb first, also went in, and he saw and *believed*" (v. 8). This is the only occasion on which he uses

---

(Phillipsburg, NJ: P&R Publishing, 2015).
    6. Ibid., 54–55.

the word *believe* in reference to himself. This is no coincidence; he is inserting his own conversion story as proof of why he writes his Gospel. Paul's conversion was like a light that flashed suddenly, as it did both literally and metaphorically; but for John it was like the slow dawning of the sunrise—much like that early Sunday morning. The drama of Paul's conversion climaxed in a single moment. John's conversion slowly built up through fits and starts of nascent faith and climaxed at the empty tomb.

What shall we make of these differences? In his book, Smallman explains Jesus' metaphor of the new birth by comparing it to the whole gestation period of pregnancy. He likens the first signs of the Spirit's work of regeneration to the point of conception. Then he likens the signs of conversion—the response of faith and repentance—to the actual emergence of the newborn babe from the womb.[7]

The labor pains for some people may be long and very pronounced. These people wrestle and deliberate until things finally make sense. It could be that their gestation period is long, perhaps even years, as they move agonizingly toward the full embrace of Christ. On the other hand, the gestation period and labor pains for others may be very short. The first time such people hear the gospel, they see the truth of it and exercise a relatively quiet and painless faith. Some converts are greatly agitated in their souls because they realize what awful sinners they are. For them, faith and repentance are more painful and powerful. They can identify with the apostle Paul (1 Tim. 1:13). Other converts see their sin for what it is in a matter-of-fact way while moving effortlessly toward Christ.

There is no single narrative of conversion.[8] John Paton (1824–1907), who worked for many fruitful years among the cannibalistic tribes of the South Pacific, understood this well. He wrote:

> Truly there is only one way of regeneration, being born again by the power of the Spirit of God, the new heart; but there are many ways of conversion, of outwardly turning to the

---

7. Ibid., 29 (see chart at bottom of page).
8. Anthony A. Hoekema, *Saved by Grace* (Grand Rapids: Eerdmans, 1989), 120.

Lord, of taking the actual first step that shows on whose side we are. Regeneration is the sole work of the Holy Spirit in the human heart and soul, and is in every case one and the same. Conversion, on the other hand, bringing into play the action also of the human will, is never absolutely the same perhaps in even two souls—as like and yet as different as are the faces of men.[9]

God works in each convert with respect to his or her own unique person, character, and circumstances. For one person, the supernatural nature of regeneration and subsequent conversion is palpable; for another, it is barely discernible. Some have a greater perception of God's work within, whereas for others the movement toward belief is perceived to be wholly a work of their own. In either case, God stands squarely behind each individual experience, and yet in a way that is free of coercive overtones. God draws sinners to himself even as they embrace Christ freely. We are never passive in the process.

Two remarkable realities encompass the wonder of conversion. First, God has designed and directed the story of salvation so that everyone enjoys the privilege of active participation in its outworking. Even God appears as a passive observer in the shadows behind the stage. Second, every believer has her own unique story that sets her apart as special in the divine playwright's script. Just as every snowflake bears a unique design and image, every believer bears the stamp of God's diverse imagination. We are not all replicas cranked out on an assembly line. Nor are we automatons, but personal beings with unique emotions and experiences that are attended by real choices freely exercised. What amazing care God has put into producing each of his precious saints!

The Regenerate Retain Vestiges of the Old Nature

One of the disconcerting realities for believers is the ongoing burden of the propensity to sin. You'd think that the reception of a

9. John G. Paton, *John G. Paton: Missionary to the New Hebrides*, ed. James Paton (Carlisle, PA: Banner of Truth, 1965), 372.

new nature would completely dispense with the troubling vices of the old nature and that it would no longer be an albatross around the neck. In many ways, the new life of a believer isn't an escape from the battle with evil, but an invitation to wage an internal war with it that previously didn't exist. Dane Ortlund writes, "Regeneration is not the elimination but the inauguration of true moral struggle."[10] Justification promises us freedom from the *penalty* of sin and sanctification promises us freedom from the *power* of sin, but only our future glorification promises us freedom from the *presence* of sin. In the meantime, we fight as never before.

So then, what happens to the old sin nature in those who are new creations in Christ? Does it disappear, or is it simply invigorated by the presence of the new nature? Curiously, the answer is yes on both counts. Regeneration means that the reception of new life together with the presence of the divine life of the Spirit (2 Peter 1:4) has dealt a mortal blow to the sin nature. The "old self was crucified with him in order that the body of sin might be brought to nothing, so that we would no longer be enslaved to sin" (Rom. 6:6; cf. Gal. 2:20). Notice that even though the sin nature was crucified, we still retain a body that sins and that will eventually be done away with. This is like being stung by a honeybee. It dies, but only after leaving its stinger to agitate its victim.

Likewise, sin no longer serves as master over the believer (Rom. 6:14). Its reign has been severed, cut down as it wallows on the ground before us. And even though its mortal wound spells its eventual doom, it reaches out in desperation to drag the regenerated follower of Christ down to the grave with it.[11] It'll never succeed in doing so, but nonetheless it retains a strength that must be reckoned with. We can't take lightly its brutish designs to make our lives miserable.

This is what prompts Paul's admonition to believers in Ephesians 4:22–24: "Put off your old self, which belongs to your former manner of life and is corrupt through deceitful desires, and . . . be renewed in the spirit of your minds, and . . . put on the new self, created after the

10. Ortlund, *A New Inner Relish*, 135.
11. Robert A. Peterson, *Election and Free Will: God's Gracious Choice and Our Responsibility* (Phillipsburg, NJ: P&R Publishing, 2007), 131.

likeness of God in true righteousness and holiness." The phrases "put off" and "put on" appear in this passage to be commands. Actually, they describe realities that the Ephesians had been "taught . . . in Jesus" (v. 21). Thus, they should read: "You were taught . . . that you *have laid aside* the old self . . . and *have put on* the new self."[12] The old sinful self was cast aside like a ragged old cloak. A new cloak has been put on in its stead.

In Colossians 3:9–10, Paul uses these same declarative phrases, indicating the decisive shift from the old self to the new self. But what are used as declarations of past fact in verses 9 and 10 are used as present imperatives in verses 8 and 12. There he says to "put off" all vices associated with the old self (v. 9; cf. Rom. 8:13) and "put on" virtues that are commensurate with the new self (Col. 3:12). What we see here is the paradox of new life in Christ. In one sense, the sinful nature has *already* been killed; but in another sense, it has *not yet* experienced its final breath.[13] We are already redeemed from the curse of sin (Gal. 3:13; 1 Peter 1:18), and yet we still await our final redemption when we will sin no more (Rom. 8:23; Eph. 4:30).

We are to be conformed in practice with what we already are in status. Both Ephesians 4:23 and Colossians 3:10 speak of a present renewal that is taking place in the believer. This indicates that the effects of regeneration have only just begun at the moment of our conception and birth. We are experiencing a lifelong metamorphosis whereby we are moving from a raw, unformed piece of clay into a glorious sculpture (2 Cor. 3:18) that mirrors the righteous perfections of Christ (Rom. 8:29). God began this good work in us, and he will not stop until Christ receives us into glory (Phil. 1:6).

But until that work is complete, the Christian is engaged in a brutal conflict. The believer feels like Gandalf battling the Balrog in the dark mines of Moria instead of Aragorn at his coronation among the bright courts of Minas Tirith. When the old nature reigned, we aligned ourselves with the kingdom of darkness, and sin was largely exercised in ease and with little thought of how it was destroying

12. Both words are aorist infinitives, not imperatives. See discussion in Harold W. Hoehner, *Ephesians: An Exegetical Commentary* (Grand Rapids: Baker, 2002), 599–602.
13. Many theologians speak of an *already/not yet* tension in the New Testament.

us. But when Christ becomes our Master and his Spirit renews our natures, the kingdom of darkness is enraged, and its dark lord (Satan) seeks to devour us by tempting us to embrace the old ways (1 Peter 5:8).

Paul's Internal Battle

In Romans 7, Paul describes this predicament as an internal battle between conflicting desires.[14] We have an innate knowledge of good and evil through the law of God. Although this law is good (v. 12), it wreaks havoc on those who cannot obey its precepts. In other words, when we were dominated by the old nature, "our sinful passions, aroused by the law, were at work in our members to bear fruit for death" (v. 5). We could do no other. But now we have been set apart to "serve in the new way of the Spirit" (v. 6).

Nonetheless, the conflict has only just begun as the Christian seeks to live life under the new identity of the Spirit. Paul laments, "For I do not understand my own actions. For I do not do what I want, but I do the very thing I hate" (Rom. 7:15). The knowledge of moral truth informs the conscience and compels us to obey its precepts, but the vestiges of the old sin nature still sting. On the one hand, Paul wants to obey and has every good intention of doing so (v. 19), but sin rears its ugly head and shapes another set of desires so that Paul ends up choosing what he hates.

This is a conflict of desires, and the prevailing evil desire too often wins out. But why? Isn't Paul adamant in saying that he has "the desire to do what is right" (Rom. 7:18)? Why does he practice the very evil that he does *not want* to do (v. 19)? It sounds like he is acting contrary to his desires.[15] On the surface, he sounds like a libertarian. But consider the uniqueness of conflicting desires in which one desire is appealing and the other is decidedly unappealing. As a Christian,

14. There is disagreement about whether Romans 7 (particularly vv. 14–25) is referring to Paul's pre- or postconversion experience. I believe the evidence favors the latter. John MacArthur writes, "The level of spiritual insight, brokenness, contrition, and humility that characterize the person depicted in Romans 7 are marks of a spiritual and mature believer, who before God has no trust in his own goodness and achievements." *The MacArthur New Testament Commentary: Romans 1–8* (Chicago: Moody, 1991), 379.

15. Lemke, "Critique of Irresistible Grace," 151.

Paul finds sin unappealing, whereas godly behavior is appealing. All things being equal, he would never choose to sin.

So what is happening?

In order for sin to make itself appealing and thus incite a stronger desire to act on it, it must deploy the weapon of deception. This is the key to understanding Paul's dilemma. In Romans 7:11, he says that "sin . . . deceived me." The power of sin lies in its subterfuge (Heb. 3:13). It tempts us to think that if we engage in what it promotes, then it will benefit us. The young man may look at that tempting ad on the otherwise innocuous Internet site. He rolls his screen past it so that he doesn't have to consider what he hates. But the sinister voice of sin whispers in his ear, telling him that he will gain a wonderful pleasure if he simply rolls back the screen and makes one simple click of the mouse. Sin is deceiving him, causing him to think that this is what is in his best interest even though his conscience tells him otherwise.

This contrary and deceptive force wields such power that Paul exclaims, "It is no longer I who do it, but sin that dwells within me" (Rom. 7:17, 20). Paul's identity as a new creation in Christ is not the source of such choices (Gal. 2:20); rather, the remaining vestiges of sin left by the old nature continue to make their dreaded presence known. It is a conflict between the new nature and what remains of the old. The untainted desires of the new nature reflect what John teaches in 1 John 3:9: "No one born of God makes a practice of sinning, for God's seed abides in him, and he cannot keep on sinning because he has been born of God." The implanted spiritual nature in a new believer at the time of the second birth is not capable of feeding the old desires because it is marked by the indwelling presence of the Spirit of holiness.

This doesn't mean that a believer never sins, because the vestiges of the sin nature remain. John makes this clear earlier in 1 John 1:8–10. Rather, it means that his primary disposition is such that sin no longer dominates him. It isn't his normal practice to indulge sinful desires. As the spiritual seed of new life matures, it crowds out the weeds of sin. Nonetheless, the battle is acute, and the Christian can never let his guard down.

But one need not be discouraged. Paul cries out, "Wretched man that I am! Who will deliver me from this body of death?" (Rom. 7:24). His response: "Thanks be to God through Jesus Christ our Lord!" (v. 25). He moves on to proclaim, "For the law of the Spirit of life has set you free in Christ Jesus from the law of sin and death" (8:2; cf. Acts 13:39). This reflects what Paul says earlier: "For if we have been united with him in a death like his, we shall certainly be united with him in a resurrection like his. We know that our old self was crucified with him in order that the body of sin might be brought to nothing, so that we would no longer be enslaved to sin. For one who has died has been set free from sin" (Rom. 6:5–7).

Slavery Is Liberty

The New Testament says much about slavery to unrighteousness and the believer's subsequent freedom in Christ. Its pages use a number of terms to describe the Christian that are useful in understanding our new identity in Christ. But as John MacArthur points out, "The Bible uses one metaphor more frequently than any of these. It is a word picture you might not expect. . . . It is the image of a *slave*."[16] Ironically, this image of slavery becomes a prominent motif for our newfound liberty.

The believer experiences a new power of freedom—not a freedom to choose whatever one wants, but a freedom to choose what truly benefits the person most. "Having been set free from sin, [we] have become slaves of righteousness" (Rom. 6:18). This means that we have a new Master, the Lord Jesus, who bought us (Acts 20:28; 1 Cor. 7:23) with the purchase price of his blood (1 Peter 1:18–19; Rev. 5:9). Christ "gave himself for us to redeem us from all lawlessness and to purify for himself a people for his own possession who are zealous for good works" (Titus 2:14). Our new owner, Jesus Christ, "has made [us] his own" (Phil. 3:12), in order that we might become his "willing captives."[17] We are now slaves of Christ (1 Cor. 7:22), yet we are free. Paul says, "For freedom Christ has set us free; stand

16. John MacArthur, *Slave: The Hidden Truth about Your Identity in Christ* (Nashville: Thomas Nelson, 2010), 12 (emphasis in original).
17. Ibid., 132.

firm therefore, and do not submit again to a yoke of slavery" (Gal. 5:1; cf. John 8:32, 36).

Our new Master invigorates our new nature so that we can freely choose that which we could never choose before—the good that never falls short of the glory of God (Rom. 3:23). MacArthur contrasts the old slavery with the new slavery:

> Sin is the cruelest and most unjust of all masters; Christ is the most loving and merciful. Sin's burden is heavy and loathsome; Christ's "yoke is easy" and His "burden is light" (Matt. 11:30). Sin traps its slaves in darkness and death; Christ brings light and life to all those who have been "made . . . alive together with Him" (Col. 2:13). Sin diverts, deceives, and destroys; Christ is "the way, and the truth, and the life" (John 14:6). Insofar as slavery to sin consists of everything hateful, harmful, dreadful, and despicable, so slavery to Christ entails everything good, glorious, joyous, and right.[18]

As liberated slaves of Christ, we are set upon an assured path of sanctification that leads to the consummation of our eternal life (Rom. 6:22). Our wills are unbound so that we can act as we were designed to act. The vestiges of the old life remain and place limitations on this freedom; nonetheless, we are privileged to enjoy a glimpse of the fullness of freedom that will soon come with the fullness of our redemption.

Chapter Summary

A compatibilist theology of the new life helps make sense of many truths regarding both conversion and sanctification. First, conversion is far from some forced profession of faith that opponents of Calvinism insinuate must be the case if God determines salvation. True believers freely embrace Christ with headlong joy and devotion. What was once unmitigated resistance in the unbeliever gives way to full acceptance. Indifference gives way to deep interest. Hatred is transformed into unbridled affection.

18. Ibid., 141.

Second, the conditions under which people experience new life in Christ make the narrative of every conversion both unique and surprising. Stephen Smallman compares the new birth to the whole gestation period of pregnancy. The first signs of the Spirit's work of regeneration correspond to the point of conception. Then the signs of conversion—the human response of faith and repentance—correspond to the emergence of the newborn babe from the womb. What happens between conception and birth is as varied as are people themselves. The labor pains for some may be long and very pronounced. These people wrestle and deliberate until the gospel finally makes sense. In other cases, the gestation period and labor pains may be very short. The first time such people hear the gospel, they see the truth of it and exercise a relatively quiet and painless faith.

Third, the work of regeneration does not suddenly cast aside all troubles and temptations, but in fact invites them with increased vigor. In the end, however, the believer's newfound freedom in Christ secures a hope undeterred by the assaults of the enemy and what remains of the old sinful self.

Glossary

old nature. See *old self*.

old self. In Paul's writings, synonymous with *flesh*. Even though believers have been granted a new nature at the moment of *regeneration*, they become engaged in a great battle with what remains of the old *sin nature*. The old self has been crucified, but it still seeks to drag us down (i.e., throughout the Christian life) while in its death throes, prompting us with sinful desires. Also termed *old nature*.

Study Questions

1. The Bible is clear that unbelievers resist God and reject the offer of the gospel. Does this mean that when sinners enter the kingdom of God, they do so kicking and screaming (i.e., against their will)? Explain your answer.
2. What do Calvinists really mean when they speak of God's *irresistible grace*?
3. Will people ever stand before God in judgment pleading innocence

because they wanted to enter his kingdom but he wouldn't allow them in? Explain your answer.

4. How does Stephen Smallman describe the process of moving from regeneration to conversion?

5. No two conversions are alike. What did your conversion to Christ look like? Was it a long or short process? Simple or complex? Painless or torturous? Quiet or pronounced? More intellectual or emotional?

6. Why do you suppose God has orchestrated every conversion to be different for each person?

7. Explain what happens to the old sin nature once a person has been regenerated.

8. When Paul describes his inner conflict with sin in Romans 7, he admits that he does the very thing that he does not want to do (v. 19). Thus, he appears to be acting contrary to his desires, which sounds very libertarian. Is Paul espousing libertarianism, or is there another explanation for what he says?

9. Read 1 John 3:9. Is the apostle John suggesting that a believer never sins? Why or why not? What does John mean by "God's seed" that "abides" in the believer?

10. What is one of the most frequent metaphors used in the Bible to describe the Christian? How does this metaphor speak of the believer's newfound freedom?

Resources for Further Study

Matthew Barrett, *Salvation by Grace: A Case for Effectual Calling and Regeneration* (Phillipsburg, NJ: P&R Publishing, 2013). An excellent treatment of regeneration, irresistible grace, and effectual calling.

John MacArthur, *Slave: The Hidden Truth about Your Identity in Christ* (Nashville: Thomas Nelson, 2010). A revolutionary look at how the word *slave* describes the liberating life of a believer in submission to Christ.

Stephen Smallman, *Beginnings: Understanding How We Experience the New Birth* (Phillipsburg, NJ: P&R Publishing, 2015). A remarkable look at the relationship between regeneration and the various ways in which people experience conversion.

12

Absolute Freedom

What is freedom? It is a question that rests heavily on the hearts and minds of the inhabitants of a planet that has little of it. People have an innate longing to experience liberation. Like Aretha Franklin in her hit song "Think," they burst out in a repeating crescendo the words "freedom . . . freedom!" But few really understand what true freedom is. In the libertarian scheme, to be free is to be unhinged from any power, any force, and any thought that might dictate what you should do. You must have the power to exercise indifference to all alternative possibilities. In order to love, you must have the equal and neutrally disposed capacity to hate. In order to give, you must also be able to take away. In order to tell the truth, you must also be able to tell a lie. Without this equanimity of choices and the unhindered power to pursue either path with equal ease, freedom is sacrificed. To have such libertarian freedom is one of the greatest virtues contained in the volumes of the Arminian library.

But is this the essence of freedom? Is this such a virtuous commodity that we must risk calamity, disaster, and the prevailing course of evil to obtain and maintain it?[1] Is this the sort of freedom that the Christian will have in heaven? If this libertarian vision of freedom holds true, then heaven could never be a place where only righteousness dwells (2 Peter 3:13). In order to have righteousness in heaven, God would have to continue to risk the presence of evil.[2] If glorified saints are

1. James S. Spiegel, *The Benefits of Providence: A New Look at Divine Sovereignty* (Wheaton, IL: Crossway, 2005), 190.
2. D. A. Carson, *How Long, O Lord? Reflections on Suffering and Evil* (Grand Rapids: Baker, 2006), 34.

confined to making only righteous choices and could never engage in an evil deed ever again, then libertarian freedom is wholly destroyed. This is a fatal blow to the notion that libertarian free will is any kind of virtue at all.

Furthermore, libertarianism consistently claims that contrary choice is the only ground for human responsibility. If that is the case, then all heavenly saints will be irresponsible ones, since they will have no freedom to sin. Likewise, if heaven harbors the freedom for saints to sin, then it becomes a thinly disguised hell that undermines the power of Christ's redemptive work in vanquishing the power of sin and death among the redeemed (1 Cor. 15:55–57). In that case, free will becomes the unconquerable enemy of Christ.[3] Since this is utterly preposterous, the existence of heaven decisively bankrupts libertarianism. The fact is, "the highest state of human existence will be a state without libertarian freedom."[4]

This book has attempted to correct this dystopian vision. When all is said and done, libertarianism demonstrates a fundamental misapprehension of the nature of true freedom. Freedom of the will is not having an array of choices before us that includes myriads of possible opposing alternatives. True freedom consists in knowing the best and right choices, in being unhindered in making them, and in experiencing the greatest joy when we do make them. The right choices are the ones that God has prescribed through the morally binding instruction of his Word. Though it is hard to believe, God's righteous law is freedom.

But wait a minute! There is a problem. Am I saying that legalism is freedom? Not at all.

The Problem of Freedom and the Law

We know that people chafe against rules and laws and the demands that they place on us. Our sin nature craves freedom from the demands of God's law. If moral precepts demand our obedience, then they seem to hinder our freedom. They become a compelling

3. John M. Frame, *The Doctrine of God* (Phillipsburg, NJ: P&R Publishing, 2002), 142.
4. Ibid., 141.

force to enslave us. And of course, there is a thorny current of truth here. The law of God exposes how out of whack we truly are (Rom. 3:20; 7:7). It arouses our sinful passions (7:5, 8). When we see "Stay off the grass!" signs, we want to stay *on* the grass. When our friend admonishes, "Now, don't covet that new BMW!," we covet the BMW. The law does nothing to free us and everything to enslave us (Rom. 7:6) and even to kill us (vv. 10–11).

With friends like the moral law, who needs enemies?

Many are tempted to say that the moral demands inherent in the commands of God are not good and maybe even positively evil (Rom. 7:7). But nothing is wrong with God's law. According to Paul, "the law is holy, and the commandment is holy and righteous and good" (v. 12). The problem is not the law; the problem is us. The only reason that the moral precepts of God written on human hearts (2:14–15) are so troublesome is that the sin nature incurs a moral inability to obey them. The sin nature causes an aversion to the law. We want to be free from its demands.

But freedom from any compelling demands of the law also means freedom from any source of authority. Moral precepts entail moral authority. Our ultimate moral authority is God. To be unshackled from the authority of God is not freedom. To be released from the authority of God's Word is to invite bondage of the worst sort. The Bible has a binding claim on the lives of God's children, and that is a blessed reality to embrace with every fiber of our being.

We must not misapprehend the nature of true freedom. Submission to authority is not contrary to freedom, nor is adherence to righteous laws. The locus of freedom is found precisely in one's submission to God's authority and his instructive will as expounded in the revelation of the Scriptures. We should be able to say, "Oh how I love your law! It is my meditation all the day" (Ps. 119:97). The problem lies neither with divine authority nor with divinely mandated moral laws; the problem lies in our inability to submit to either. This is why the center of the Christian faith is found in the redemption of Christ. Freedom comes through grace extended to those unable and unwilling to embrace the lordship of Christ and to adhere to God's moral demands for our lives.

The Freedom of the Gospel

In the gospel, Christ met the demands of God's law on our behalf. He not only met the sanctions leveled against us as violators of the law by absorbing the wrath of God on the cross, but also lived a life of perfect righteousness by which he met the positive demands of the law on our behalf. He became sin for us so that we might obtain God's righteousness in him (2 Cor. 5:21). God initiated a great exchange in the two account ledgers of Christ and the children of God. The full sin that marks our debit column has been imputed to Christ's empty debit column. Our account is full of sin; his is bereft of any sin. Likewise, the full righteousness that marks his merit column has been imputed to our empty merit column. His account is full of righteousness; ours has none. See fig. 12.1.

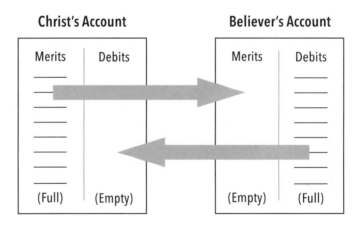

Fig. 12.1. The Great Exchange

We are justified by Christ and freed from the demands as well as the sanctions of the law. This is a forensic work of God on the believer's behalf—a legal declaration of pardon from guilt and an affirmation of righteousness that is foreign to our actual moral achievements. Believers did nothing to satisfy God and prompt this declaration. It was all secured by Christ's labor. That is why it is of grace and accepted by simple faith (Eph. 2:8–9).

God's purpose is not merely to justify us, however, but also to sanctify us. Justification frees us from the legal demands of the law that prevented us from gaining God's stamp of salvific approval. But that does not free us from the need to be conformed to the righteousness reflected in the law and in Christ. This is the point at which the importance of regeneration enters. Redemption entails a twofold change in our identity. It involves a change in our *status* through justification, but also a change in our very *being* through regeneration for the purpose of sanctification. When God justifies us, he also promises to conform us to the image of Christ and his righteousness in a very real and practical way. This can happen only when we have been born anew with a spiritual nature suited to equip us with the power of the Holy Spirit to joyfully obey the precepts of our Lord. And this leads us to set the stage for the final proposition in our understanding of human freedom and responsibility.

Freedom, the Fall, and Freedom Restored

In order to see this last truth in its proper context, we need to turn to a helpful guide from church history. The great theologian Augustine (354–430) developed a way to think about the shifting and progressing plight of humanity's original freedom in righteousness, then bondage to sin, and then freedom regained—the freedom that God's redeemed children are privileged to enjoy. Augustine's insights have been further developed in the subsequent history of Reformed theology. The work of redemption is chronicled in four stages using a series of Latin phrases to identify and describe each stage (pay careful attention to the order of the terms).[5]

First, in the prefall state of mankind, we speak of "Adam's freedom" (*libertas Adami*). In this case, our first human parents were "able to sin" (*posse peccare*) as well as "able not to sin" (*posse non peccare*). In other words, Adam and Eve had the capacity to act with God-pleasing righteousness when they chose to do so; nonetheless, they retained the potential to sin. Of course, they succumbed to sin, which resulted in the great fall of mankind.

Second, the postfall state of man changed everything. Adam's sin thrust humanity into a curse that forfeited the freedom that Adam had enjoyed. There remains a freedom, but only a "sinner's freedom" (*libertas*

---

5. See Richard A. Muller, "Libertas Naturae," in *Dictionary of Latin and Greek Theological Terms* (Grand Rapids: Baker, 1985), 176.

peccatorum). Present fallen humanity is now in a state in which our cursed nature limits our liberty only to corrupted choices. Fallen creatures are "not able not to sin" (*non posse non peccare*). The unregenerate can do nothing to prevent the predicament of actually sinning. None of the sinner's deeds can be God-pleasing. Even those deeds that have a low-grade virtue always fall short of glorifying God (Rom. 3:23).

Third, those who have been the recipients of God's gracious work of election enter the next stage, called the "freedom of the faithful" (*libertas fidelium*). As part of the firstfruits of redemption, and as new creations in Christ, we have undergone a partial transformation. While the regenerate are still "able to sin" (*posse peccare*), yet as those in a state of rebirth we are like Adam once again and "able not to sin" (*posse non peccare*). As believers, we have a renewed liberty to act in ways that are truly pleasing to God. What we lacked before the new birth is now restored, but only in a limited capacity. The fact is that sin still afflicts us in disconcerting ways.

But this is not the end.

Our definitive triumph comes when, fourth, we enter the "liberty of glory" (*libertas gloriae*) in heaven, a permanent state of existence in which our final redemption is consummated. This means that our transformation as new creations in Christ will become fully realized. In heaven, the redeemed will exist in a state whereby we are "not able to sin" (*non posse peccare*) at all. In other words, not only will we be capable of fully pleasing God with undefiled righteousness, but we will have no capacity to sin ever again. Therefore, "heaven will not be a matter of Paradise regained. Heaven will be better than that which Adam enjoyed in Eden prior to the fall."[6] It will be Paradise extraordinaire.

We Are Ultimately Free Only When Sin Is Absent and Our Joy Is Made Full in God

This picture of the fourfold state of human freedom frames God's beneficent design for the redemption of his creatures. The apex and goal of this plan is represented by our final proposition. Let us unfold its significance.

---

6. R. C. Sproul, *Willing to Believe: The Controversy over Free Will* (Grand Rapids: Baker, 1997), 53.

It starts by understanding that God's moral and spiritual precepts reflect his own character, which in turn represents the highest and greatest good that exists. The moral atmosphere encompassing God is the pinnacle of all that is right and true and beautiful. There is no more wonderful state of existence than to have one's being immersed in the fullness of such righteous perfection. God's design for his lowly creatures is to enjoy fellowship with him in the unbridled glory of his holiness, where we can be holy as he is holy (1 Peter 1:16), unhindered by the shackles of sinful corruption.

Adam and Eve enjoyed this holy bliss as they walked with God in the garden of Eden. The fall destroyed Adam and Eve's freedom. They could no longer enjoy and participate in God's goodness. Their sin brought about the curse that placed subsequent humanity in bondage and has kept us from fulfilling God's design in creating us. But redemption is the work of God to reverse the curse, to purchase us from sin's slavery, and to restore the freedom of divine fellowship and the joy of holiness that marks it.

This freedom means embracing God and his moral will as our highest good. John Piper declares, "The highest, best, final, decisive good of the gospel, without which no other gifts would be good, is the glory of God in the face of Christ revealed for our everlasting enjoyment."[7] Put more simply, Piper is fond of saying, "God is most glorified in us when we are most satisfied in him." This means that God himself and the pursuit of all holiness that brings him glory is what brings us greatest satisfaction. Piper has adapted this perspective from the well-known question that opens the Westminster Shorter Catechism: "What is the chief end of man?" The answer: "Man's chief end is to glorify God, and to enjoy him for ever."[8] David, who is ever worshiping his Lord, puts it this way:

O God, you are my God; earnestly I seek you;
　　my soul thirsts for you;

---

7. John Piper, *God Is the Gospel* (Wheaton, IL: Crossway, 2005), 13.

8. Piper rewords the answer to the catechism's question this way: "The chief end of man is to glorify God BY enjoying him forever." *Desiring God* (Sisters, OR: Multnomah, 1996), 23.

my flesh faints for you,
  as in a dry and weary land where there is no water.
So I have looked upon you in the sanctuary,
  beholding your power and glory.
Because your steadfast love is better than life,
  my lips will praise you.
So I will bless you as long as I live;
  in your name I will lift up my hands.

My soul will be satisfied as with fat and rich food,
  and my mouth will praise you with joyful lips. (Ps.
  63:1–5)[9]

Apart from new life in Christ, all that we perceive to be in our best interest is sinful, distorted, and deceptive inasmuch as it brings us glory—making much of ourselves. What is in our best interest is what brings God glory—all that makes much of him. This brings us the greatest satisfaction. Kelly Kapic notes that when "we stop worrying exclusively about *our* world, and we start caring about *God's* world,"[10] then we experience the life-giving power whereby God restores our purpose as his creatures. We live according to the new self and not the old self (cf. Col. 3:8–12). Again Piper observes, "The power of sin is the false promise that it will bring more happiness than holiness will bring."[11] What the heart treasures the most becomes our god (Matt. 6:21). If we treasure anything other than God as our highest good, we will be paupers indeed.

As long as Christians suffer from the aftershocks of the old nature, however, this freedom is never fully experienced. Certainly the regenerate person participates in the firstfruits of this sort of freedom. Thus, our *moral inability* has given way to a *moral ability* empowered by the Holy Spirit. We are no longer utterly crippled by sin, but our ability to freely walk is still restricted. The remnants of the sin nature

9. See also Pss. 16:2–6, 11; 20:4–5; 27:4; 37:3–6; 73:25–28; 1 Peter 2:6–7.
10. Kelly Kapic, "The Egocentric Predicament," *Tabletalk* 36, 3 (March 2012): 22 (emphasis in original).
11. John Piper, *Future Grace* (Sisters, OR: Multnomah, 1995), 386.

stand in our path and trip us up along our daily pilgrimage to the Celestial City.[12]

The full harvest of moral and spiritual freedom will not be experienced until our final redemption and glorification. This is what creation itself earnestly yearns for. "For the creation waits with eager longing for the revealing of the sons of God. For the creation was subjected to futility, not willingly, but because of him who subjected it, in hope that the creation itself will be set free from its bondage to corruption and obtain the *freedom* of the glory of the children of God" (Rom. 8:19–21). Paul describes the future glory of the children of God as something marked by "freedom." Heaven holds for us absolute freedom, the place in which all the vestiges of sin and the old self will have completely disappeared. No longer will we suffer conflicting desires between good and evil. No longer will sin distort our perception about what is good and what lies in our best interest. Deception is part of the curse. In heaven, the curse is destroyed (Rev. 22:3). Satan, the father of lies (John 8:44), will be cast into the lake of fire, never to deceive the nations again (Rev. 20:3, 8, 10).

Instead, the absolute freedom of which we gain only a glimpse now will bloom into the fullness of its radiant beauty. Part of the motivation that dictates our choice to fight against the sin that restricts us now lies in the hope of this greater freedom. We strive for this freedom now so that we can have more of it in the future. Heaven's glory eradicates all presence of sinful desires so that we can act with unhindered freedom for the glory of God. We will finally and only act in our best interest. Our experience will be the joy of always longing to choose according to the holy precepts that God has set forth as good and right and true (cf. Ps. 19:7–11). We will be fully conformed to Christ, who on the earth was always doing the will of his Father and pleasing him (John 4:34; 8:29).[13] We will gladly and fully submit to Christ as our benevolent Master with such perfected obedience that unbridled holiness will be our most cherished mantle.

---

12. The allusion here is to John Bunyan's classic allegory of the Christian life, *Pilgrim's Progress*.

13. Carson, *How Long, O Lord?*, 191.

Abraham Kuyper has said: "In heaven God's children will not stand still—their joy and glory will ever increase, but not their holiness which lacks nothing. And to be more holy than perfectly holy is impossible. Their development will consist in drinking ever more copiously from the life of God."[14] But they will be enabled to drink so freely because they will have been made so holy. Our relationship with God will experience its fullest restoration. We will see him face to face and know him as we have been fully known (1 Cor. 13:12). We have loved the Lord Jesus ever so weakly in his absence now (1 Peter 1:8). But in that day as we behold his presence, he will become the object of our unwavering love unhindered by sin forever.[15]

A Bold Vision of Freedom

The heart of this study has been to demonstrate that human freedom is not destroyed by determinism. All our choices have causes that necessarily dictate what we will choose, yet we freely choose what we want and bear responsibility for those choices. Our freedom is enhanced when we are free from hindrances that constrain the voluntary exercise of our wills. This is obvious by a careful examination of human experience.

More importantly, Scripture testifies that God's absolute sovereignty is compatible with human freedom and responsibility. God can and does dictate all the paths that shape the map of history and our personal lives while working in concert with every step we freely take (Prov. 16:9). Furthermore, God's sovereignty does not eviscerate our freedom. Quite the opposite, in fact: God's absolute sovereignty magnifies our absolute freedom.

This is not a brand of fatalism, as many misguided inquirers have erroneously imagined. As God superintends the course set before us, he never interferes with our capacity to choose what we most want to choose. Rather, he achieves his purposes precisely through the confluence of his will and ours. God did not have to create us this

14. Abraham Kuyper, *The Work of the Holy Spirit* (Grand Rapids: Eerdmans, 1975), 248.
15. Robert A. Peterson, *Election and Free Will: God's Gracious Choice and Our Responsibility* (Phillipsburg, NJ: P&R Publishing, 2007), 131.

way. Nothing suggests that he could not have exercised his sovereign purposes apart from the power of free agency. Even now, he could frequently bypass our choices and manage the world without our participation.

But he does not.

Instead, he makes us instruments of purpose. He tethers his plans to our own intricate deliberations and intentional acts. He condescends to us like a father who plays with his children on the playground. He guides us through a path in the woods even when it appears from our vantage point that we forge every new direction without him. He does this because he wants our participation in his plans to matter. He wants our lives to have meaning, and meaning comes from the responsibility attended by freely made choices.

Every one of God's creatures exercises a broad freedom of choice in the ordinary matters of life. This *general* freedom concerns morally neutral decisions of a relatively inconsequential nature. We choose our habitations and vocations. We choose our labor and our leisure. We open the pantry and choose the green cup or the blue cup based on which desires prevail the most. We make important decisions and trivial ones, and God grants us this freedom of inclination.

Yet when it comes to *spiritual* and *moral* freedom, we encounter a far different scene. Here our choices matter a great deal more. In this scene, the landscape is colored by a strange irony—people who are both free and in bondage at the same time. Mankind is shackled to desires dictated by morally corrupted natures, and yet pleased to be held captive to this awful condition. As Francis Turretin comments, unregenerate man is an imprisoned soul who "kisses his chains and refuses deliverance."[16] Since the fall of our first parents, generation upon generation of the world's inhabitants have freely indulged the passions of their sinful flesh, yet this is no freedom at all. Under this curse, a greater transcendent spiritual freedom beyond anything that we have ever conceived in this world remains elusive.

But there is hope.

---

16. Quoted in Thaddeus J. Williams, *Love, Freedom, and Evil: Does Authentic Love Require Free Will?* (New York: Rodopi, 2011), 126.

Here is the only freedom that the "Scripture portrays as worth having."[17] It is a bold vision of unleashed liberation unparalleled by the lesser trifles of our weak imaginations. It begins by humbled creatures' being burdened under the weight of sin that crushes our will and our power to do what is in our best interest—to glorify the God of heaven. But God, who is rich in mercy and power, liberates imprisoned wills from sin. He frees us from guilt, shame, powerlessness, and ultimately death. He renews dead spirits with his Holy Spirit. The Creator fashions within us a new heart with new affections directed toward the wonder of Christ so that we would follow and worship him. We know that God has done this the moment we freely pour out our confessions of rebellious failure before him, entrust ourselves to his Son, our appointed Redeemer, and embark on the course to obey all that he has commanded.

Charles Wesley, an ardent Arminian, has captured well the spiritual liberation that biblical compatibilism embraces through his hymn "And Can It Be That I Should Gain":

> Long my imprisoned spirit lay
> Fast bound in sin and nature's night;
> Thine eye diffused a quick'ning ray;
> I woke, the dungeon flamed with light;
> My chains fell off, my heart was free;
> I rose, went forth, and followed thee.

This is our blessed lot, and it only increases as eternity draws near. Our heavenly Father directs our paths for his name's sake (Ps. 23:3) as we make it our ambition to desire Christ as our food and drink—our very life and sustenance (John 6:55). God glorifies himself in us, his willing instruments, to choose the very best for our every good revealed in his holy Word. We live now with but a few appetizers. Soon we will be ushered into the full banquet hall of freedom that our Lord has prepared for us in his coming kingdom. At that time,

17. Mark R. Talbot, "True Freedom: The Liberty That Scripture Portrays as Worth Having," in *Beyond the Bounds*, ed. John Piper, Justin Taylor, and Paul Kjoss Helseth (Wheaton, IL: Crossway, 2003), 109.

our freedom will be forever exalted as it finally bursts forth from all the remaining chains of our present malevolent existence, still reeling from the curse. Curse will give way to unimaginable blessing.

Oh, what a splendid day that will be—to eternally live for, serve, obey, enjoy, and freely worship before our glorious Sovereign as we cast our crowns before his magnificent throne (Rev. 4:10)!

Chapter Summary

Genuine freedom consists in knowing the best and right choices, being unhindered in making them, and experiencing the greatest joy when they are made. The right choices are the ones that God has prescribed through the morally binding instruction of his Word. God's righteous law is freedom, and this is not legalism. Rather, in the gospel, Christ met the demands of God's law on the believer's behalf through justification, which frees us from having to gain God's salvific approval by our own merit. But that does not free us from the need to be conformed to the righteousness reflected in the law and in Christ. When God justifies believers, he also promises to sanctify us. Redemption entails a twofold change in our identity. It involves a change in our *status* through justification, but also a change in our very *being* through regeneration for the purpose of sanctification.

The new nature that transforms believers compels us to live righteous lives for the glory of God. This is in our best interest—advancing our greatest benefit and fullest joy. As long as we suffer from the aftershocks of the old nature, however, this freedom is never fully experienced until our final redemption and glorification. Although believers are no longer utterly crippled by sin, our ability to freely walk is still restricted. The remnants of the sin nature stand in our path and trip us up along our daily pilgrimage to the Celestial City. But a glorious day is coming when we will burst free from all the remaining chains of our present malevolent existence, and curse will give way to unmitigated blessing in heaven.

Study Questions

1. Why would having libertarian freedom become a problem in heaven?

2. What sorts of choices bring the greatest freedom to human beings?

3. Why do people chafe against rules and laws? Why is obedience to God's moral precepts so troublesome to people?

4. The author explains the doctrine of justification by using the illustration of two account ledgers—one for Christ and one for the sinner. How does this illustration clarify the doctrine of justification?

5. The author states that the redemption of sinners involves a twofold change in one's identity. What is that twofold change, and why are both elements so important?

6. The great theologian Augustine used different Latin phrases to describe four different stages in the work of redemption in humanity. How do these stages help to clarify both the bondage and the freedom of the human will?

7. What does John Piper say is the highest good of humanity? His answer draws on the first question of the Westminster Shorter Catechism: "What is the chief end of man?" The answer: "Man's chief end is to glorify God, and to enjoy him for ever." Do you believe that Piper has reframed the catechism's answer in a satisfactory way?

8. Why does heaven hold for the believer the greatest freedom imaginable—an absolute sort of freedom?

9. Why does God's sovereignty magnify true freedom instead of hindering it?

10. How has this study enhanced or changed your view about God's sovereignty and human freedom and responsibility? Has it answered looming questions? Has it raised more questions than you had before? What impact has it had on you?

Appendix 1:

Comparing Libertarian and Compatibilist Beliefs on Free Agency[1]

Libertarian (Arminian) Beliefs	Compatibilist (Calvinist) Beliefs
Free agency or the freedom to choose **is the ability to choose contrary to a choice** that is made. This is sometimes called the *freedom of contrary choice.*	**Free agency** or the freedom to choose **is the ability to make a choice voluntarily.** This is sometimes called the *freedom of inclination* because one is always inclined to make particular choices.
Choices are sufficiently **determined by a person's power of willing** and nothing else, including God.	**Choices are** necessarily and sufficiently **determined by God as well as by a person's nature** and most compelling desires or motives.

1. This chart compares the common Christian beliefs about free agency—in particular, the views of Arminians (libertarians) and Calvinists (compatibilists). Secular libertarians and compatibilists would not hold to the distinctive Christian beliefs depicted in the chart.

God can influence choices, but he cannot determine choices without violating one's free will. One can always resist God's influence. **If God determined choices, then people would be coerced** to act with no other choice available.

God ultimately determines choices, but he uses secondary means, including human nature, desires, and motives. Secondary means can include coercive influences, **but God himself never directly coerces a person** to act against his will, thus violating the voluntary nature of his freedom.

Being free from all influences directing the will toward particular choices **is freedom from coercion.** Since all influences would be coercive if they causally determined choices, in that case they would hinder free will.

Choices are more voluntary if freed from coercive influences determining choices. But not all prior influences are coercive. Coercive influences prevent choosing what one most wants to otherwise choose. The coercive influence provides a more compelling motive, causing one to willingly make another (unappealing) choice instead.

One's desires and motives can influence choices, but they cannot sufficiently **determine them.** One can always act against them.

One's desires and motives are the immediate cause of the **choices** that a person makes, and he cannot act against them.

Conflicting or competing motives are deliberated over, **but have no** sufficient causal **bearing on what one** finally **chooses.**

Conflicting or competing motives are deliberated over **until** the **most compelling motives determine** the **choice** made.

Choices are contingent. No alternative is more compelling than another. Thus, alternative choices can be made regardless of prior influences.

Choices are certain. Given all prior influences determining choices, only one choice can be made.

Choices can be contrary in any given situation. One can act against all influences inclining one to a particular choice, including one's desires, motives, and nature.

Choices are never contrary to prior determining influences. One never acts against his most compelling desires, motives, and nature. The choice made is always what is most compelling, even if it is not the most appealing choice otherwise.

People are free to the extent that they can rise above their desires, motives, and nature and choose alternative possibilities.

People are free to act only according to their desires, motives, and nature. They are never indifferent to alternative possibilities.

Greater possibilities for alternative choices exist because choices are not necessarily dependent on prior causal influences. If one wants to choose differently than he does, he can, as long as no particular influences prevent him from doing so.

Fewer possibilities for alternative choices exist because choices are limited by prior causal influences. If one wants to choose differently than he does, he can, if a different set of causal influences precedes the choice.

Choosing one alternative over another (A or B) risks the possibility of **being arbitrary,** since no prior causal influences are sufficient for either choice.

Choosing between alternatives (A or B) is never arbitrary because prior causal influences are always necessary and sufficient for particular choices made.

Choices do not necessarily correspond to typical patterns of behavior because choices can be made contrary to all prior causal influences.

Choices often correspond to typical patterns of behavior because there is always a necessary cause-effect relationship to prior causal influences.

Choices are largely unpredictable, since no prior causal influences are necessary for choices made.

Choices are predictable only to the degree that all the influences determining choices can be ascertained, which is not always possible.

Human responsibility for choices is maintained only when a person has the ability to act contrarily in any given situation (i.e., allowed to act equally with alternative choices).

Human responsibility for choices is maintained the more voluntarily (i.e., willingly/intentionally) a person makes a particular choice.

If choices are determined by anything other than the person who wills, then they are coerced, and coercion nullifies human responsibility.

To the degree that choices are determined by coercive influences, then responsibility is correspondingly reduced because the voluntary nature of such choices is reduced.

If all choices are ultimately determined by God, then that must include evil choices. Therefore, God is culpable for evil.

All choices are ultimately determined by God, including evil choices. Yet culpability for evil lies in one's intentions. Since God always has good intentions for the evil he determines, then he is never culpable for evil. Likewise, men are culpable for evil choices because their intentions (desires and motives) are evil.

Unbelievers have freedom to make moral and spiritual choices. They are not necessarily constrained by their sin nature. God's grace allows them this freedom.

Unbelievers have no freedom to make God-pleasing **moral and spiritual choices** because they are constrained by their sin nature.

God's prevenient grace is supplied to all men and is necessary in order to choose (believe) Christ for salvation. But when further divine *saving grace* is supplied to sinners so that they might choose Christ, this grace can be resisted.

God's grace is necessary in order to choose (believe) Christ for salvation. **Divine saving grace is supplied only to the elect** so that they can voluntarily choose Christ. This grace is irresistible, so they will certainly choose Christ.

God's saving grace helps sinners to exercise saving faith (if they so choose) in order that their natures might be regenerated.

God's saving grace regenerates a sinner's nature in order that he can voluntarily **exercise saving faith**.

If a person is **not given the ability to resist God's saving grace, then** any **choice** exercised to believe Christ is not free. If this grace is irresistible, then it **is coercive, and** the choice to believe is **not free**.

A person who receives **God's irresistible saving grace** exercises faith in Christ voluntarily because this grace **is not coercive**. God does not force people to believe Christ against their will. Left to themselves, they willingly reject him.

If God's saving grace were not extended to sinners, giving them the opportunity to believe, then **God would be unfair**, since people deserve equal opportunity to believe or reject Christ for salvation.

By definition, **God's saving grace is undeserved. He is under no obligation to extend his grace** to anyone because all have sinned and rejected God willingly. Thus, God is not unfair in not supplying what people already do not want. God does not force people to reject him against their will; they do so willingly.

Spiritual freedom is achieved when one is completely **free of all determining influences** interfering with his ability to choose contrarily in any situation. **This** sort of **freedom will not exist in heaven,** however, because believers will have no ability to choose contrary to righteous choices.

Spiritual freedom is achieved only **when** the **sin nature and** its attending **desires** and motives **preventing** people from acting in **their best interest have been mitigated.** Regenerated believers have a glimpse of this freedom now. But **only believers in heaven will have full freedom** when sin is fully eradicated. Then they will act in full accordance with God's moral commands and precepts of truth, which are in their best interest.

Appendix 2:

A Review of Randy Alcorn's *hand in Hand: The Beauty of God's Sovereignty and Meaningful Human Choice*

When I first decided to write *What about Free Will?*, I did so believing that the topic of biblical compatibilism needed a full-length treatment written in a comprehensible manner. Such a book didn't exist. When the manuscript was completed, I discovered to my dismay that Randy Alcorn had just released his book *hand in Hand: The Beauty of God's Sovereignty and Meaningful Human Choice* (Colorado Springs: Multnomah, 2014). My fear was that he had beaten me to the punch and written the book I intended. I knew immediately that I needed to read his book in order to compare it to my own before submitting my manuscript for publication. I soon discovered that the version of compatibilism to which he holds doesn't resemble my own or that held by virtually all other self-identifying Calvinistic compatibilists since Jonathan Edwards.[1] Thus, I believe that there is a need to distinguish his view from the standard view I hold to.

1. Edwards did not identify himself as a *compatibilist*, since that term is largely a twentieth-century invention in philosophical debates about determinism and free agency. But it accurately reflects what Edwards taught in *Freedom of the Will*—the first systematic articulation of this idea from a Christian perspective. Before Edwards, theologians such as Augustine, Calvin, and Luther did not argue in compatibilistic categories when discussing free will, although some suggest that Calvin (and others before Edwards) held views that could be construed as compatibilist. See Paul Helm, *John Calvin's Ideas* (Oxford: Oxford

To begin, let me say that Alcorn's book makes many commendable points. He has a good overview of the basic distinctions between Calvinism and Arminianism and treats both views fairly. Alcorn describes himself as a former Arminian who has slowly gravitated toward Calvinism, but not fully. He self-identifies as a four-point Calvinist (21) or an "80 percent Calvinist" (210). His chapters on divine sovereignty (chapter 3) and trusting God in the midst of suffering (chapter 10) are very helpful. His critique of open theism and hyper-Calvinism are right on target. Making the book unique is its numerous charts and diagrams that seek to clarify the complex issues that plague this topic. Alcorn passes along many encouraging truths to the reader, and his book will generate a lot of constructive reflection on the issues.

Defining Free Agency

The key to understanding Alcorn's perspective is his definition of *free agency*. Although he identifies himself as a compatibilist, the distinguishing features of his view are somewhat novel. Alcorn has a few scattered quotes from a couple of compatibilists, but he never interacts with standard compatibilist accounts of divine sovereignty and free agency. At times he sounds like he embraces compatibilism while distancing himself from libertarianism. Yet throughout the book he assumes only one definition of *free agency*, which happens to be that of libertarianism, not compatibilism.

This is evident across most chapters of the book. For example, Alcorn quotes descriptions of human freedom approvingly from Alvin Plantinga (55) and C. S. Lewis (56), both of whom are libertarians. Libertarians hold to what is called *contrary choice*. Even though a person chose A, without qualification he could have chosen B instead. Alcorn affirms this basic definition when he states that "'choice' by definition involves selecting between alternatives" (135). Like most libertarians, he says that God "gives us the power to tell the truth or to lie. . . . Real choices are nearly always open to us" (74). He states forthrightly, "I believe compatibilism leaves room for limited or

---

University Press, 2006), 164–71; Paul Helm, "Edwards and the Freedom of the Will," available at http://paulhelmsdeep.blogspot.com/2011/02/edwards-and-freedom-of-will.html.

qualified contrary choice" (135). To distinguish his view from others, he calls it "meaningful human choice" throughout the book.

On page 60, Alcorn declares:

> While some will argue that [divine] determinism means only one choice is possible, compatibilism holds that determinism and free choice can coexist. Isn't the mind of God big enough to determine some things or many things while granting genuine choice to his creatures? If contrary choice simply implies the existence of more than one possible choice, isn't that what choice means in the first place? If our view of God is sufficiently large, this kind of contrary choice is no threat to his sovereignty.

Alcorn seems to be unaware that no compatibilist defines *free will* in such libertarian terms.

Alcorn's "limited or qualified" view of libertarianism means that humans sometimes have libertarian freedom and sometimes they don't. He seeks to straddle the fence between Arminian and Calvinist theologies. He suggests that libertarian freedom is the default mode for human choosing. He also says, "Compatibilists believe God is free to overrule creatures' choices but is also free to choose not to, whenever he can accomplish his sovereign plan through their freely made choices, right or wrong" (81).[2] The first part of the statement conflicts with libertarianism, which says that choices cannot be causally determined by God without being coerced against one's will. This would eviscerate not only our freedom, but also our responsibility. But I'm not aware of any compatibilist who has said anything like what appears in the second part of the statement.

Historically, compatibilists have defined their position in the following way. First, God determines every choice of every person, yet every person voluntarily chooses according to his most compelling motives and desires. He cannot act contrary to his prevailing motives or God's decree of the person's actions. Second, God's causal determination of human actions is remote and primary, whereas human choices of the

2. See also pages 71, 88, 128, 138, 165, 173 for other statements of divine overruling.

same actions are immediate and secondary. Furthermore, God acts so that he neither coerces people to choose as they do nor directly causes them to carry out evil. As long as no other outside constraints are placed on humans, they freely and responsibly act according to their desires. I have sought to demonstrate that this explanation of compatibilism best coheres with the scriptural data (see especially chapters 5 and 6), and it is the prevailing way in which compatibilists argue. But Alcorn seems unaware of this way of thinking.

Decretive and Permissive Wills

So in what other ways does Alcorn's position differ from traditional compatibilism? He clarifies matters in the following statement:

> God's choices and creature choices all exist within his sovereign rule. The evils done by God's creatures are their choices, not his. He chooses to permit evils—and could have prevented them—but he doesn't *cause* them; he's not the author of evil. Nonetheless, his creatures' wrong choices exist within his decree and unlimited circle of his sovereignty, and they don't defeat his ultimate purpose and plan. He could have chosen to not permit them, and his permission reflects both purpose and plan. Indeed, he uses at least some of his creatures' disobedience, if not all of it, to accomplish that plan. (133)

Alcorn is concerned to demonstrate that God doesn't stand behind the evil choices that people make. God "permits" them but does not "cause" them in any way. Alcorn affirms the standard Calvinist distinction between God's decretive (sovereign) will and his preceptive (moral) will (81).

But he limits God's decretive will by supplementing it with an Arminian view of God's permissive will. He writes:

> There are direct decrees and permissive decrees. The incarnation of Christ is a direct decree, while the fall of Adam and Eve is an indirect or permissive decree. God didn't make sin happen, in the sense that he made the incarnation happen. He didn't

merely permit the incarnation; he caused it. Permission and causation are not the same. Yet, God decreed both the sin he permitted and the incarnation he caused. (143–44)

Distinguishing permission from causation is an Arminian maneuver. When Calvinists use the term *permissive will*, they usually mean that God is passive in the unfolding of evil while active in the accomplishing of good. In either case, God remains in full control of all the evil that transpires through his overarching decretive will and through his providential causal determination. Thus, when Alcorn claims that God doesn't "cause" evil, if he means that God doesn't directly act on the hearts, minds, and wills of humans so that they operate as passive instruments of some evil intention in God, then classic Calvinists would agree. Nonetheless, the Bible often speaks of people acting as God's instruments when they perform acts of evil (e.g., Pharaoh in Exodus 4–14; the king of Assyria in Isaiah 10:5–19). In several places Alcorn seems to agree with this perspective, and in other places he doesn't.

Conflicting Positions

Let us consider Alcorn's conflicting positions further. On page 161, he discusses God's predestination of Christ's death through the collusion of human participants described in Acts 4:27–28. He states, "Did Herod and Pilate and the others have sufficient contrary choice to have acted differently to the extent that they could have thwarted the plan God predestined? Clearly not." In making this statement, is Alcorn denying the perpetrators' libertarian freedom or merely limiting it? It would seem the latter, since he says that the power of their free will was not "sufficient" to overcome God's plans. This corresponds to what he states elsewhere: "If someone believes contrary choice means freedom to choose contrary to God's decree, I obviously disagree" (60).

But this raises another question. Was the crucifixion of God's Son part of his "direct decree" or his "permissive decree"? I think Alcorn would say that it was God's direct decree. Perhaps he believes that God "overruled" the perpetrators' libertarian freedom in this instance and causally determined their evil actions. Now, if this is the case, does Alcorn believe that God was culpable for their sinful actions? Elsewhere he says, "God is certainly capable of overruling me, and he's entitled to do so whenever he wishes. But if God predetermines every choice I make, then when I sin, he's causing me to do evil" (71). Alcorn has a serious problem here. He must either consistently adhere to libertarian freedom or abandon the idea that such freedom is necessary to exonerate God from culpability for evil.

Again, on page 83 Alcorn correctly states, "Compatibilists believe that much that happens in this fallen world violates God's moral will, but everything that happens is in accord with his decretive will (defined as 'the sovereign, efficacious will by which God brings to pass whatever He pleases by His divine decree')." Here he quotes the popular Calvinist R. C. Sproul. When Sproul uses the word *efficacious* to describe God's sovereign will and decree, he means that God causally brings about that will in all that transpires. This contradicts what Alcorn has said about God's permissive will on pages 143–44. Alcorn seems to embrace mutually exclusive ideas. He cannot affirm God's immutable decree and libertarian freedom at the same time. One is either free from God's sovereign control or subject to it. To suggest that God wholly determines the outcome of history while making room for contrary choice invites contradiction. It doesn't appear that Alcorn has fully thought out what libertarian freedom entails.

In other places, Alcorn writes that compatibilism teaches that God uses evil choices "after the fact to accomplish his purposes" (89). In this case, Alcorn appears to be saying that humans use libertarian free will (at least part of the time) to choose evil and then God mitigates these choices afterward to accomplish a prior goal. Perhaps this is what he means by divine "overruling" whereby this divine intervention retains libertarian freedom instead of short-circuiting it. But how does God do this without violating further instances of libertarian freedom? Why doesn't God just prevent the evil choices from happening in the first place? This is not the position of traditional compatibilism. When Joseph's brothers sold him into slavery, God did not react to this situation by rectifying their bad choices "after the fact." Rather, the text of Scripture makes it clear that he predetermined their evil actions all along (Gen. 45:5, 7–9; 50:20; Ps. 105:17), in the same way that he predetermined the actions of Herod, Pilate, and the other instigators of Jesus' crucifixion.

God's decree is comprehensive and exhaustive and speaks of the causal determination of all things. Ephesians 1:11 tells us that God "works all things according to the counsel of his will." There is no reason to restrict the universality of "all things." The concept of working (*energeo*) here speaks of causation. There is no room for a brand of permissive willing that does not at least involve indirect or passive causation. Thus, we can say that God is the ultimate cause of evil in the sense that it conforms to his immutable active decree. But one cannot entertain a sanguine attitude. This is a difficult pill to swallow, and most Calvinists admit that we run into mystery at this juncture. It explains why D. A. Carson calls God's relationship to good and evil *asymmetrical*. God stands behind good in such a way that he is the direct cause of it and stands behind evil in such a way that he is not the direct cause of it. Thus, God is not culpable for evil's violation of his moral character and precepts.[3] I have argued that this position is more faithful to the biblical text (see chapters 3 and 6).

Ship Illustration

Perhaps the most poignant illustration that Alcorn uses to describe his position is his analogy of a ship crossing the ocean (152–53). God is the owner and captain of the ship, and he determines its ultimate destination. Nobody can do anything to alter the destination. Alcorn then likens human beings to passengers who roam about on the ship. He paints several different scenarios that correspond to different views about human freedom. First, the hard determinist (i.e., hyper-Calvinist) would say that each passenger is a "preprogrammed automaton with no true freedom." Each is destined for a particular task as he roams about the ship's confines. "There's no permission; everything is mandated. Meaningful human choice is illusory." Second, what Alcorn calls the "extreme libertarian" position (perhaps to distinguish it from his own)

---

3. D. A. Carson, *How Long, O Lord? Reflections on Suffering and Evil* (Grand Rapids: Baker, 2006), 189.

involves such a radical freedom that the people in this scenario can roam about the ship wherever they want. Furthermore, they can "get off this ship and captain [their] own, sailing to any harbor [they] choose."

In the third scenario—the one that Alcorn adopts—he lumps "compatibilists and moderate libertarians" together, making little distinctions between the two. These sorts of passengers are allowed to freely roam the ship like extreme libertarians; the difference is that they can never get off the vessel. Compatibilists (Calvinists) have less freedom than the moderate libertarians (Arminians); nonetheless, each possesses the freedom of contrary choice.

Alcorn's first two scenarios make sense with hard-determinist and standard libertarian positions. But his third scenario makes much less sense given his acceptance of basic libertarian notions. Libertarians consistently define *free agency* as the ability to make contrary choices in an unconstrained manner. If freedom truly comes about, then one must have the capacity to choose genuine alternatives in any given situation. All live options are open. Yet if someone in Alcorn's illustration *really* did want to get off the ship and go against the will of the captain (God), he could not do so. He would be absolutely constrained. No matter how much freedom he had within the confines of the ship, he would still end up going to the destination determined by the captain for the ship to go. So even though Alcorn is granting the passengers limited libertarian freedom, that freedom itself is no less illusory than the hard-determinist position, and I think most libertarians and Arminians would agree. Most compatibilists would reject the illustration as well because it assumes libertarian freedom, which cannot be compatible with a God who exercises meticulous providence in accordance with his absolute decrees.

Conclusion

I believe Randy Alcorn's book is a valiant attempt to reconcile God's sovereignty with human freedom and responsibility. I sympathize with his approach only because I once tried to entertain some space for a limited exercise of libertarian free will in wrestling with the issues. But I ended up abandoning such an approach for three reasons. First, the scriptural evidence for God's meticulous providence leaves no room for libertarianism. Second, the more I came to understand libertarian arguments, they did not really make sense of the way in which people make choices and how the Bible conceives of our responsibility. Third, classic compatibilism makes far greater sense of the scriptural examples of divine and human action and the doctrines and practices that flow from reconciling the two.

There is no question that Alcorn's book contains much that is helpful to the Christian struggling with this issue. But in the end, I think it falters under the effort to navigate between what Alcorn perceives to be the Scylla of undiluted Calvinism and the Charybdis of his former Arminianism. In a conciliatory tone Alcorn remarks, "People on both sides of the issue can sometimes make sense" (32). But he cannot have it both ways. Either God is fully sovereign in the causal determination of history and our personal lives or he is not. Either humans have libertarian freedom or they do not.

Alcorn sometimes appears to lean toward a classic compatibilist explanation but never quite comes around to offering an account that coheres with what most other biblical compatibilists have offered. This surely explains why he embraces a novel explanation of the issues. He proffers only one definition of human freedom (i.e., libertarian) and distinguishes the different views as existing along the continuum of this definition. On the one end, you have extreme libertarianism that perhaps flirts with Pelagianism; and on the other end, you have hyper-Calvinism that denies any freedom at all and borders on fatalism. In between, you have various Arminian and Calvinist views all holding to the same libertarian perspective, but with the Calvinist views placing more restrictions on its exercise. In contradistinction to this unsatisfying narrative, the more widely held view of classic compatibilism offers an entirely different account of human freedom, one that is far more consistent with Calvinism. Yet more importantly, it is far more consistent with the data of Scripture.

Glossary

accommodation. A doctrine concerning God whereby he condescends to his creatures in such a way that he is able to communicate and interact with them on a level that they can relate to. God often appears to be a finite creature like us, even though he is the transcendent Creator of all. See also *anthropomorphic*, *immanence*, and *transcendence*.

anthropomorphic. Of or relating to attributing human characteristics to God. Combines the Greek words for *human* (*anthropos*) and *form* (*morphe*). Anthropomorphic language is used in the Bible. See also *accommodation*.

Arminianism. A theology associated with the teachings of Jacob Arminius (1560–1609). Arminianism teaches five basic ideas. First, God has predestined to save those whom he foreknows will exercise faith in Christ. Second, Christ's death was an atonement for all mankind regardless of who believes on Christ for salvation. Third, humans in their natural state do not have *free will* or the capacity for saving faith. But, fourth, God has supplied *prevenient grace* to all humans so that they can recover free will and exercise saving faith. This prevenient grace enables them to either cooperate with God's saving grace or resist it if they choose. Fifth, the grace of God assists the believer throughout his life, but this grace can be neglected. Subsequently, the believer can incur the loss of salvation.

Calvinism. A theology that embraces a broad spectrum of ideas associated with the teachings of the Protestant Reformer John Calvin (1509–64). Calvinism, however, is often identified by the five points of Calvinism, traditionally represented by the acronym *TULIP*. The *T* stands for *total depravity*, which indicates that humanity is in bondage to sin. The *U* stands for *unconditional election*, which indicates that God chooses people for salvation wholly apart from anything they do. The *L* stands for *limited atonement*, which indicates that Christ's death secured atonement only for the elect. The *I* stands for *irresistible grace*, which indicates that God draws chosen sinners to salvation irresistibly. The *P* stands for *perseverance of the saints*, which indicates that the elect will certainly persevere in their salvation until the end.

compatibilism. The biblical view that divine *determinism* is compatible with human *free will*. There is a dual explanation for every choice that humans make. God determines human choices, yet every person freely makes his or her own choices. God's causal power is exercised so that he never coerces people to choose as they do, yet they always choose according to his sovereign plan. People are free when they voluntarily choose according to their most compelling desires and as long as their choices are made in an unhindered way. While God never hinders one's choices, other factors can hinder people's freedom and thus their responsibility. Furthermore, moral and spiritual choices are conditioned on one's base nature, whether good or evil (i.e., regenerate or unregenerate). In this sense, one is either in bondage to his or her *sin nature* or freed by a new spiritual nature. See also *soft determinism*.

competing desires. Apposite (but not opposing) desires that are nearly equal in their positive or negative appeal, making it difficult to act on one or the other. For example, which favorite cereal shall I choose—Lucky Charms or Cap'n Crunch? See also *conflicting desires*.

concurrence. The doctrine of God's providential action in the world whereby he is the *primary* but *remote cause* of all human actions. Likewise, humans are the *secondary* but *proximate cause* of their own actions.

conflicting desires. Opposing desires that battle with each other. Usually the conflicting desires arise in situations in which external coercion influences someone toward a choice that under normal circumstances the person wouldn't make. For example, a person might not normally give all his money to a stranger. But he might if the stranger held a gun to his head. The second scenario produces a conflicting desire. One doesn't want to part with his money, but neither does he want to part with his life. See also *competing desires*.

conscience. The human faculty that reveals to us the knowledge of moral right and wrong. God stamped his moral law on the conscience of every human being, and this serves to indicate our accountability before him. The moral signals that the conscience provides can be heeded or suppressed.

contrary choice. A basic idea in *libertarianism* that humans can always choose contrary to any prior influences that might direct their choices. Given exactly the same set of circumstances, no particular choice or outcome is guaranteed.

conversion. The voluntary act of repenting from sin and exercising faith in Christ for salvation, neither of which is possible unless one has experienced the prior gracious work of *regeneration* by the power of the Holy Spirit.

decretive will. God's sovereign will whereby he ordains or decrees all events that transpire in space, time, and history, including all human actions. God ensures that his decrees will certainly take place. Sometimes this is called God's *secret will*, since he does not normally reveal what he intends to do.

determinism. The idea that all events and human choices are necessarily and causally determined by prior conditions. The world operates in a definitive cause-effect reality. Calvinists believe that God's sovereignty is deterministic and stands behind all that transpires in the world. Arminians deny that God's sovereignty is deterministic. See also *divine sovereignty* and *hard determinism*.

divine sovereignty. The biblical doctrine that God controls time, space, and history. Calvinists usually hold that God meticulously determines all events that transpire, including human choices. Arminians teach that God limits his sovereign control of events, giving humans significant freedom of choice, which is defined as *libertarianism*. See also *determinism*.

extraordinary providence. Rare instances in which God's superintendence of events involves miracles or supernatural occurrences (e.g., Jesus' turning water into wine). See also *ordinary providence*.

fatalism. An aberrant form of *determinism* stating that future events are fixed in such a way that human choices are irrelevant. What will be will be, and there is nothing that anyone can do about it.

foreknowledge. In classic theism, God's exhaustive knowledge of all future events before they transpire. Arminians embrace simple foreknowledge or divine prescience: God looks down the corridors of time and sees all that will happen. Calvinists agree, but add that God predetermines all that he foresees.

free will (free agency). The idea that humans are designed by God with the capacity for freely making choices for which they are responsible. Most Calvinists and Arminians agree that some kind of free agency is necessary for *moral responsibility*. But each branch of theology defines it differently. Arminians embrace a libertarian notion of free agency. Many Calvinists embrace a compatibilist notion of free agency. See also *compatibilism* and *libertarianism*.

general freedom. In *compatibilism*, the concept that humans have the freedom to choose what they most want to choose with regard to morally inconsequential actions, but that they remain in bondage to sin unless they are liberated by the work of *regeneration*. See also *moral/spiritual freedom*.

hard determinism. The concept that all human choices are necessarily determined by prior conditions, which may include God's sovereignty. Hard determinists believe that human freedom is incompatible with *determinism* and that it is therefore an illusion. Some hard determinists reject *moral responsibility*, while others say that human freedom is not necessary for responsibility. See also *hyper-Calvinism*.

human responsibility. See *moral responsibility*.

hyper-Calvinism. A deviant form of *Calvinism* that denies any human freedom or *moral responsibility*, usually with respect to matters of faith and repentance. Hyper-Calvinists embrace *hard determinism* and discourage open invitations to sinners to believe on Christ for salvation. God's love is restricted only to the elect.

immanence. The attribute of God in which he draws near to his creatures even though he is distinct from his creation as the

Creator. He makes his presence known by becoming directly involved in the lives of human beings. See also *transcendence*.

incompatibilism. The idea that human freedom is incompatible with *determinism*. *Hard determinism* and *libertarianism* are incompatibilist views. Hard determinists believe that every human choice is determined and that this is incompatible with human freedom, which is an illusion. Libertarians say that human choices are free and that this is incompatible with determinism of any kind.

instructive will. See *preceptive will*.

irresistible grace. Is represented by the *I* in the traditional Calvinistic acronym *TULIP*. It refers to the grace of God as it draws sinners to Christ through the work of *regeneration* so that they come to him irresistibly. It is a gracious work because without it no one is either willing or able to come to Christ on his or her own. See also *Calvinism*.

libertarianism. The view that *free will* is incompatible with divine *determinism* (i.e., God's meticulous decreeing of all things), which undermines human freedom and *moral responsibility*. God's sovereignty is exercised so that he does not causally determine human actions. Freedom of choice comes about when one has the ability to choose contrary to any prior factors that influence the choice, including external circumstances, one's motives, desires, character, and nature, and, of course, God himself. If these prior influences decisively determine choices, then the freedom and responsibility of those choices are undermined.

monergism. In *Calvinism*, the idea that salvation is the result of "one (*mono-*) agent working (*ergon*)." In this case, salvation is solely the work of God's grace. See also *synergism*.

moral ability. In *compatibilism*, the ability of a regenerate person to conform to God's standard of righteousness. The unregenerate person has a moral inability to act in any God-pleasing manner. All moral actions of the unregenerate fall short of the standard of righteousness that God sets. See also *natural ability*.

moral responsibility. Humans' culpability for their moral choices. A person who does good deserves praise or reward. A person who does evil deserves blame or punishment. Most Calvinists and Arminians believe that some kind of human freedom is necessary for moral responsibility. Also termed *human responsibility*.

moral/spiritual freedom. In *compatibilism*—which teaches that in their natural state human beings remain in bondage to their *sin nature*—the state of the sinner in which the work of *regeneration* liberates him or her from this bondage. See also *general freedom*.

moral will. See *preceptive will*.

natural ability. The ability that a person has or does not have to act in some way. People may have natural abilities that allow them to act in some way as well as disabilities that prevent them from acting in some way. Also, external natural restraints may hinder one from acting in some way. See also *moral ability*.

necessary condition. A prior condition that is necessary in order for something to come about. While something may be necessary in order to bring about a particular outcome, it may not be sufficient. Gasoline is necessary for a car to run, but it is not sufficient, since other conditions are also necessary. See also *sufficient condition*.

new nature. See *regeneration*.

old nature. See *old self*.

old self. In Paul's writings, synonymous with *flesh*. Even though believers have been granted a *new nature* at the moment of *regeneration*, they become engaged in a great battle with what remains of the old *sin nature*. Even though the old self was crucified, it still seeks to drag us down (i.e., throughout the Christian life) while in its death throes, prompting us with sinful desires. Also termed *old nature*.

open theism. A radical form of *Arminianism* that embraces *libertarianism* but denies orthodox doctrines that classical theism embraces. Namely, open theists deny that God has exhaustive *foreknowledge* of the future. The future is "open." God acts and reacts in response to what humans do and changes his plans accordingly.

ordinary providence. Everyday instances in which God's superintendence of events involves predictable patterns that are normally identified in scientific parlance as laws of nature. See also *extraordinary providence*.

Pelagianism. A belief system derived from the teachings of the British monk Pelagius (c. 354–415). Pelagius taught that divine grace was not necessary for humans to achieve salvation. Rather, people are born morally neutral and with their *free will* are able to equally choose between sinful and righteous actions. Pelagianism is regarded as heretical by both Calvinists and Arminians.

preceptive will. God's revealed will in Scripture whereby he declares or instructs us what he has established as righteous, wise, good, and true. Some call this God's *moral will, instructive will*, or *will of command*.

prevenient grace. In *Arminianism*—which teaches that mankind is morally depraved due to our *sin nature* inherited from Adam, thus placing our wills in bondage to sin—the grace that God bestows on unbelievers that restores their free will (i.e., defined as *libertarianism*) and allows them to cooperate with or resist further effusions of God's grace.

primary cause. In *compatibilism*, God as the orchestrator of all human actions. His eternal decrees determine all that transpires in human history. See also *concurrence, secondary cause, proximate cause*, and *remote cause*.

proximate cause. In *compatibilism*, the immediate source of human choice; the near cause. While humans are the *secondary cause* of their own actions, they are also the immediate cause, acting in response to their most compelling motives and desires. See also *concurrence, primary cause*, and *remote cause*.

regeneration. The extraordinary work of the Holy Spirit whereby he causes a *new nature* to arise in the souls of those whom God chooses to redeem. This new nature is inhabited by the Spirit, who works to transform unregenerate people. It is marked by the implantation of spiritual life where none existed before and generates godly desires and a *moral ability* to make choices that are truly God-pleasing. *Conversion* (i.e., the exercise of faith and repentance) and subsequent sanctifying actions in the regenerate person are not possible apart from this preceding gracious work of God.

remote cause. In *compatibilism*, God as distant initiator of human actions, working through secondary means. While God is the *primary cause* of all human actions, he is not the *proximate cause* of those actions. In other words, he does not normally act directly upon humans, bypassing their freely made choices. See also *concurrence* and *secondary cause*.

secondary cause. In *compatibilism*, humans as the orchestrators of all their actions. God is the *primary cause* of all human actions, but he accomplishes his purposes through the means of secondary human agents. See also *concurrence*, *proximate cause*, and *remote cause*.

secret will. See *decretive will*.

self-determining choice. The idea in *libertarianism* that choices are self-determined or self-caused. Nothing outside the person making the choice can be the decisive cause for choices made. Humans are the sole originators of their own choices.

self-interest. In *compatibilism*, the motivation that people have to always act in a way that they perceive will serve their own best interest or what will benefit them the most. Also termed *self-love*.

self-love. See *self-interest*.

sin nature. The corrupted nature that all people are born with that has a propensity for sin. The core moral and spiritual condition of all human beings is to be dead in sin. Their wills are in bondage to sin, and they are unable to perform God-pleasing actions apart from the work of *regeneration*. See also *old self*.

soft determinism. Another name for *compatibilism*, the idea that choices are necessarily determined, yet compatible with human freedom and responsibility.

sovereign will. See *decretive will*.

sufficient condition. A prior condition that is sufficient in order for something to come about. While something may be sufficient in order to bring about a particular outcome, it may not be necessary. A rainstorm may be sufficient to wet a lawn, but it is not necessary. Gasoline can wet a lawn as well. See also *necessary condition*.

synergism. In *Arminianism*, the idea that salvation is the result of "multiple agents (God and man) working (*ergon*) with (*syn-*) one another." Humans must cooperate with God's grace in order to be saved. See also *monergism*.

transcendence. The attribute of God as Creator indicating that he is wholly distinct from the creation and his creatures. He is above and beyond the created universe even though he interacts with it directly. See also *immanence*.

will of command. See *preceptive will*.

Select Bibliography

Alcorn, Randy. *hand in Hand: The Beauty of God's Sovereignty and Meaningful Human Choice*. Colorado Springs: Multnomah, 2014.

———. *If God Is Good: Faith in the Midst of Suffering and Evil*. Colorado Springs: Multnomah, 2009.

Barrett, Matthew. *Salvation by Grace: A Case for Effectual Calling and Regeneration*. Phillipsburg, NJ: P&R Publishing, 2013.

Basinger, David. *The Case for Freewill Theism*. Downers Grove, IL: InterVarsity Press, 1996.

Basinger, David, and Randall Basinger, eds. *Predestination and Free Will: Four Views of Divine Sovereignty and Human Freedom*. Downers Grove, IL: InterVarsity Press, 1986.

Beale, G. K. "An Exegetical and Theological Consideration of the Hardening of Pharaoh's Heart in Exodus 4–14 and Romans 9." *Trinity Journal* 5, 2 (1984): 129–54.

Boettner, Loraine. *The Reformed Doctrine of Predestination*. Philadelphia: Presbyterian and Reformed, 1932.

Byl, John. *The Divine Challenge: On Matter, Mind, Math and Meaning*. Carlisle, PA: Banner of Truth, 2004.

Calvin, John. *The Bondage and Liberation of the Will*. Edited by A. N. S. Lane. Translated by G. I. Davis. Grand Rapids: Baker, 1996.

———. *Institutes of the Christian Religion*. Edited by John T. McNeill. Translated by Ford Lewis Battles. Philadelphia: Westminster, 1960.

Campbell, Joseph Keim. *Free Will*. Malden, MA: Polity Press, 2011.

Carson, D. A. *The Difficult Doctrine of the Love of God*. Wheaton, IL: Crossway, 2000.

———. *Divine Sovereignty and Human Responsibility: Biblical Perspectives in Tension*. Atlanta: John Knox, 1981.

———. *How Long, O Lord? Reflections on Suffering and Evil*. Grand Rapids: Baker, 2006.

Ciocchi, David M. "Reconciling Divine Sovereignty and Human Freedom." *Journal of the Evangelical Theological Society* 37, 3 (September 1994): 395–412.

Cottrell, Jack W. "The Nature of the Divine Sovereignty." In *The Grace of God and the Will of Man*, edited by Clark H. Pinnock. Minneapolis: Bethany House, 1989.

Cowan, Steven B., and James S. Spiegel. *The Love of Wisdom: A Christian Introduction to Philosophy*. Nashville: B&H Publishing Group, 2009.

Dennett, Daniel C. *Freedom Evolves*. New York: Viking, 2003.

DeYoung, Kevin. *Hole in Our Holiness*. Wheaton, IL: Crossway, 2012.

———. *Just Do Something*. Chicago: Moody, 2009.

Edwards, Jonathan. *The Freedom of the Will*. Vol. 1 of *The Works of Jonathan Edwards*, edited by Paul Ramsey. New Haven, CT: Yale University Press, 1957.

Feinberg, John S. *The Many Faces of Evil: Theological Systems and the Problem of Evil*. Wheaton, IL: Crossway, 2004.

———. *No One Like Him*. Wheaton, IL: Crossway, 2001.

Forlines, F. Leroy. *Classical Arminianism: A Theology of Salvation*. Nashville: Randall House, 2011.

Frame, John M. *Apologetics: A Justification of Christian Belief*. Phillipsburg, NJ: P&R Publishing, 2015.

———. *The Doctrine of God*. Phillipsburg, NJ: P&R Publishing, 2002.

———. *No Other God: A Response to Open Theism*. Phillipsburg, NJ: P&R Publishing, 2001.

———. *Systematic Theology: An Introduction to Christian Belief*. Phillipsburg, NJ: P&R Publishing, 2013.

Friesen, Garry. *Decision Making and the Will of God*. Colorado Springs: Multnomah, 2004.

Geisler, Norman L. *Chosen but Free: A Balanced View of Divine Election*. Minneapolis: Bethany House, 1999.

Grudem, Wayne. *Systematic Theology*. Grand Rapids: Zondervan, 1994.

Hafemann, Scott J. *The God of Promise and the Life of Faith*. Wheaton, IL: Crossway, 2001.

Harris, Sam. *Free Will*. New York: Free Press, 2012.

Helm, Paul. *Eternal God: A Study of God without Time*. Oxford: Oxford University Press, 1988.

———. *The Providence of God*. Downers Grove, IL: InterVarsity Press, 1994.

Hoekema, Anthony A. *Created in God's Image*. Grand Rapids: Eerdmans, 1986.

———. *Saved by Grace*. Grand Rapids: Eerdmans, 1989.

Holmes, Stephen R. "Strange Voices: Edwards on the Will." In *Listening to the Past: The Place of Tradition in Theology*. Grand Rapids: Baker Academic, 2002.

Kane, Robert. *A Contemporary Introduction to Free Will*. New York: Oxford University Press, 2005.

Kapic, Kelly. "The Egocentric Predicament." *Tabletalk* 36, 3 (March 2012): 20–23.

Lawson, Steven J. *Foundations of Grace: 1400 BC–AD 100*. A Long Line of Godly Men 1. Orlando, FL: Reformation Trust, 2006.

Lemke, Steve W. "A Biblical and Theological Critique of Irresistible Grace." In *Whosoever Will: A Biblical-Theological Critique of Five-Point Calvinism*, edited by David L. Allen and Steve W. Lemke. Nashville: B&H Publishing Group, 2010.

Luther, Martin. *The Bondage of the Will*. Translated by J. I. Packer and O. R. Johnston. Grand Rapids: Fleming H. Revell, 1957.

MacArthur, John. *Found: God's Will*. Colorado Springs: David C. Cook, 2012.

———. *Slave: The Hidden Truth about Your Identity in Christ*. Nashville: Thomas Nelson, 2010.

Manta, Paul. *Free Will, Moral Responsibility, and Reformed Theology: A Contemporary Introduction*. Paul L. Manta, 2011. Available at http://analytictheologye4c5 .files.wordpress.com/2011/07/free-will-and-moral-responsibility-intro11.pdf.

Moreland, J. P., and William Lane Craig. *Philosophical Foundations for a Christian Worldview*. Downers Grove, IL: InterVarsity Press, 2003.

Morley, Brian. *God in the Shadows: Evil in God's World*. Fearn, Scotland: Christian Focus, 2006.

Murray, John. *Redemption Accomplished and Applied*. Grand Rapids: Eerdmans, 1955.

Olson, Roger E. *Against Calvinism*. Grand Rapids: Zondervan, 2011.

———. *Arminian Theology: Myths and Realities*. Downers Grove, IL: InterVarsity Press, 2006.

Ortlund, Dane. *A New Inner Relish: Christian Motivation in the Thought of Jonathan Edwards*. Fearn, Scotland: Christian Focus, 2008.

Packer, J. I. *Evangelism and the Sovereignty of God*. Downers Grove, IL: InterVarsity Press, 1991.

Peterson, Robert A. *Election and Free Will: God's Gracious Choice and Our Responsibility*. Phillipsburg, NJ: P&R Publishing, 2007.

Peterson, Robert A., and Michael D. Williams. *Why I Am Not an Arminian*. Downers Grove, IL: InterVarsity Press, 2004.

Picirilli, Robert E. *Grace, Faith, Free Will*. Nashville: Randall House, 2002.

Pink, A. W. *The Sovereignty of God*. Grand Rapids: Baker, 1984.

Pinnock, Clark H. "Responsible Freedom and the Flow of Biblical History." In *Grace Unlimited*, edited by Clark H. Pinnock. Minneapolis: Bethany House, 1975.

Piper, John. "Are There Two Wills in God?" In *Still Sovereign*, edited by Thomas R. Schreiner and Bruce A. Ware. Grand Rapids: Baker, 2000.

——. *Desiring God*. Sisters, OR: Multnomah, 1996.

——. *Finally Alive*. Fearn, Scotland: Christian Focus, 2009.

Plantinga, Alvin. *God, Freedom and Evil*. Grand Rapids: Eerdmans, 1989.

Reichenbach, Bruce R. "Freedom, Justice and Moral Responsibility." In *The Grace of God and the Will of Man*, edited by Clark H. Pinnock. Minneapolis: Bethany House, 1989.

Schreiner, Thomas R. "Does Scripture Teach Prevenient Grace in the Wesleyan Sense?" In *Still Sovereign*, edited by Thomas R. Schreiner and Bruce A. Ware. Grand Rapids: Baker, 2000.

Smallman, Stephen. *Beginnings: Understanding How We Experience the New Birth*. Phillipsburg, NJ: P&R Publishing, 2015.

Spiegel, James S. *The Benefits of Providence: A New Look at Divine Sovereignty*. Wheaton, IL: Crossway, 2005.

Sproul, R. C. *Chosen by God*. Wheaton, IL: Tyndale, 1986.

——. *The Invisible Hand*. Phillipsburg, NJ: P&R Publishing, 1996.

——. *Willing to Believe: The Controversy over Free Will*. Grand Rapids: Baker, 1997.

Steele, David N., Curtis C. Thomas, and S. Lance Quinn. *The Five Points of Calvinism*. Phillipsburg, NJ: P&R Publishing, 2004.

Storms, Sam C. *Chosen for Life*. Wheaton, IL: Crossway, 2007.

——. "Jonathan Edwards on the Freedom of the Will." *Trinity Journal* 3, 2 (1982): 131–69.

——. "The Will: Fettered Yet Free." In *A God Entranced Vision of All Things*, edited by John Piper and Justin Taylor. Wheaton, IL: Crossway, 2004.

Tada, Joni Eareckson, and Steven Estes. *When God Weeps*. Grand Rapids: Zondervan, 1997.

Talbot, Mark R. "All the God That Is Ours in Christ." In *Suffering and the Sovereignty of God*, edited by John Piper and Justin Taylor. Wheaton, IL: Crossway, 2006.

——. "True Freedom: The Liberty That Scripture Portrays as Worth Having." In *Beyond the Bounds*, edited by John Piper, Justin Taylor, and Paul Kjoss Helseth. Wheaton, IL: Crossway, 2003.

Tiessen, Terrance L. *Providence & Prayer: How Does God Work in the World?* Downers Grove, IL: InterVarsity Press, 2000.

Walls, Jerry L., and Joseph R. Dongell. *Why I Am Not a Calvinist*. Downers Grove, IL: InterVarsity Press, 2004.

Ware, Bruce A. "The Compatibility of Determinism and Human Freedom." In *Whomever He Wills: A Surprising Display of Sovereign Mercy*, edited by Matthew M. Barrett and Thomas J. Nettles. Cape Coral, FL: Founders Press, 2012.

———. *God's Greater Glory: The Exalted God of Scripture and the Christian Faith*. Wheaton, IL: Crossway, 2004.

———. *God's Lesser Glory: The Diminished God of Open Theism*. Wheaton, IL: Crossway, 2000.

———, ed. *Perspectives on the Doctrine of God: 4 Views*. Nashville: B&H Publishing Group, 2008.

Wellum, Stephen J. "The Importance of the Nature of Divine Sovereignty for Our View of Scripture." *Southern Baptist Journal of Theology* 4, 2 (Summer 2000): 76–90.

Williams, Thaddeus J. *Love, Freedom, and Evil: Does Authentic Love Require Free Will?* New York: Rodopi, 2011.

Wright, R. K. McGregor. *No Place for Sovereignty: What's Wrong with Freewill Theism*. Downers Grove, IL: InterVarsity Press, 1996.

Index of Scripture

Index of Subjects and Names

synergism, 8, 22, 28, 97–99, 97n8, 144,
    150–51, 186, 188, 192, 197, 253,
    259–60. *See also* monergism

Tada, Joni Eareckson, 5n10, 54, 74, 142
Talbot, Mark R., 92
Templeton, Charles, 61–62
Tennet, William, 106n20
theodicy, 71n29. *See also* evil, problem of
Thomas, Curtis C., 4n10, 11, 186n14
Tiessen, Terrance L., 126n25, 133
Tolkien, J. R. R., 83, 89
Toplady, Augustus, 189
Turretin, Francis, 234
Twelve Angry Men (1957 film), 93

Vines, Jerry, 24
Voyager 1 spacecraft, 71

Walls, Jerry L., 11, 29
Ware, Bruce A., 5n12, 49n43, 92
Wells, Brian, 163–64
Wellum, Stephen J., 111
Wesley, Charles, 235
Wesley, John, ix, 145
Westminster Confession of Faith, 78,
    78n8, 188
Westminster Shorter Catechism, 230, 237
Whitefield, George 107n20
Williams, Thaddeus J., xiii, 33–37,
    53–54, 67
Wurmbrand, Richard, 68

Your God Is Too Small (Phillips), 55

Zamperini, Louis, 23n25
Zwemer, Samuel, 106